HOW
DEVELOPMENT
PROJECTS
PERSIST

D1713887

ERIN BECK

HOW DEVELOPMENT PROJECTS PERSIST

Everyday Negotiations
with Guatemalan NGOs

Duke University Press   Durham and London   2017

© 2017 DUKE UNIVERSITY PRESS
All rights reserved
Printed in the United States of America on acid-free paper ∞
Cover design by Matt Tauch; interior designed by Courtney Leigh Baker
Typeset in Minion Pro by Copperline Books

Library of Congress Cataloging-in-Publication Data
Names: Beck, Erin, [date] author.
Title: How development projects persist : everyday negotiations
with Guatemalan NGOs / Erin Beck.
Description: Durham : Duke University Press, 2017. | Includes
bibliographical references and index.
Identifiers: LCCN 2016053085 (print)
LCCN 2016058225 (ebook)
ISBN 9780822369615 (hardcover : alk. paper)
ISBN 9780822363781 (pbk. : alk. paper)
ISBN 9780822372912 (ebook)
Subjects: LCSH: Non-governmental organizations—Guatemala. |
Guatemala—Social conditions. | Guatemala—Economic
conditions. | Women in development—Guatemala. | Fundacion
Namaste Guatemaya. | Fraternidad de Presbiteriales Mayas (Guatemala)
Classification: LCC HN143 .B435 2017 (print) | LCC HN143 (ebook) |
DDC 306.097281—dc23
LC record available at https://lccn.loc.gov/2016053085

Cover art: The chaotic process of taking attendance in the Fraternity.
Photograph by the author.

CONTENTS

ACKNOWLEDGMENTS

After my first year of graduate school, I decided to spend the summer in Latin America, practicing Spanish and relaxing at the same time. I was on a graduate student's budget and flights to Central America were cheap, so I booked a flight to Guatemala City without much thought. Little did I know that I would be challenged and inspired over the following decade by what I found.

I spent my first few weeks in Guatemala in the style of so many foreigners, volunteering and attending classes and seminars with a left-leaning language school in Quetzaltenango. Early on, I was asked to translate for a guest presenter while he discussed his personal experiences during the U.S.-backed coup (1954) and the subsequent armed conflict (1960–96). I was unprepared for the task and struggled to find the words to respectfully translate the detailed story of this man's capture by members of his own community (organized into state-sponsored civil defense patrols) and his subsequent torture. At the time, he was living in an impoverished town lacking basic services. When he organized his peers to undertake an irrigation project, he was labeled a guerrilla and was subsequently kidnapped, beaten, and thrown into a pit, where he was starved and periodically urinated on. Translating his firsthand account left me emotionally exhausted, wondering how any person, or any country, could recover from such trauma.

A few weeks later, I accompanied a group of foreigners to a small community associated with the language school. The community's residents were mostly former refugees who had returned to the country from Mexico after the democratic opening in the mid-1980s. One of the residents puffed up in pride, telling me that they had built the community, the school, the clinic, and the homes on their own. "The only thing the government provided was the road," he said, pointing to the narrow brick road running through the center of the small town. They relied on support from foreign nongovernmental organizations (NGOs), small-scale agricultural projects, and selling locally manufactured goods to gringos like me. *Poco a poco* (little by little) they were leveraging local and foreign connections to build a new community for themselves, bypassing the racist, corrupt state that had previously driven them from the country.

Thereafter, traveling around the country, I was repeatedly struck by two observations that arose from these initial encounters. First, I was impressed by Guatemalans' creativity and resilience in their daily struggles to *salir adelante* (get ahead), even in the face of dramatic events like armed conflict and genocide and of hidden but equally dramatic structures that marginalized them. These were not passive recipients of social, economic, and political forces but agents adeptly navigating and actively shaping (although in a constrained way) their local realities.

Second, I was struck by the impressive number of mostly foreign-funded NGOs claiming to contribute to democracy, empowerment, and development. I became interested in how the visions of these NGOs were interacting with local understandings of progress. Additionally, I could not help but wonder how foreign-funded projects were being incorporated in a national context that had previously been so dramatically influenced by foreign interventions, including interventions that interrupted efforts at redistribution and oppressed even seemingly harmless grassroots development efforts, such as irrigation projects.

Many people and organizations have helped me to translate these initial impressions into a defined research project about the daily interactions in and around development interventions in Guatemala; they have animated my thinking and buoyed my spirits over the subsequent decade. I have been fortunate enough to locate my intellectual "homes" in two institutions—Brown University and the University of Oregon—in which important questions were valued over disciplinary bounds. At Brown University, Richard Snyder helped to nurture the initial seeds of this research project and pushed me to think about how different NGOs embody varying visions of development—a key insight that contributed to the analysis presented here. Pauline Jones Luong had the unique capacity to find insight in even the most jumbled ideas as well as to offer substantive critique coupled with sincere encouragement. I am glad that Jane Jaquette agreed to work with me after only one meeting, as I now consider her to be one of my most important mentors and a close friend. Her expertise in gender politics has been immensely valuable, and observing her commitment to conducting research that focuses on, and contributes to, gender equity has been an inspiration. The mentorship of Patrick Heller ensured that my research would always be interdisciplinary at its core. Patrick consistently challenged me to ask "bigger" questions, and I have become a more ambitious scholar as a result.

Also at Brown University, members of a writing group—Sukriti Issar, Shruti Majumdar, Esther Hernández-Medina, Dikshya Thapa, Sinem Adar, Myungji Yang, Christopher Gibson, Oslec Villegas, and Angélica Durán-Martinez—provided insightful feedback throughout the early stages of my research. I especially would like to thank Jennifer Costanza for her friendship and intellectual companionship over the years. Our shared passion for Guatemala, along with Jennifer's detailed feedback, has served as a constant source of motivation.

At the University of Oregon, my colleagues in the Department of Political Science, the Center for the Study of Women in Society, and the Center for Latino/a and Latin American Studies (CLLAS) have provided intellectual homes in which I feel inspired and supported daily. From my first year at the University of Oregon, Lynn Stephen provided crucial mentorship and friendship, helping me to navigate the university while pushing me to stay true to my values and vision. I thank her profoundly. Ron Mitchell, Karrie Koesel, Craig Kauffman, Burke Hendrix, Craig Parsons, David Steinberg, and Will Terry all read and gave comments on early drafts of chapters included here. Gerry Berk read multiple versions of the entire manuscript and gave me the intellectual push I needed to draw out the book's broader implications for the field of development. Cary Fontana helped compile data on trends in international funding over time and was a delight to work with. The Department of Political Science generously funded a book workshop, which was instrumental to my success and profoundly shaped this book's theoretical framework. I am forever grateful for those who participated, including Yvonne Braun, Gerry Berk, Craig Parsons, Jocelyn Viterna, Phil Oxhorn, and David Lewis. I thank them for dedicating so much time and energy to this project and for their continued encouragement. Their enthusiasm pushed me through the final stages of this project and motivated me when I felt discouraged. Elizabeth Bennett and Kyle Lascurettes helped me put the finishing touches on the book when I felt too overwhelmed to make any more choices.

Most people can point to at least one teacher in their lives who changed the way that they saw the world and expanded their sense of what was possible. For me that was Doug Blum, who also happens to be the reason I am a political scientist. He taught the first class in political science that I took, hired me as a research assistant, pushed me to go to graduate school, and continues to cheer me on to this day. I hope one day to be even half as effective and compassionate a mentor as he has been for so many.

Friends and family have been instrumental to my sanity during this process. Sarah Jane Smith saw me through the emotional ups and downs of fieldwork and writing and continues to surprise me with her generosity and intellectual curiosity. Elizabeth Bennett and Huss Banai rooted for me, laughed with me, and believed in me even when I did not. Allyson Vinci, Pablo Paniagua, Álvaro León, Michael Tallon, and Rayza, Angelica, and Carlos Chava provided much-needed support and friendship during my time in Guatemala. Jake and Danea DeGlee helped me get my feet wet (literally) in all things Oregon and have given me a sense of family on the West Coast. The fierce females of Oregon—Shelley Harshe, Martina Ferrari, Julia Mahncke, and Shabnam Akhtari—have given me a sense of community. The loving support of my East Coast family—my grandparents, cousins, aunts, and parents—has been constant throughout many intellectual and personal roller coasters. As they are supposed to do, family members assured me that I was brilliant even when I felt like a complete fraud. My parents, Bernadette and James Krueger, are perhaps the world's most generous people. My father, William Beck, and my sister, Julie Beck, stepped out of their comfort zones and onto Guatemala's precarious roads to explore the country that I love so much. My aunts, Roselle Ricotta and Julie Ricotta Gusmerotti, prove that one can never have too many mothers. The animals in my life—Weezy, Maxine, and Taco—have reminded me to take time to revel in the present. They cannot read (yet), but I will acknowledge that rare gift just the same.

The research for this book would not have been possible without generous funding from the Fulbright-Hays Doctoral Dissertation Fellowship, Brown University Dissertation Fellowship, and CLLAS. It was a pure delight to work with Gisela Fosado and Lydia Rose at Duke University Press. Gisela believed in this project from the very beginning, pushed me to find my voice, and has been critical to the book's realization.

I am grateful to those involved in Namaste and the Fraternity (funders, policymakers, and workers) for opening up their organizations to a gringa with too many questions. Most importantly, I am indebted to the many Guatemalan women who invited me into their homes and businesses and trusted me with their personal stories. A decade later, Guatemalans' creativity, humor, and resilience continue to challenge and inspire me to ground even the "biggest" questions in the everyday lives of those people from whom we rarely hear but have much to learn.

CHAPTER ONE

SOCIAL ENGINEERING
FROM ABOVE
AND BELOW

In the village of Santana[1] in southwestern Guatemala, Mariana placed chairs under the shade of a crooked tree so that we could sit and talk. Old Toyota pickup trucks rumbled past us, heading south to the large fields of sugarcane, cotton, coffee, or cacao that populated the nearby export agricultural zones. Mariana was a seventy-four-year-old widow, mother to six children who were grown with children of their own. Like her, most of her children were uneducated and had difficulty finding secure work. When I asked how many grandchildren she had, she flashed a smile missing a few teeth and sighed, "*Ay*, who knows? Many." When I asked her about her business, she looked over her shoulder into the small store that she managed out of the front room of her cinderblock house. Shiny bags of chips and small packages of sweets hung from the plastic strip dangling from the ceiling. A refrigerator with a condensation-covered glass door was sparsely stocked with bottles of Coca-Cola and Sprite. "I hope God allows me to pay back what I borrowed," she said.

For almost a year and a half, Mariana had been receiving loans from an NGO called Fundación Namaste Guatemaya (Namaste). Namaste offered women small loans accompanied by classes on business and financial literacy and one-on-one meetings with business advisers who helped the women calculate their profits or losses and discuss strategies to improve sales or reduce costs.

Namaste was the brainchild of a Californian businessman who valued special-ization and the application of a business mentality to nonprofit work. Reflecting this history, Namaste focused "exclusively on helping women make profits from their businesses," as the founder explained in a 2010 staff meeting. This special-ization was based on a model of "bootstrap development," which entailed a fo-cus on the individual and a belief that, given the opportunity and resources, the poor could lift themselves out of poverty through their own entrepreneurship.

Roughly forty miles north of Santana lived Lorena, a thin Maya K'iche' woman who participated in a very different NGO. She wiped the dust off a plastic chair for me to sit on while she gathered items from a chest of drawers that divided her concrete house in two. She proudly displayed her products: colorful scarves from Taiwan that she bought in bulk to sell in the market; long strips of cloth that K'iche' women wrap around their waists as belts; reams of fabric that she sewed into aprons with the help of her daughter's dexterous fingers. Lorena was able to purchase these goods using a loan from a NGO called Fraternidad de Presbiteriales Mayas (the Fraternity). She needed every penny she earned to support her two daughters' studies because her husband was not there to contribute to their expenses. He was incarcerated about a decade previously, thus ensuring that the day-to-day struggles to provide for the family fell squarely on Lorena's shoulders. Shouldering the weight was difficult; because of an illness that affected her hands, Lorena was unable to perform agricultural or factory work, and because she only reached the third grade, steady employment in a nonmanual job had been hard to find.

Like Namaste, the Fraternity provided women with loans and classes. But whereas Namaste focused on business and financial literacy, the Fraternity required women to attend classes on a variety of topics, including Bible study and lessons about self-esteem, caring for the environment, and recapturing Mayan culture. Other classes taught women handicrafts, composting, and how to make and use organic fertilizers and prepare nutritious meals. The orga-nization's roots informed its multifaceted approach. Indigenous women had previously organized in the Presbyterian Church to fight ethnic and gender discrimination and eventually separated to establish the Fraternity as an in-dependent NGO. The NGO's policymakers believed one could not separate indigenous women's economic well-being from their emotional, spiritual, and physical well-being, or from that of their families, churches, and communities. They therefore pursued a holistic model of development—one that taught women to recapture their Mayan identities, value themselves, care for the environment, participate actively in their faiths and communities, and earn incomes in ways that were consistent with their cultural and spiritual beliefs.

Mariana and Lorena represent the very type of beneficiaries that many development interventions today target, especially those that incorporate microcredit, or the provision of small loans to impoverished borrowers who lack collateral. As women, they are seen as having greater levels of need because of unequal access to schooling, resources, and decision-making authority. Targeting women like Mariana and Lorena with loans is additionally seen as more efficient than targeting men. Based on their reproductive roles and gender stereotypes, it is assumed that women will channel economic benefits to their families and communities and manage their money more responsibly.

Namaste and the Fraternity represent distinct approaches to development that are common the world over. Namaste is a foreign-founded and foreign-managed NGO that operates according to a bureaucratic structure, leverages the market, and values specialization and quantifiable results. It embodies the push toward professionalization, results-based management, and social entrepreneurship in the field of development. The Fraternity, on the other hand, is a grassroots organization that adopts a multifaceted approach, criticizes neoliberal policies, and seeks environmental sustainability, cultural recuperation, and personal transformations—goals that cannot be easily quantified. It embodies the call for grassroots alternatives and culturally appropriate development. The contrasts between Namaste and the Fraternity inevitably lead to the question, Which type of NGO and which development model works better? Which more effectively empowers women, contributes to development from the "bottom up," and has the more meaningful impact in the lives of women like Mariana and Lorena?

This book makes the case that although these questions are central to the study and pursuit of development, they are the wrong questions with which to start. For too long, scholars and practitioners studying NGOs' development interventions have fixated on outcomes and have seen development projects as phenomena that *happen to* people like Mariana and Lorena, thus ignoring the ways that these people transform projects in practice. As a result, many have ignored questions that are analytically prior, namely, How are NGOs' development projects constituted in the first place? What determines what actually happens on the ground? Answering these questions requires delving into the sources of development models, the relationships between these models and the actual practices and meanings, and the ways that development projects are embedded in, and transformed by, particular environments and lives.

Once we get inside them, it becomes clear that development NGOs are not neatly bounded and fixed organizations, and their projects are neither linear nor predetermined. Long-term comparative ethnographies of Namaste and the Fraternity reveal the interactional origins of development projects and demonstrate that international trends, development models, and organizational characteristics influence, but do not determine, actual practices and experiences on the ground. This suggests that abstract debates about the "best" development models or approaches, detached from close analyses of practices and experiences, are misplaced. Thus, this book does not arbitrate debates about the value of different development models. Moving away from binary assessments of success or failure, it does not reveal the "best" strategy for development or empowerment, nor does it universally condemn or celebrate NGOs and microcredit. Instead, it addresses a significant gap in the literature between "increasingly grandiose vision[s] of international development" and "relatively low levels of transparency and clarity about how development institutions work" (Lewis and Mosse 2006, 15).

To that end, this book explores the diverse meanings, motivations, and strategies that are continuously unfolding under the label "NGO" and under the guise of development. It focuses on the interactions among international trends, local histories and contexts, and developers' experiences, alongside the quotidian interactions between development workers and beneficiaries. This analysis reveals that development interventions are not merely the implementation of technical plans or expressions of hegemonic tendencies. Instead, they are interactive processes in which multiple dispositions, interests, and meanings conflict, interlock, and interpenetrate, and in which accommodation, reinterpretation, struggle, and adjustment are ongoing (Lewis and Mosse 2006). What happens on the ground in the context of development is not only the product of international trends, development models, and formal policies; it is also shaped by the ways that various stakeholders creatively interact with each other and with materials (paperwork, databases, evaluation reports, and technologies) over time in a given context. Thus, we cannot ask what development does for people without also asking what people do for development.

This book focuses on various "types" of people as they affect and are affected by development interventions. Tracing the development "chains" created by Namaste and the Fraternity, it explores the meanings and practices of funders and policymakers, which in turn shape development and organizational models and strategies. Funders are those who contribute resources but who do not make organizational decisions themselves, even if they influence them explicitly or implicitly, whereas policymakers are those who craft NGOs' formal policies (regardless of the degree to which these formal policies reflect on-the-ground practices) and have final say over evaluation and hiring processes, among others. Tracing development chains to the ground, the book also focuses on NGO leaders, workers, and beneficiaries. NGO leaders (directors and upper-level management) often spend most of their time in offices and oversee operations acting as key brokers between workers and policymakers. Workers carry out development strategies in offices or communities, often interfacing with communities and aid recipients on a regular basis but having little say over formal policies or operations. When grouped together, these people—funders, policymakers, NGO leaders, and workers—are labeled "developers" in this book. Those whom developers target with goods or services are referred to as "beneficiaries." The degree to which developers actually induce development (however defined) is debatable, and of course, the degree to which those targeted by development interventions actually benefit varies. What is more, the term "beneficiary" implies an assumption of passivity this book is actively attempting to combat. Thus, although these terms appear throughout this book, readers should remain aware of these notes of caution.[2]

Although they cannot reveal the "best" development model, case studies of particular interventions and organizations are still able to reveal generalizable conclusions about the nature of development. The comparative ethnographies at the heart of this study demonstrate that development projects represent social engineering from above and below. Those involved in development projects—developers and beneficiaries alike—leverage their respective expertise, networks, and meanings in attempts to bring about their visions of the good life, either for themselves or for others. Because there is always room for diverse actors to maneuver in pursuit of their own goals and meanings, and because those goals and meanings never completely overlap, development projects will inevitably be characterized by incoherencies and contradictions that interrupt clear, predictable paths between inputs and outputs or between plans and practices. Development is not one thing but many things to many people; that is why it is always decidedly "messier" in practice than on paper, and perhaps why it persists even when it fails to develop communities and countries.

DEVELOPMENT PROJECTS AS ONGOING INTERACTIONS

This book focuses exclusively on development as project-based, intentional activity with roots in the post–World War II intervention into the global south and NGOs geared toward development rather than advocacy and activism. However, some scholars focus on development as a long-term, ongoing process that alters the organization of economies, social relationships, and politics. These scholars often dismiss projects as irrelevant practically and theoretically because after six decades of internationally funded development interventions, "no country in the world has ever developed itself through projects" (Nyoni in Edwards 1989, 118; Cowen and Shenton 1996; Hart 2001; Banks and Hulme 2012). While initially there was hope that development NGOs could buck this trend by advocating for structural change, more recently, scholars have found that at best, development NGOs simply support alternative forms of project-based intervention (Bebbington, Hickey, and Mitlin 2008). Others have emphasized that governments, not NGOs and projects, develop countries, and have thus focused their attention on national economic policies relating to trade, fiscal policy, and the like, alongside state institutions, rather than development projects and NGOs.

If NGOs and their development projects do not contribute to national economic development and poverty reduction, why study them? Although they may have failed to live up to their stated goals, development projects and NGOs continue to exist, proliferate, and generate numerous effects. Regardless of the degree to which development "works" (i.e., does what funders and policymakers intend), it endures—affecting local economies, formal and informal institutions, social relations, and subjectivities (Viterna and Robertson 2015; Babb 1996; Schofer and Hironaka 2005; Leve 2014; Sanyal 2009; Swidler and Watkins 2009). And just as development affects people's lives in multiple, contradictory ways, people in the global south (NGO workers, beneficiaries, communities) transform development interventions and NGOs by interacting with them and assigning them new meanings and goals. Understanding how development projects and NGOs are transformed, leveraged, and appropriated, how developers and beneficiaries interact, and how interventions affect and are affected by local social relations is therefore key to understanding social reality across the global south.

Development projects of the kind explored here are often studied in one of two ways. Some scholars highlight the global politico-economic power structures in which projects emerge, and explore the various ways that development interventions involve technical solutions for inherently political problems, thus distracting from structural change and reproducing hegemony. Others focus less on structural conditions and more on local-level effects in the short and medium term. This latter group of scholars evaluates the effectiveness of development projects in achieving their stated goals with the hopes of distilling best practices. Yet both of these contrasting approaches risk reifying development projects and thus obscuring development's messy, power-laden processes and the diverse ways they interact with people's lives on the ground.

This book, by contrast, conceptualizes development projects not as prepackaged products that arrive in the global south from the global north, but rather as ongoing series of interactions in which diverse actors in the global north *and* the global south play an active role. In so doing, it demonstrates that by focusing on what development projects are supposed to do (whether it be reproducing neoliberal hegemony according to some, or lifting significant portions of the population out of poverty according to others), we overlook what development projects really do: namely, become imbricated in the daily strategies and meanings of diverse beneficiaries and developers operating in particular contexts in significant but unexpected ways.

When scholars and practitioners insist on reifying development projects and focusing on their (presumed or stated) goals alone, they blind themselves to the tensions inherent in development that allow projects, even those that fail to meet their intended goals, to be reproduced. Instead, by exploring development projects as emergent interactions among diverse actors, this book is able to uncover that even when international discourses shift, underlying mentalities and practices may persist, allowing development projects to endure in repackaged forms even if they have not led to widespread community or international development. Projects are repackaged, but not as the result of a worldwide conspiracy or because they are particularly effective. Rather, they are perpetuated as the accidental result of various actors pursuing their own goals in the context of development projects and casting a variety of outcomes as "success," thus obstructing critical reflection on the value of particular development projects, or of development projects generally. Policymakers and NGO leaders draw on their existing habitus (often shaped in previous development projects) to craft future projects and point to evaluations that leverage various measures of success to keep their jobs, get promoted, secure future funding, or feel like they are making a difference. The NGO workers look to projects as, among other things, a relatively rare source of steady or prestigious employment and often draw on and replicate strategies and meanings honed in their previous experiences in other projects. Meanwhile, beneficiaries attempt to leverage the latest projects to their benefit, learning how to skillfully manipulate developers' expectations, express the appropriate form of gratitude, or sidetrack projects to their own benefit so that they can view their participation as "successful" even when policymakers' stated goals are not met.

Reifying development projects is also problematic because it generates unrealistic expectations that a particular development schema will produce similar effects across widely varying contexts and people. It also encourages inadequate systems of evaluation and measurement that cannot capture what development projects *really* do (positive or negative)—whether that be increasing divisions or inequalities between beneficiaries or providing steady employment and prestige to NGO workers in contexts in which both jobs and status are in short supply. As the findings presented here demonstrate, viewing development projects as emergent interactions encourages us to abandon quests for the "best" development model, to rethink our evaluation strategies, and to question our ends rather than merely reforming our means, all while simultaneously opening up new lines of inquiry.

THE FAILURES OF GUATEMALA'S DEVELOPMENT PROJECTS

Guatemala is representative of many countries in which development has generated a variety of effects, even as it has fallen short of transforming economic and political power structures. Despite a long history of development projects undertaken by a variety of actors (described in chapter 2), Guatemala remains one of the most unequal countries in the world. While it is home to 235 "ultra high net worth" individuals, with a combined net worth of $28 billion (Wealth-X 2013), over half of the population lives in poverty. In rural areas, rates of poverty climb to roughly three-quarters of the population. Despite the country's abundance in agricultural products, half of Guatemalan children under the age of five nationwide and 70 percent of children in indigenous areas are undernourished—the highest rates in the Americas (World Food Programme 2014).

Inequalities rooted in ethnicity, geography, and gender intersect. Roughly half of Guatemala's population is indigenous—belonging to one of twenty-three distinct ethnolinguistic groups, most of them of Mayan descent. Guatemala thus appeals to international funders who wish to promote the now-popular goal of "culturally appropriate development." Indigenous populations are concentrated in rural areas, where poverty and malnutrition are rampant and state services are missing, weak, or privatized. During Guatemala's protracted armed conflict (1960–96), these areas were most affected by human rights abuses and acts of genocide, committed by government agents.

Women in Guatemala have long endured discrimination and marginalization. Historically, educating girls was seen as a waste. Many adult Guatemalan women describe the tendency to celebrate the birth of a son but not the birth of a daughter, and to keep girls home to cook, clean, or work in the markets and fields while their brothers attend school. Today, women have limited access to property in their name and are overrepresented in the informal sector and the maquiladora industry, ensuring that when they undertake wage labor, they receive low wages, limited job security, and little to no benefits.

Politically, women continue to be underrepresented in local and national political institutions, making up just 13 percent of the national legislators. Even in the face of peace accords and recent legislation that address indigenous and women's rights, racism and sexism continue to be widespread, and discrimination based on gender and ethnicity magnifies social exclusion. Indigenous women therefore experience a dramatically different reality than nonindigenous men. For instance, while the average nonindigenous Guatemalan man has received seven and a half years of schooling, the average indigenous woman has received just two and a half years (Inter-American Development Bank 2012).

Yet those who are most marginalized are in many ways central to Guatemala's economic well-being. The labor of the rural poor is central to the production of coffee, sugar, bananas, African palm, and other key agricultural exports. The informal sector—employing three-quarters of the population, mostly women—fuels local economies and feeds the tourist industry. Tourism, the country's second-largest earner of foreign currency, rests on images of Mayan women, who are more likely to wear traditional clothing and produce handicrafts that attract and delight foreigners from around the world. In the context of tourism, but also missionary work, Spanish schools, voluntourism, NGOs, and academic research, Guatemalans and foreigners participate in the "economy of desire" and the "economy of humanitarianism," in which culture, gender, and poverty are precious commodities (Nuñez 2009, 113). Local and foreign NGOs alike rely on images of indigenous populations and poor women in order to secure international funding and support, tapping into the global popularity of culturally appropriate and women-empowering development.

A long history of persistent inequality and poverty, state weakness, privatization, and waves of international funding, alongside the legacies of collective action and religious outreach, has established a patchwork of development NGOs spread unevenly across the country. As a result, NGOs have been said to represent the "face" of development for many Guatemalan communities (Rohloff, Díaz, and Dasgupta 2011) and to be "one of the most prevalent features of [Guatemala's] late capitalist landscape" (Way 2012, 186). Guatemalans, like citizens of most countries in the global south, are increasingly accustomed to interacting with NGOs, especially small NGOs like those at the center of this book, which are more numerous and are more likely to engage in sustained action than larger, better-studied NGOs. As elsewhere, many of these NGOs have religious origins or ties, although these types of NGOs tend to be overlooked in the literature on development and NGOs, influenced as it is by a secular bias (Hofer 2003; Bornstein 2005; Clarke 2007).

Postwar Guatemala encounters various challenges that other countries face: poverty, inequality, ethnic and gender discrimination, political corruption, and uneven state reach. It has long been influenced by international actors, discourses, and practices that have also influenced countries around the globe and is home to development actors who are present the world over—government agents, international agencies, social movements, religious organizations, and local and international NGOs. Development projects in Guatemala are characterized by the same tensions that characterize development projects everywhere. Thus, while the stories told here are intimately embedded in the Guatemalan context and shaped by the lives of particular people, the book's conclusions remain global in scope.

NAMASTE AND THE FRATERNITY:
DIFFERENT ENDS ON MULTIPLE DEVELOPMENT SPECTRUMS

This book's central findings about development's constitution are based on comparative ethnographies of Namaste and the Fraternity. These two NGOs are similar sizes, working with between four and six hundred beneficiaries, depending upon the time in question. They target similar populations—poor women living in mostly rural and semirural communities. They also deploy similar technologies, providing women small loans (known as microcredit or microfinance) accompanied by education. Both have managed to secure relatively stable international funding and long-term partnerships. Yet, despite their similarities, Namaste and the Fraternity are located at opposite ends of various spectrums in the field of development: they embody distinct development models, NGO types, and international trends that are popular in many areas of the world. Their comparison therefore stands to illuminate the origins, expressions, and effects of varied development and NGO models. It also reveals how these different international ideas and development models are translated into practices on the ground, as well as how the poor subsequently experience, react to, and transform them.

Development Models: Bootstrap versus Holistic

Namaste and the Fraternity operate according to development models that are popular across the globe. I define development models as comprising ideas about the sources of underdevelopment, a vision of what development entails, and beliefs about the most appropriate means of moving from one to the other. Even when they are implicit, these models influence decisions about the resources or services to be provided (Should we focus on loans, grants, clinics, or consciousness-raising?), the intermediary and end goals to prioritize (What is immediately necessary and what should be postponed?), and the appropriate targets of interventions (Should we target communities, businesses, or individuals? Men or women or both?). Models therefore affect (but do not determine) practices on the ground by informing views of beneficiaries and developers, as well as strategies, formal policies, and organizational values.

Namaste operates according to a development model that I label bootstrap development. Bootstrap development relies on resource-based definitions of underdevelopment and development and focuses on the individual. It is based on the assumption that given the opportunity, the poor are able to lift themselves up "by their bootstraps." Although Namaste's policymakers recognize nonmaterial aspects of development and human well-being, they specialize in increasing women's incomes because they believe that doing so will contribute to broader goals and ensure stability by helping the poor help themselves. This reflects a popular trend in the field of development in which, while scholars and practitioners recognize the multifaceted nature of poverty, they see limited access to health, education, and political power as consequences, rather than the causes, of resource deficiency (Kabeer 2004, 2).

In this model, development can be reduced to a technical challenge of providing the poor access to resources in the most efficient and effective way possible. Bootstrap development therefore has an elective affinity with a focus on "expertise" (narrowly defined) and fits well with the new managerialism that values results-driven action and quantifiable goals. Those who pursue bootstrap development, like Namaste, often target women because women are assumed to give them more "bang for their buck." Policymakers highlight that women are less likely to have access to resources and are more likely to channel resources toward their children's and community's well-being, producing positive spillover effects.

The Fraternity, on the other hand, operates according to a model that I label holistic development. This model challenges resource-based definitions of underdevelopment and development and instead argues for addressing multiple obstacles to development at once—including the relational and institutional sources of social exclusion, as well as people's identities and capabilities (Sen 1999; Nussbaum 2001). The Fraternity, as a NGO run by and serving Christian Mayan women, operates according to the belief that "it is not enough [for Mayan women] to have food to eat," as the Fraternity's director explained in a 2009 interview. In its vision, Mayan women should also be physically and psychologically healthy, educated in their rights and obligations as women and citizens, active in their churches and communities, and connected to their

Christian values, Mayan spirituality, and nature. The Fraternity's development model reflects a broader trend in which development is seen as entailing personal, internal transformations alongside other changes in the poor's environments (Rowlands 1997; Nussbaum 2001; Appadurai 2004).[3]

In this model, development is viewed as a political challenge of transforming individuals and communities and entails internal transformations alongside other changes. Because they often seek to address the relational nature of poverty and social exclusion, those applying holistic models of development are more likely to see their beneficiaries as members of excluded groups, rather than as individuals, and value their inclusion in key institutions in their lives (families, churches, development councils, political parties, etc.). Holistic models of development imply comprehensiveness over specialization and the pursuit of multiple, long-term goals that are often difficult to quantify.

Organizational Origins and Networks:
Foreign versus Grassroots

Namaste and the Fraternity each have origins that are common among development NGOs. Namaste is a foreign transplant that is similar to many other foreign-founded NGOs operating in developing countries. Its roots are in social entrepreneurship, an increasingly significant force in the field of development that encourages applying business mentalities to philanthropy and leveraging the market (Edwards 2010). Like other social entrepreneurs, Namaste's policymakers champion specialization, efficiency, measurement, innovation, and "results-driven" action. Successful North American businesspeople themselves, Namaste's early policymakers applied the "strategies of action" that they learned in business to the nonprofit world when designing and managing Namaste. These origins continue to influence the NGO, informing its "audit culture" (characteristic of many development organizations today) and providing it with many foreign, but few local, connections, such that beneficiaries see it as a "gringo bank."

On the other hand, the Fraternity, like many NGOs in Latin America, grew out of social mobilization. A small group of Mayan women in the Presbyterian Church mobilized for participation and leadership opportunities for indigenous women in local and national churches. They received funds from international sister churches and religious organizations, which they distributed to groups of Mayan Christian women for small projects such as raising chickens or cultivating small plots of land. In the face of resistance from nonindigenous and male members of the church, the Fraternity eventually separated to become an independent NGO providing small loans and classes to groups of indigenous women. These origins led policymakers to view women's participation, internal transformations, and inclusion as intrinsically valuable. They also provided the Fraternity with relatively stable international funding through religious networks while embedding it in local religious and ethnic networks and imbuing it with a local identity.

Organizational Norms: Faith in the Market versus Faith in God and Culture

Namaste's and the Fraternity's organizational norms, which are intimately connected to their origins, also diverge. Although Namaste's central founder was called to social entrepreneurship through a spiritual awakening, the "faith" that influences Namaste's development model and policies is not religious. The framework established by Namaste's policymakers and formal policies is rooted instead in a faith in the market. The NGO is designed to provide women small loans to be used in their businesses based on the assumption that one of the key obstacles to development is the poor's lack of access to capital. Once this obstacle is overcome, the policymakers believe, women can help themselves and their families by engaging in and leveraging the market. They think this contributes not only to women's well-being but also to the development of local economies. To integrate women into the market, Namaste's interest rates have been aligned with those of commercial banks, and limits have been placed on the number of loans women can receive from the NGO, so that women can prepare themselves to move seamlessly from nonprofit to market-based borrowing.

By contrast, the Fraternity's origins in the Presbyterian Church imbue the organization with Christian practices and beliefs. The NGO incorporates required and optional Bible study and theology classes, NGO leaders and workers include prayer and Bible verses and stories in the vast majority of their activities, and the organization's goals are informed by Christian values. In addition to its religious nature, the Fraternity's organizational norms are influenced by policymakers' interpretations of Mayan culture, which emphasize recapturing traditional practices, caring for the environment, eschewing foreign products, and focusing on the community rather than the individual. Drawing on both Mayan *cosmovision* and Protestant values and beliefs, the NGO promotes an alternative development that includes nonquantifiable goals such as community well-being, culturally different citizens, and indigenous women's voice and inclusion, as well as a revalorization of nonhuman life that results in "communities that are green, with crystal waters [and] pure air."[4] In this way, the Fraternity represents localized, indigenous understandings of development championed by post-development scholars and indigenous movements across Latin America, which challenge Western conceptions of progress (Escobar 1995; Acosta 2010; Gow 2008).

Bureaucratic versus Charismatic Organizational Structures

Namaste and the Fraternity are also influenced by distinct organizational structures that are emblematic of contrasting NGO types. Namaste is typical of professionalized NGOs. Its structure is bureaucratic, organized internally according to impersonal rules and valuing technical capacity, efficiency, and measurement. Decisions are made at the top with little to no input from workers or beneficiaries, and NGO staff members specialize in a limited number of activities. Meticulous files and internal feedback mechanisms contribute to a high degree of institutionalization.

The Fraternity, on the other hand, is typical of many NGOs that grew out of grassroots collective action. I label its structure charismatic (Beck 2014), drawing on Weber's description of charismatic authority (Weber 1921). The Fraternity is organized hierarchically—the director has historically made the majority of decisions with little input from workers or beneficiaries, and there is an informal hierarchy among workers and beneficiaries. Unlike in Namaste, however, this hierarchy is not based on technical capacity or task differentiation, but rather on personal relationships, valuing loyalty and personal characteristics over formal training or technical expertise. The organization's larger-than-life director has traditionally made decisions based on her personal judgments and relationships rather than impersonal rules.

THEORIZING DEVELOPMENT: AN AGENT-BASED APPROACH

How, then, are we to move forward comparing these contrasting organizations? The existing literature provides surprisingly scant direction because while social scientists are generally interested in the fine-grained nature of people's lives, meanings, and motivations, this has not always been the case when it comes to those involved in NGOs or development projects. Instead, many researchers have unintentionally relied on caricatures of the people involved in development, assuming or imputing the meanings and motivations of beneficiaries and developers rather than taking them as objects worthy of social science inquiry.[5] And in contrast to their detailed studies of other institutions, researchers have all too often promoted simplistic views of development interventions themselves, seeing them as arriving, more or less fully formed, in communities in the global south, rather than springing from or interacting with national and local-level histories and actions (Lewis 2014). The result has been sparsely populated depictions of NGO-led development interventions, curiously lacking any sense of living, breathing human beings dealing with the "incoherences, uncertainty and contradictions" (Olivier de Sardan 2005, 5) inherent in their social, political, and organizational contexts (Beck 2016).[6]

As a corrective, this book explores the socially constructed nature of development interventions, investigating how developers and beneficiaries exercise agency by reflecting on their experiences, assigning various goals and meanings to development projects, and acting in diverse ways in the face of given development models and policies (Giddens 1984; Long and Long 1992; Olivier de Sardan 2005). It brings to the forefront human agency rooted in ongoing practices and webs of meaning, interactions between people and things, and multiple forms of power. It demonstrates that those involved in development strategize, negotiate, and collude, and through acts of translation they enroll human and nonhuman actants in pursuit of their projects. As a result, the book shows, development projects are never linear and policymakers' hopeful predictions are rarely fulfilled.

Starting at the top of the development chain, this book views policymakers as social actors. As such, it moves past simplistic images of them as cogs in an "anti-politics machine" (Ferguson 1994) or as simply searching for the most efficient solution to an obvious problem, in order to explore the interactional origins of their worldviews and models of development. Doing so allows us to understand the processes by which these actors, often motivated by good intentions, come to define "messy, indeterminate situations" (Schön 1987, 4) as problems that require their expertise and intervention (Shore and Wright 1997; Apthorpe 1997; Escobar 1995; Fairhead and Leach 1997; Li 2007). Analyzing policymakers' somewhat idiosyncratic personal trajectories and dispositions reveals that, both Namaste's and the Fraternity's organizational values, structures, and models of development fit well with founders' and policymakers' habitus (Bourdieu 1990): their dispositions, values, and strategies of action, informed by their previous experiences and interactions. Through their subsequent efforts to materialize their positions, values, and visions, founders and early policymakers contributed to the "organizational habitus" of Namaste and the Fraternity in ways that influenced various actors' meanings and behavior well into the future (Ebrahim 2003; Lewis 2008; Yarrow 2011; Venkatesan and Yarrow 2012).

The agent-based approach adopted by this book predicts at best a loose coupling between workers' and beneficiaries' meanings and actions and those inscribed in written policies, based on the reality that even the most meticulously developed policies cannot account for the diversity and agency of implementers (NGO leaders and workers) and beneficiaries (Olivier de Sardan 2005; Rottenburg 2009; Fechter and Hindman 2011). We will see that actors involved in Namaste's and the Fraternity's projects come to these projects with multiple goals and meanings that often diverge from the projects' stated rationales. They subsequently act in ways not predicted by policymakers, sidetracking and transforming development interventions in the process.

Such an approach not only helps us explain why development projects are unlikely to proceed linearly toward "successful" development; it also forces us to prioritize people's multiple goals and experiences of development and thus abandon neat assessments of project outcomes as success or failure. Projects have many more effects than those sought by policymakers and funders because people use projects for their own purposes. Outcomes are never uniform across beneficiaries, and assessments of project success depend on whom you ask and whose definition of success gets prioritized (Pigg 1992; Pawson 2006; Mowles 2013). When we reject the assumption that people join NGOs or development projects for the same reasons that policymakers design them, we open ourselves up to the very real possibility that some may judge an intervention as successful even when the goals established by policymakers are not met, and some may judge an intervention as a failure even when the goals established by policymakers are met.

POWER IN AN AGENT-BASED APPROACH

It is important to note that although this book highlights the agency of diverse actors, it does not imply that anything is possible in the context of development. Macrophenomena, such as international trends and political and economic structures, shape project trajectories and possibilities, and some actors exercise much more power than others. Yet its findings highlight that macrophenomena are themselves the result of a "complex interplay of specific actors' strategies, 'projects,' resource endowments (material/technical and social/institutional), discourses and meanings" (Long 2004, 15), and power inequalities themselves result from processes of translation and composition.

In the context of development NGOs, policymakers often leverage relations with actors and materials to further entrench their positions, visions, and values through the creation and manipulation of organizational structures, employment guidelines, evaluation procedures, documentation and calculation techniques, and databases, with lasting effects. In these contexts, knowledge does not involve the "simple accumulation of facts" about the global south, poor women, and "best practices," but rather a way "of construing and ordering the world" to the benefit of some over others (Long 2004, 15; see Foucault 1980; Sletto 2008). As a result, development projects are akin to living games of chess, "where some control many more pawns, some are only allowed a few moves, whereas others can change the rules to their advantage" (Bierschenk 1988, 146; Gareau 2012). In the chapters that follow, we will see that despite their differences *both* Namaste's and the Fraternity's developers seek to govern women's economic, social, and political behavior. By leveraging relationships and material and by reinforcing ideas about "good" entrepreneurs or "good" Christian Mayan women, they encourage women to work on themselves.

Still, power in development projects is not limited to that of developers deploying power over and through their beneficiaries. Power may be uneven, but it is also diffuse, and "government is a congenitally failing operation" (Rose and Miller 1992, 190). Even though developers and beneficiaries possess unequal resources (status, time, money, valued expertise, networks, or alternatives), beneficiaries are able to exercise power, at the very least because they can "refuse to do what is expected of them or to do it another way" (Friedberg in Olivier de Sardan 2005, 186). Indeed, the diversity of goals, meanings, and criteria for evaluation involved in projects provide actors with opportunities to do much more than resist or comply (Mosse 2013; Olivier de Sardan 2005). Often, workers and beneficiaries alike exercise agency through collaboration, manipulation of dominant rhetoric, aid seeking, or undertaking small acts of reinterpretation (Olivier de Sardan 2005; Bending and Rosenda 2006; Rossi 2006). Even when developers appear to succeed in enlisting beneficiaries in their projects, we cannot assume that beneficiaries are mere dupes. When beneficiaries support top-down narratives, it is often a legitimate strategic response that expands their room for maneuver in the short term, even if it further reinforces the existing order in the long term (Rossi 2004; Mosse 2005; Bending and Rosendo 2006; Beck 2016).

In both Namaste and the Fraternity, women learn NGOs' "lessons" but also reappropriate, resist, or reinterpret them. Some women "go through the motions," use NGO spaces for their own purposes, or reinterpret NGO lessons in creative ways. Their actions demonstrate that although developers write development scripts, beneficiaries are active (although not equally powerful) characters in those scripts, jointly recrafting the plot and able to improvise.

LONGITUDINAL, COMPARATIVE ETHNOGRAPHIES
OF DEVELOPMENT INTERFACES

Because people practice, experience, and transform development interventions in concrete settings, it follows that a researcher interested in these processes must embed herself within these settings. But given that even small NGOs are embedded in webs of relations that cross multiple borders and are affected by international, national, and personal trajectories, where then does one locate the "field"? Following in the tradition of actor-oriented sociology, I conducted ethnographies at the interfaces of developers, beneficiaries, and their material reality (technologies, office space, credit), where different and often contrasting lifeworlds intersected and ongoing series of negotiations over resources, meaning, legitimacy, and control took place (Long 2001, 1; Gareau 2012).

What did ethnographies at development interfaces look like in practice? During my time with Namaste and the Fraternity, I spent some of my days in the NGO offices, attending staff meetings and planning sessions, taking part in informal conversations, and analyzing NGO databases, office space, and paperwork. I spent the rest of my time observing NGO activities with beneficiaries that unfolded in NGO offices, community buildings, and women's homes. In this way, I was able to analyze the ways that NGO policymakers, leaders, and workers talked about their work and beneficiaries, as well as the quotidian ways that developers enacted and transformed development models through their interactions with beneficiaries, communities, paperwork, and databases. I supplemented informal conversations with formal interviews of fifty-two beneficiaries. Through observations of and conversations with beneficiaries in the context of NGO activities and outside of them, I was also privy to the ways that beneficiaries themselves pursued their own diverse goals and meanings, along with the multiple ways that they accommodated, reinterpreted, resisted, or leveraged NGO discourses and strategies.

All told, the findings presented in this book are based on twenty months of field research in Guatemala and regular engagement from afar, spread out over the course of over seven years. During this time, in addition to ethnographies and interviews with beneficiaries, I undertook formal and informal interviews with Namaste's and the Fraternity's policymakers, leaders, funders, and workers (in person in Guatemala, Toronto, and Oakland and via email, Skype, and phone). The longitudinal nature of this study allowed me to study the experiential learning curves of developers and beneficiaries, investigate the nature of individual and organizational change, and thus more fully understand the interactional, dynamic nature of development and NGOs. Observing NGOs and beneficiaries over time allowed me to explore not only the ways that NGOs affected women's identities, strategies, and well-being, but also the multiple ways that women in turn affected NGOs and their projects.

Development interfaces are not self-contained spheres of interaction—they are embedded in personal, local, national, and international landscapes and histories. In order to situate the interactions I observed in Namaste and the Fraternity in a broader history and context, I drew on national and NGO archives; newspaper searches; interviews with a wide variety of NGO leaders, journalists, and government officials; and life histories of policymakers, leaders, and workers. To situate these two NGOs in the reality of women's lives, I additionally conducted surveys with over 250 women not participating in Namaste and the Fraternity about their experiences with NGOs and microcredit organizations (known as microfinance institutions, or MFIs) and drew on life histories of beneficiaries at each NGO. Combined, this research highlighted the importance of international trends, national histories, and local institutional landscapes for present-day development projects. But it also demonstrated that personal histories and dispositions, alongside memories and knowledge of other development projects, informed the expectations, meanings, and goals that developers and beneficiaries assigned to development interventions (see the appendix for further discussion of research methods and the ethical and practical issues they raised).

GENERALIZING USING AN AGENT-BASED APPROACH

Because the two NGOs represented radically different development models applied to similar technologies, reflected contrasting organizational "types" that figured prominently in debates about NGOs, and embodied distinct, noticeable trends in development, I originally saw the comparison between Namaste and the Fraternity as ideal for arbitrating debates about the value of competing development models, NGO types, and development trends—debates that were intimately linked to the field's focus on outcomes. Yet once I got inside these organizations to observe their quotidian practices, I realized that such abstract models and debates did not capture the reality of these organizations, nor did they translate seamlessly and predictably into the NGOs' outcomes. The realities of these NGOs and their projects were not merely products of development models, organizational types, and international trends. They were also products of the emergent interactions between real people, who acted and assigned meaning creatively, and sometimes unpredictably. These interactions transformed NGOs and their projects and served as the critical link between development models, organizational types, and international trends on the one hand and NGOs' mixed outcomes on the other. Thus, abstract questions about the "right" or "wrong" development model or NGO type were misplaced, because models and types did not convert predictably into actual practices and experiences.

I concluded that despite my original hopes to the contrary, case studies of particular projects could not arbitrate abstract debates about the "best" development or NGO models. The contingent nature of the NGOs' respective projects indicated that the best I could do was to generalize about development's interactional terrain, rather than the value of particular development technologies, approaches, or organizations. Applying an agent-based approach to the comparison between Namaste and the Fraternity revealed generalizable tensions that result from the plurality of dispositions, goals, and meanings that exist within *any* given NGO-led development intervention, even those (like Namaste and the Fraternity) that embody diverging development models, organizational types, or international trends.

In subsequent conversations, scholars who study very different projects, from those focused on disaster relief to those focused on assisting former sex workers, have reported that the tensions I identified for development NGOs resonate with them as well. Thus, I suspect that the tensions uncovered here are common even beyond the field of development. I do not believe resources need to be changing hands for these tensions to occur, as the coming together of diverse lifeworlds and multiple, at times contrasting, organizational goals characterize a wide variety of internationally stretched projects, which can be seen as various forms of "global social engineering" (Bierschenk 2014) that, while influential, are never coherent.

These tensions—resulting from intersecting lifeworlds and the confluence of NGOs' organizational and developmental goals—may be inevitable, but they are not resolved in predictable ways. Rather, they are productive in the sense of generating multiple potential meanings and actions, enabling some forms of agency while constraining others. They thus ensure room for maneuver in even the most meticulously planned projects and challenge attempts at prediction and "scaling up."

When Simplified Views of the Other Collide

Development insiders and scholars alike have noted the tendency of policymakers to rely on stereotypical views of beneficiaries, creating reified categories for people or places as part of the process of rendering development "technical" (Trinh 1989; Mohanty 1991; Pigg 1992; Mosse 2003, 2005; Olivier de Sardan 2005; Soss 2005; Korf 2006; Li 2007). Project frames that represent beneficiaries according to social, demographic, or economic categories such as "the landless poor," "indigenous women," or "informal workers" serve to "stabiliz[e] and homogeniz[e] specific people within a larger group" (Craig and Porter 1997, 52). Doing so overlooks the diversity and ongoing dynamics within these groups and assumes subjectivities and cohesion that may not exist. While developers draw on simplified views of beneficiaries (often associated with a degree of powerlessness), they also draw on their own experiences and perceptions to imagine beneficiaries' needs and desires. Often these align with the needs and desires of developers themselves (Long 2001, 85–8). It is assumed that women in the global south wish to engage in paid labor outside the home and seek independence from their husbands (Pearson 2007; Kabeer 2011) or that informal workers want to expand their businesses.

In parallel fashion, those targeted by development interventions construct simplified conceptions of developers (Olivier de Sardan 2005), drawing on their own experiences to judge developers' power, needs, and desires. They compare development institutions to others with which they are familiar, generating expectations about what participation in them will entail. Based on their previous experiences with other developers, they are likely to ask for things that they expect developers to be willing and able to provide (Olivier de Sardan 2005). Indeed, ethnographers have found that "even in the most remote village of the third world, people have developed an impressive capacity for decoding the language of the project offers on hand. . . . They rapidly sense whether to talk of 'poverty,' 'gender,' 'care for the environment,' or 'small business dynamism'" (De Herdt and Bastiaensen 2007, 877). In this context, "participatory sessions" may act as "schools" where the poor develop expectations of developers and "learn to speak in the global language of poverty and development" (De Herdt and Bastiaensen 2007, 877). Thus developers' and beneficiaries' meanings and expectations alike are grounded in simplified views of each other, informed by their respective past experiences and sociomaterial surroundings, and in many cases contribute to the reproduction and repackaging of past projects.

Simplified views of the other are also connected to varying views of development interventions themselves. Based on their views of beneficiaries' levels of need, policymakers and NGO leaders often see interventions as "central, omnipresent, unique" (Olivier de Sardan 2005, 33) and ask workers and beneficiaries to give projects more time, energy, and importance than they are willing or able to give. Funders and policymakers often suffer from "amnesia" (Lewis 2009, 34; Bierschenk 2014, 89) when it comes to previous projects (Bierschenk, Elwert, and Kohnert 1993; Richards 1985), living in the "perpetual present" (Lewis 2009, 33) in part because they tend to be embedded in their own cognitive structures, knowledge systems, and communication channels that exist apart from those of local contexts and subjectivities (Bierschenk 2014). As a result, failed technologies or approaches often reappear as "new" development in the eyes of "experts." In other cases, projects may simply be repackaged using the latest rhetoric (Bierschenk 2014, 91).

Policymakers and funders may be prone to amnesia, but beneficiaries are not. Instead, they consider interventions in light of their previous experiences and knowledge of other projects (Hilhorst 2003) and are thus likely to see interventions as "temporary, relative, and incidental—just another link in a chain of consecutive interventions" (Olivier de Sardan 2005, 33). Development workers are likely to have their own views of the intervention, seeing it as philanthropy, a job similar to previously held positions, or a stepping-stone to something more prestigious. Some may be motivated by altruism, but others may not even believe in the principles of the intervention at hand.

In sum, when different lifeworlds meet at development's interfaces, developers and beneficiaries alike construct and act on simplified conceptions of each other while maintaining more nuanced views of themselves, thus assigning various meanings and goals to development projects and experiencing these projects differently. Because their goals, expectations, and meanings arise from their different histories and networks, communication and relational practices at development's interfaces proceed through series of "mutual misunderstanding[s]" that open up room for negotiation and interpretation (Rossi 2004, 559; see Marsland 2006).

When simplified views of the other collide—both with their opposition and with real people—it can lead to a variety of interactions: beneficiaries may talk back to stereotypes, act in ways that challenge policymakers' assumptions, or play into higher-ups' simplified views of them in order to access benefits which they assume developers are able to distribute. Policymakers, for their part, may readjust their policies to better fit the complexity of the social reality they find on the ground or allow for a decoupling of policy and practice to simultaneously satisfy funders and beneficiaries, among other responses (Meyer and Rowan 1977). Workers might leverage stereotypes of the "backward" beneficiaries to NGO leaders to explain unsatisfying results while simultaneously relying on stereotypes of "prestigious" or "demanding" policymakers/NGO leaders to pressure beneficiaries to comply with expectations (Sharma 2014; Lewis and Mosse 2006).

When Developmental Goals Meet Organizational Goals

In the field of development NGOs, tensions additionally arise from the intersection of NGOs' developmental and organizational drives. Development NGOs are value-based organizations that are guided by distinct worldviews (Lissner 1977; Kilby 2006), including visions of development, *and* by typical organizational pressures. Yet developmental goals and organizational pressures often run in opposite directions. Development NGOs of *all* stripes— foreign and grassroots, Western and indigenous, bureaucratic and charismatic, secular and religious, bootstrap and holistic—seek to "help" but also to govern their beneficiaries. Their desire to govern beneficiaries is understandable because even when NGOs control the distribution of resources, their ability to achieve their particular visions of development depends on beneficiaries utilizing these resources in ways that advance their broader, long-term goals (Li 2007). Thus, they work to create subjects that are both instrumental to and constitutive of their visions of development (Mosse 2005, 6; Adams and Pigg 2005; Li 2007; Swidler and Watkins 2009). The result is that NGOs inevitably undertake moralizing and managing work in the process of helping.

What is more, as organizations generally accountable to external donors, NGOs inherently face high demands for effective management, requiring central control and meeting pre-established objectives. These demands often run counter to the messy reality of interactions on the ground and to the inefficient, uncertain, and undisciplined nature of bottom-up participation, helping to explain why behind participatory rhetoric, one often finds "projects as usual" (Craig and Porter 1997; Mosse 2003, 2005; Quarles van Ufford 1993; Nauta 2006).[7] In their desire to help, development NGOs aim for lofty goals but, unlike firms, lack "specific technologies with known relationships between inputs and outputs" (Watkins, Swidler, and Hannan 2012, 289). These lofty goals often include transforming beneficiaries' lives in ways that make further projects unnecessary. Yet, as organizations, they crave predictable, reproducible, manageable processes and are influenced by system goals of their own long-term survival and growth (Bob 2001; Olivier de Sardan 2005; Watkins, Swidler, and Hannan 2012; Fox 2014; Krause 2014).

Developers may address this tension in a variety of ways, leveraging materials (forms, contracts, photographs) and monitoring and evaluation technologies (site visits, databases), as well as adjusting the ways that they frame their goals to make the situation more manageable. They may enlist ritualistic documentation and measurement techniques like logframes (logistical frameworks) to create a virtual reality in which cause-and-effect relationships predominate, unknowns are knowable, and projects are coherent and manageable (Craig and Porter 1997; Chambers 2010; Rossi 2004; Eyben 2007). By relying on reports, evaluations, databases, and surveys, policymakers and NGO leaders attempt to provide their funders and themselves a semblance of linearity, certainty, and coherence. Quantitative measurements, surveys of beneficiaries, headcounts at NGO activities, photographs, and detailed reports give the impression of certain relationships between inputs and outputs. Alternatively (or even simultaneously), they may leverage ignorance by neglecting to verify certain project characteristics or to measure particularly problematic outcomes (Quarles van Ufford 1993; Mosse 2003; see Bierschenk, Elwert, and Kohnert 1993; Arce and Long 1993). They may reframe goals in processual rather than "outcome-based" terms, or select measurable outcomes that are unproven proxies for those that are not so easily measured.

These conflicting developmental and organizational drives affect many aspects of NGOs' trajectories, including learning processes. As such, the relationship between "feedback" and subsequent policies and practices is neither automatic nor linear. Even policymakers, NGO leaders, and workers who believe deeply in an NGO's vision of development have a host of other goals, including status, job security, and a sense of purpose. Because these other goals are tied up with management and organizational survival, it is quite rare that evaluation leads to recognition of contingency or questioning the "whole idea of planned intervention and the rationality of planning," much less the project itself. Instead, one may interpret ambiguous feedback as proof of success, attribute failure to outside forces, or see failure as "the starting point for the elaboration of the next round of interventions" (Long 2001, 37). As a result "single-loop learning," concerned with improving organizational performance, is more common than "double-loop learning," concerned with questioning underlying power relations and worldviews (Ebrahim 2003, 109–10).

The tension between NGOs' development and organizational drives manifests in a number of ways, generating inconsistencies in NGO discourses and practices that in turn open up significant room for maneuver on the part of those involved in development. Beneficiaries may leverage discourses of helping in order to make claims on NGOs, hold workers to account, shift NGO activities to meet their own needs, or resist developers' attempts to govern their behavior. Workers may rely on anecdotes, headcounts, or quantitative measure to prove their effectiveness in order to keep their jobs. Leaders and policymakers may decouple policies, practice, and evaluation, maintaining distinct "frontstage" and "backstage" scripts (Lund 2001).

The agent-based approach applied in this book, and its recognition of development's central tensions, has implications for the ways we go about studying and pursuing development in the global south. Such an approach forces researchers and practitioners to view development interventions as a set of ongoing, contingent relationships rather than one-sided, static interventions on the part of the global north into the global south. In the face of development's inherent tensions, even workers and beneficiaries are afforded significant room for maneuver. By navigating and expanding that room to maneuver, they co-create development practices and experiences on the ground. This insight should lead researchers and practitioners to question their desire to locate best practices or scale up the best development models, because these models will never convert predictably into practices, experiences, and outcomes. It also means that researchers and practitioners should *expect* gaps between policies and practices and view them as valuable sources of information rather than flaws to be eliminated.

Finally, an agent-based approach and appreciation of development's central tensions help to explain why development projects persist even when they fail to live up to our expectations: operating based on multiple meanings and assigning various goals to development interventions, developers and beneficiaries' often interact to produce something not quite intended but something that can be recast by various agents as success (Long and Long 1992; Mosse 2005).

PLAN FOR THE BOOK

Chapter 2 provides a historical overview of development projects in Guatemala, demonstrating the multiple ways that international discourses and practices influenced but did not dictate local development efforts. Instead, they interacted with the sociopolitical context in which local actors (military and government forces, religious organizations, indigenous movements, grassroots NGOs, credit unions, and private businesses) exercised varying degrees of agency. This chapter demonstrates that these interactions often resulted in the repackaging of past projects, strategies, and discourses, contributing to projects' endurance even in the face of changing buzzwords. It also explains how NGOs came to be one of the key faces of development in many Guatemalan communities and how organizational diversity was able to persist even in the face of international pressures such that NGOs as different as Namaste and the Fraternity could coexist.

Chapters 3 through 6 focus on the organizational and individual levels of analysis, first for Namaste and then for the Fraternity. These chapters explore the NGOs' interactional prehistories, organizational trajectories, and resulting organizational characteristics, before delving into interactions at Namaste's and the Fraternity's interfaces to explore the processes by which beneficiaries form expectations of the NGOs and the quotidian and power-laden interactions between and among developers and beneficiaries.

Chapter 3 analyzes Namaste, demonstrating how its prehistory, rooted in Western business practices and social entrepreneurship, contributed to its model of bootstrap development, which focuses on resources, individuals, and cultivating self-sufficiency through engagement with the market. This history also informed Namaste's other organizational characteristics, including its values, bureaucratic structure, and embeddedness in foreign, rather than local, networks.

Chapter 4 zooms in further, focusing on the spaces that Namaste creates in carrying out its activities as concrete sites where employees and beneficiaries enact and transform bootstrap development, and where attempts to create entrepreneurial subjects are undertaken and reinterpreted. It highlights how women's initial interactions with Namaste inform their perception that Namaste is more or less just another MFI, which in turn shapes their expectations of the NGO and their participation. Once they enter Namaste, their expectations remain relatively unchallenged—Namaste values efficiency, specialization, and women's participation instrumentally. Women, for their part, continue to see Namaste as similar to other MFIs and their participation as a "cost" to access a loan; they thus participate at minimal, relatively uniform levels. Namaste attempts to cultivate "good entrepreneurial subjects" by using future loans as incentives and by offering explicit lessons about "good" behavior. Women in turn respond in a variety of ways—with hidden transcripts, guile, and accommodation. The chapter concludes by connecting the ongoing interactions in Namaste to the NGOs' mixed outcomes. Women participating in Namaste generally reap short-term economic benefits but rarely experience the positive spillover effects that are often attributed to NGOs generally, and to microcredit NGOs particularly.

Chapter 5 provides an organizational analysis of the Fraternity, a foreign-funded but locally founded and locally managed NGO that grew out of indigenous women's collective action in the Presbyterian Church. Connecting this prehistory with its subsequent trajectory, the chapter demonstrates how NGO leaders' fight for greater inclusion in religious spheres informed the NGO's holistic model of development and view of indigenous women's participation as intrinsically valuable. It then details the Fraternity's other organizational characteristics—its charismatic organizational structure and its strong international and local ties.

Chapter 6 begins by demonstrating that the Fraternity's local identity informs women's view of the Fraternity as not just another MFI but rather an extension of religious or ethnic networks. This means that women join for a greater variety of reasons than those who join Namaste, and carry with them diverse expectations for participation. Thereafter, the Fraternity struggles to balance its multiple, overlapping goals in ways that allow for creativity and numerous interactions, but also lead to a good deal of inefficiency and frustration. The Fraternity's policymakers and leaders view women as having intersecting identities and as members of groups rather than individuals and see their participation as intrinsically valuable. However, only some women share this view of their own participation—some see it as a cost, others see it as valuable, and still others enter the organization seeing their participation as a cost but eventually come to see it as valuable in its own right. This variety leads to diverse levels and forms of participation across women and across time. Throughout, the NGO attempts to cultivate "good, Christian, Mayan women" subjects, although women respond in multiple and sometimes unexpected ways to these attempts. The chapter concludes by connecting women's diverse experiences in the Fraternity to their uneven and mixed outcomes. The Fraternity has questionable effects on women's incomes but is able to significantly transform *some* women's self-esteem and identity. Yet the benefits of participation are uneven and at times the organization actually reinforces economic and social hierarchies among its members—demonstrating that empowerment and disempowerment can unfold simultaneously.

The concluding chapter reflects on the implications of an agent-based approach for the ways we study and pursue development in the global south. It demonstrates that an agent-based approach like the one pursued here shifts how we conceptualize development interventions, what we can expect of them, and what types of generalizations and normative questions we can address. Rather than viewing development as a northern intervention into the passive global south, we should instead see it as a set of relationships being worked out in a particular terrain that is characterized by inherent tensions and is navigated by people using different conceptual and experiential "maps." Therefore researchers and practitioners should not be surprised when they encounter gaps between policy, practice, and outcomes but should rather expect these gaps as the inevitable result of human agency and interaction. Rather than asking if development is successful or unsuccessful, we should ask what kinds of agency particular relationships constrain and what kinds of agency they enable.

CHAPTER TWO

REPACKAGING DEVELOPMENT IN GUATEMALA

Modern development's roots can be traced to the post–World War II period when the global north became concerned with postwar reconstruction, the status of newly independent colonies, and preventing communism in countries like Guatemala in the context of the Cold War. The world quickly became divided not just between East and West, but also between North and South, between developed and underdeveloped countries. Since that time, international trends in development thinking and practice have influenced communities around the globe. Yet, as this chapter demonstrates, even though Guatemala's political and economic trajectories were dramatically shaped by foreign influence, international discourses and practices did not enter barren landscapes, nor did they erode all that came before. Instead, they were filtered through Guatemala's unique national and local contexts—which were characterized by racism, entrenched agro-industrial elites, armed conflict, religious missions, and social mobilization—and were interpreted by a variety of actors who maintained significant room for maneuver on the ground. Even in the face of shifting international trends, Guatemala's past strategies and contradictions were often simply recycled and repackaged using the latest development buzzwords. The layering of old and new strategies and discourses, alongside the creative maneuvering of various actors, in turn have shaped the development landscape that NGOs like Namaste and the Fraternity inhabit today.

GUATEMALA'S BOLD NEW PROGRAM OF DEVELOPMENT
AND DEMOCRACY, CUT SHORT

In January 1949, when President Truman was announcing the United States' "bold new program" to extend the benefits of progress to "underdeveloped areas" (Truman in Esteva 1992, 6), Guatemala was undertaking a bold new program of its own. Juan José Arévalo Bermejo (1944–51) was introducing political and economic reforms that were unprecedented in the small country with a long history of dictatorship, inequality, and racism. Previously, Guatemalans had witnessed a long line of strongman leaders who had courted foreign investment by providing cheap land, control over the country's infrastructure and services, and special tax exemptions. These authoritarian leaders used repression to quell opposition and create a cheap, flexible labor force for the agro-export sector. They had instituted vagrancy laws, forced recruitment, and day labor laws that coerced indigenous and *ladino* (mixed indigenous and Hispanic) peasants to work on plantations or infrastructural projects for little or no pay, creating a system that "approximated slavery" (Way 2012, 30).

Guatemalans, however, had grown restless. Inspired by Roosevelt's Four Freedoms, land reform in Mexico, and the defeat of the Salvadoran dictator, a group of Guatemalans rebelled. The October Revolution ushered in "ten years of democratic spring" starting with Arévalo, the country's first president elected in free and fair elections. The Arévalo administration undertook a number of reforms based on democratic ideals, generating "perhaps the most liberal constitution in Latin America" (Immerman 1980, 631–32). He and his elected successor, Jacobo Árbenz Guzmán (1951–4), pursued largely capitalist policies aimed at diversifying the economy and encouraging investment through agricultural modernization and industrialization. They coupled these policies with social guarantees including a minimum wage, equal pay for men and women, union and collective bargaining rights, and public health and literacy programs. For his part, Árbenz undertook the most comprehensive land reform the country had ever seen.

These reforms inspired strong labor unions and the beginnings of land expropriation and redistribution, both of which threatened local elites and foreign firms. At the time, the country had one of the most unequal landholdings in the world, with just 2 percent of the population controlling 72 percent of the arable land (Trefzger 2002). By far the largest landholder was the United Fruit Company (UFCO), a U.S. firm whose tentacle-like influence had earned it the nickname *el pulpo* (the octopus) (Bucheli 2003). Árbenz made slow progress toward compensated expropriation and redistribution of land and began establishing Guatemalan-controlled services and infrastructure to compete with their foreign-controlled counterparts. In the context of the Cold War, these changes were enough to raise the specter of communism (Schlesinger and Kinzer 2005).

Before he could finish his term in office, Árbenz was overthrown in a U.S.-orchestrated and U.S.-sponsored coup that left him humiliated, stripped to his underwear, and paraded before the press before being sent into exile. Guatemala, the first among many countries in Latin America to experience U.S. intervention in the context of the Cold War, would not experience another democratic opening for three decades. Although the 1954 coup was perhaps the most dramatic expression of foreign actors' influence in Guatemala's trajectory, in fact this influence manifested itself in numerous other ways throughout the country's history, ensuring that Guatemala's fate (including its development) did not rest solely in its own hands (Chase-Dunn 2000). Unfortunately, international pressures often intertwined with national policies in ways that reinforced, rather than challenged, long-standing inequalities and contradictions.

MODERNIZATION THEORY INTERTWINES WITH COUNTERINSURGENCY IN GUATEMALA

Following the 1954 coup, subsequent Guatemalan governments reversed land redistribution and implemented agrarian policies that once again focused on accumulating wealth for the agro-exporting sector. The result was increasing rates of poverty in the countryside and rural-to-urban migration that put pressure on the swelling capital city. Fearing a leftist backlash in the context of the Cold War, the United States provided post-coup governments with substantial support in the form of security training and funding (to the tune of roughly $45 million) for military and development efforts—efforts that were in practice linked. Security training and military support produced the most effective military machine in Central America (Copeland 2012, 976). Meanwhile, Guatemalan and US leaders aimed at sapping the potential energy of leftist movements by targeting the urban and rural poor with development projects, often leveraging the themes of self-help through training and entrepreneurship and the development potential of credit and technology—themes that would later be reproduced and repackaged under neoliberalism. Central to international and national development strategies was the goal of transforming Guatemala's poor into modern subjects that were both instrumental to, and constitutive of, their visions of development.

Despite efforts to thwart oppositional forces, by 1960 discontented Guatemalans had taken to the hills to form guerrilla groups, marking the start of what would become thirty-six years of armed conflict. Thereafter, military leaders came to power through fraudulent elections and sent state forces to combat guerrilla forces, organized opposition, and innocent civilians. Throughout this long period of violence, state officials and their foreign partners alike "used globally discussed practices and technologies to bend development to help achieve their political goals" (Way 2012, 92). Rather than passive recipients, national actors actively engaged and transformed international ideas to achieve their own, often violent, ends.

Like efforts around the world at the time, development projects in Guatemala in the 1950s and 1960s were heavily influenced by modernization theory. Modernization theory posited that development was a teleological process of change from premodern societies with traditional social and cultural characteristics to modern, industrialized societies with Western values. Modernization-inspired development policies focused on macroeconomic growth, the benefits of which were assumed to trickle down to the poor. Large-scale, state-sponsored projects focused on industrialization and income-producing infrastructure in the 1950s and 1960s and agriculture and integrated rural development in the 1960s and 1970s, each relying heavily on external expertise and technological advances. The Green Revolution in particular promised to radically transform agriculture and combat famine through technology such as high-yield seeds, synthetic fertilizers, and improved irrigation infrastructure. In Guatemala, though, the Green Revolution and later development strategies took on a unique flavor as military leaders working with foreign counterparts combined modernization theory with anticommunism, weaving together militarization, development, and counterinsurgency (Way 2012).

In the area of agriculture, the Guatemalan government undertook half-hearted attempts to address land inequality through a number of underfunded programs that offered peasants technical support and credit and, occasionally, access to unused land (through the 1956 Agrarian Statute and 1962 Law of Agrarian Transformation). This strategy fell in line with the U.S. Alliance for Progress's gradual approach to land reform as an alternative to more radical redistributive policies (Copeland 2012). Within months of the 1954 coup, the idea emerged among organizations such as the Ford Foundation that Green Revolution technology could be "a valuable weapon in the battle against communism" (Carey 2009, 292). Soon after, Catholic Action,[1] the military government, Peace Corps volunteers, and the United States Agency for International

Development (USAID) began promoting synthetic fertilizers, pesticides, and nontraditional crops among Guatemalan peasants, which became widespread by the early 1960s. Successive Guatemalan military governments came to incorporate these into their civic action campaigns, which promoted development projects and controlled citizen participation as a central weapon in pacifying and "modernizing" the population and penetrating rural areas (Way 2012; Copeland 2012; Smith 1990).

By the early 1970s, USAID and the Guatemalan government had developed a series of initiatives to resolve Guatemala's agrarian problem that reflected the assumptions of modernization theory as well as the increasing pressure to focus on individuals' basic needs, a movement that arose globally in the 1960s and 1970s. Initiatives encouraged the cultivation of unused land in northern Guatemala by peasants and small- and medium-scale farmers, the commercialization of agriculture in the western Mayan highlands, and diversification of agricultural products nationally. These programs emphasized credit, technology (pesticides, fertilizers, and high-yield seeds), and training (in farming techniques, new inputs, home economics, and entrepreneurialism), and they focused on the cultivation of nontraditional crops for export. Funding for infrastructure projects that were meant to support these and similar development projects came from the World Bank and USAID (before 1961, under its precursor, the International Cooperation Administration), among others. As in other third world countries, meaningful land reform, which would have inevitably entailed extensive redistribution, was notably absent from these efforts.

Instead, the focus was on ways to improve productivity through utilizing previously undeveloped land, implementing technological innovation, and changing indigenous and ladino farmers' "backward" practices (Copeland 2012). These efforts reflected the dominant global understanding of poverty as resulting from poor resource use and coordination rather than structural inequality (Ebrahim 2003, 35–8). Just as in the context of some later microfinance programs, expanding market access through credit and training in the areas of agriculture was assumed to be modernizing and liberating—assisting in the cultivation of productive subjects and fomenting "the active and calculative aspects of market citizenship" (Copeland 2012, 988). These programs, like the NGOs and microfinance institutions (MFIs) that would follow, often relied on the organizing capacity of the poor—in this case by leveraging newly formed cooperatives or local "promoters" to disseminate technologies, modern methods, and ways of thinking alongside credit and resources (Way 2012; Copeland 2015).

At the macro level, implementation of agricultural modernization programs appeared to be successful. By the end of the 1970s, Guatemala had made substantial gains in agricultural production and was said to be on the brink of becoming an important exporter of nontraditional crops. Alongside attempts to address the agrarian problem, post-coup Guatemalan governments focused on industrialization, passing the Industrial Development Law (1959), and, with the aid of the Alliance for Progress, joining the Central American Common Market (1960). In so doing, Guatemala successfully attracted transnational corporations such as Coca-Cola, General Mills, and Cargill Central Soy. Foreign and domestic investment in manufacturing increased significantly, largely channeled into the capital-intensive production of consumer goods (Booth 1984). Throughout the 1960s and even late into the 1970s, Guatemala saw positive per capita GDP growth rates, fueled by agricultural diversification and gains in manufacturing.

Yet, because it failed to challenge the economic and political power of the agrarian-industrial-financial oligarchy, macroeconomic growth during this period was unevenly shared and had little effect on social indicators. Indeed, agricultural diversification and industrialization were actually accompanied by an increased concentration of wealth and rising inequality. The promotion of Green Revolution technology and nontraditional exports led to a concentration of land ownership, with medium- and large-scale farms benefiting the most from expansion policies for nontraditional, export-oriented crops. Those who could not afford expensive agricultural technologies and inputs could not compete and were often pressured to sell their land and migrate to urban areas. Agricultural strategies also contributed to cycles of famine and unemployment as agricultural goods were diverted to external markets and seasonal variations in labor requirements became more extreme. Perhaps more significantly, the focus on Green Revolution technology allowed the Guatemalan government and its U.S. allies to "increase economic growth without recognizing small-scale farmers' demands and strategies as legitimate" (Carey 2009, 293). It thus permitted national and international elites to focus on development as a technical challenge while simultaneously ignoring its political nature.

In urban areas, Guatemalans rarely found steady employment, despite the growing manufacturing sector. Manufacturing was largely based on foreign capital, faced a relatively small market, lacked significant ties to the agricultural sector, and was relatively capital-intensive. It therefore tended to generate too few jobs, was unable to absorb a growing population, and failed to make a meaningful dent in poverty.[2] Indeed, between 1970 and 1982, even in the face of significant gains in manufacturing, unemployment doubled (Booth 1984, 361). As a result, manufacturing growth in the 1960s and 1970s, "conditioned by the needs of monopoly capitalism" (Chinchilla 1977, 55), was accompanied by increased inequality of wealth and opportunity. Real wages and the working-class share of the national income declined, and ownership of industrial production in the country became more concentrated, to the benefit of a small group of foreign and national capitalists. The working class in Guatemala ended the period of macroeconomic growth both relatively and absolutely worse off.

Women in particular were hurt: even though they made significant contributions to production prior to industrialization, female industrial employment actually declined during this period, against the expectations of modernization theory (Chinchilla 1977, 54–5). Like modernization-inspired policies around the globe, development interventions in Guatemala were by and large targeted toward men. The assumption was that modernization would either be gender neutral or benefit women through their relationships with men (Kabeer 1994). Thus interventions were focused on macroeconomic growth, designed with male farmers or workers in mind, and ignored women as valid economic actors or agents of development. This was despite the fact that Guatemalan women had long been involved in agriculture and represented the driving engine behind the informal sector. Indeed, a 1970 survey of informal street vendors in Guatemala City found that 80 percent were female single heads of household (Way 2012, 75). Macro-level gains in the areas of agricultural technology and diversification and manufacturing did not trickle down to women and actually served to increase the importance of the informal sector in women's daily survival strategies.

Thus, the macroeconomic growth in the 1960s and early 1970s that resulted from the unique braiding together of war and development benefited only a small group of elite Guatemalans and a number of foreign enterprises. The vast majority of Guatemalans, especially the very poor and women, saw little to no improvement, and they often saw their socioeconomic situation worsen (Fischer 1996; Way 2012). The results of top-down, modernization-inspired development in Guatemala reflected the disappointing outcomes in other parts of the world.

ALTERNATIVE DEVELOPMENT BLOCKED
BY MILITARY REPRESSION IN GUATEMALA

The damning evidence of modernization-inspired projects' failure world-wide left many searching for alternatives. There was a growing recognition among international actors, academics and practitioners alike, that despite previous efforts, inequality and poverty seemed to be on the rise, and women and children were increasingly overrepresented among the poor. Dependency theorists had by this point convincingly called modernization theory into question, arguing that interactions with the global north systematically underdeveloped the global south. Liberation theology and critical pedagogy called for the poor to be actively involved in the struggle for a more just future (Freire 1970), and feminists highlighted the differential effects of development for women and men. The ideas of feminist scholars and practitioners coalesced in the global stage around the fields of women and development and later gender and development (Boserup 1970; Tinker 1976, 1982; Buvinic 1983; Staudt 1986; Jaquette and Staudt 1988; Moser 1989; Tinker 1990; Kabeer 1994). They successfully added gender equity and women's empowerment to the list of development goals.

Proponents of alternative development drew on these changes to push for radical projects of empowerment and social transformation. Instead of the top-down approach that had dominated mainstream development, they pushed for bottom-up approaches that "focused on building countervailing power to enable otherwise excluded social groups to mobilize collectively to define and claim their rights" (Cornwall and Brock 2005, 6). They looked to local NGOs, community-based organizations, and grassroots networks to push forward this bottom-up approach. Yet in the context of armed conflict and under a militarized state, bottom-up projects inspired by alternative development in Guatemala faced serious obstacles.

Previously, most Guatemalan NGOs had formed alongside religious missions or to capture funds funneled through USAID projects under the Alliance for Progress. But in the 1970s, when visions of alternative development were being articulated globally and social mobilization around socioeconomic demands in Guatemala increased, a number of NGOs began breaking with USAID and the conservative elements of the Catholic hierarchies to focus on work with the base (urban workers and peasants). They implemented popular organization and education aimed at social change. Although the number of Guatemalan NGOs remained small at this time, the NGO sector in the country began demonstrating "a considerable level of organization," and "the movement around NGOs was quite dynamic." Perceived links between "radical" clergy, guerrilla groups, civil society groups, and NGOs drew the attention of the military government. While progressive NGOs attempted to distance themselves from the state, government actors "conscious of the organizational power that these NGO managed" resisted their autonomy (AVANCSO-IDESAC 1990, 24).

The 7.5 M_w earthquake of February 4, 1976—which killed 23,000, injured 76,000, and destroyed whole towns—increased international funding and "shook a population that was already relatively radicalized" (Levenson 2002, 61). Many international organizations and foreign governments channeled humanitarian aid through NGOs instead of the Guatemalan government, which was perceived as corrupt and inefficient. The sudden influx of aid, increased levels of need, and religious discourses that focused on the plight of the poor stimulated the foundation of new NGOs and the strengthening of existing NGOs. Many civil society groups, especially those based in the capital city, mobilized around the state's failed response to the earthquake—turning the natural disaster into an event with political repercussions.

Increased activism on the part of civil society organizations in the wake of the 1976 earthquake, the Sandinistas' victory in Nicaragua (1979), and the unification of Guatemalan guerrilla forces (1982) threatened the military government in the late 1970s and early 1980s. At the same time, the country was experiencing a dramatic economic downturn sparked by the Latin American debt crisis, contributing to authoritarian leaders' sense of insecurity. Governments under Presidents Fernando Romeo Lucas García (1978–82) and Efraín Ríos Montt (1982–3) responded with brutal crackdowns on all forms of associational life, dramatically reducing the possibility of bottom-up development. Community groups undertaking infrastructure projects, "all local leaders, mayors, teachers, traditional Mayan leaders," and even people who had been named to cooperatives by government agents themselves became targets as the government's list of suspicious activities became more extensive (Thorp, Caumartin, and Gray-Molina 2006, 463; North 1998).

During this time, the military turned its attention from urban centers to the rural highlands, coupling acts of genocide against civilians with targeted development schemes. Armed forces carried out scorched-earth campaigns in which entire communities were massacred and their houses, animals, and crops were burned to the ground. Roughly six hundred communities were completely eliminated. One million people were displaced and at least fifty thousand were forced into permanent exile during this period alone. Many NGOs, community associations, and progressive churches fled or suspended

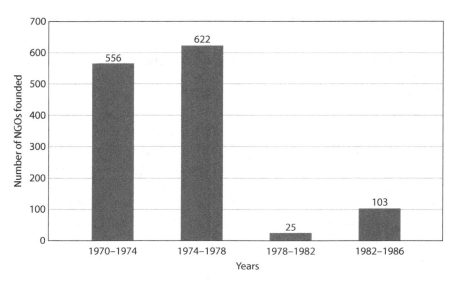

FIGURE 2.1. Number of NGOs founded by period (CEIDEC 1993, 130).

their operations out of fear of government crackdowns. As a result, only twenty-five NGOs were founded between 1978 and 1982, compared to 622 founded in the previous four-year period (figure 2.1).

In the aftermath of the violent counterinsurgency campaign of the early 1980s, the military state embarked on a new phase in which it attempted to deal with the "human and economic wreckage it had wrought in three years of burning, looting, and murdering of highland peasants" (Smith 1990, 10). Lucas García had by and large ignored development initiatives in favor of counter-insurgency; but Ríos Montt's program of *frijoles y fusiles* (beans and rifles) linked the two. At the center of these efforts were development poles—areas targeted for development projects and controlled citizen participation. Model villages in these areas served as new towns for displaced Guatemalans, where development projects could be pursued and populations could be monitored. As part of this plan, the military governments invested in strategic roads, es-tablished work-for-food programs, promoted export-oriented agriculture, and introduced agricultural training and technology in the final phase of Gua-temala's "military-led, blood-soaked Green Revolution" (Way 2012, 8). While the military itself provided limited direct development aid, the creation of model villages effectively served to extend its reach, militarizing the country-side and altering highland economies (Smith 1990).

Now more than ever, the military depicted itself as the creator of a new Guatemala; indigenous communities organized into development poles were seen as children "needing to be disciplined, 'ladinoized,' entrepreneurialized" (Schirmer in Ybarra 2011, 800). Part of this process included inculcating values of self-improvement and self-help. As General Hector Gramajo (defense minister from 1987 to 1990) explained, "we must forge *el pueblo* to force it to study, forge it to excel. . . . We in Civil Affairs don't give away anything [free]; *el pueblo* must earn everything [it receives]. There is no paternalism [involved]. But when they forge themselves, they do so by themselves, they are going to be free" (Schirmer 1999, 114). Later, while earning his degree at Harvard University, Gramajo explained that his "70 percent–30 percent civil affairs program, used by the Guatemalan government during the 1980s to control people or organizations who disagreed with the government . . . provide[d] development for 70 percent of the population, while [killing] 30 percent." He argued that this was a "more humanitarian, and less costly strategy" than murdering 100 percent of the population (Gramajo in Chomsky 2015, 40).

Óscar Humberto Mejía Victores overthrew Ríos Montt in a coup in 1983 and, as president, allowed for the controlled entry into conflict areas of NGOs that were affiliates of foreign organizations, most notably USAID and right-wing North American fundamentalist churches. He saw these types of NGOs as modern imports and significantly safer than other NGOs, which he viewed as potential threats to the government's authority. With guerrilla forces effectively decimated, and in the face of mounting international pressure for peace, military forces allowed for a gradual democratic opening in 1985. Democratization in Guatemala occurred at the same time that neoliberal priorities were becoming firmly entrenched internationally, influencing the subsequent contours of Guatemalan development.

The strategies adopted during periods of economic growth in the 1960s and 1970s and the subsequent downturn in the 1980s, rather than tackling the root causes of conflict, combined militarization and repression with development efforts. They resulted in, and indeed depended on, increased ethnic, class, and gender inequality (Fischer 1996; Way 2012). Rather than representing a break with past patterns and contradictions, development strategies in the subsequent neoliberal era would often simply repackage them using the latest development trends and buzzwords.

NEOLIBERAL DEVELOPMENT IN GUATEMALA

Proponents of alternative development in the 1970s may have faced serious obstacles in Guatemala, but elsewhere they had succeeded in placing the goals of poverty alleviation and human resources onto many mainstream development agendas, if only rhetorically. Yet by the 1980s, the mounting oil and debt crises, developing countries' balance of payment problems, and the political developments in the United States and United Kingdom under Reagan and Thatcher refocused attention on macroeconomic growth and reinstated technical and economist solutions to development that harkened back to the days of modernization theory (Cornwall and Brock 2005). This time, however, neoliberal prescriptions positioned the state as the problem, rather than the solution to development. By the end of the 1980s, structural adjustment plans that enforced neoliberal prescriptions across the global south had dramatically reduced public expenditures as the market replaced the state as the locus of development.

Worldwide, governmental and nongovernmental initiatives alike were influenced by the tenets of new public management, which sought to reform social service delivery by leveraging markets, incentives, and targets—fitting well with the neoliberal agenda. In the field of development, it encouraged such principles as "purchaser/provider split in public service provision" (ensuring beneficiaries contributed to the costs of social goods) and improving accounting transparency by using quantifiable indicators (Lewis and Kanji 2009, 41–2). In this atmosphere, feminist practitioners and scholars were forced to make their arguments for women's inclusion in development initiatives based on efficiency. They argued that including women would maximize returns on development investments. Rather than arguing that "women needed development," they argued that "development needed women" (Kabeer 1994, 25). Women's empowerment thus became an acceptable mainstream objective in the neoliberal era, not because of its radical connotations of shifting power relations but because it was linked to a "'do-it-for-yourself' ethos" that aligned with neoliberalism's emphasis on individual responsibility (Cornwall and Brock 2005, 7).

Guatemala's democratic opening in the mid-1980s, and the signing of the peace accords a decade later (in 1996), brought dramatic increases in international funding (see figures 2.2 and 2.3). Because democratization and the peace process occurred at the same time that neoliberal priorities were becoming firmly entrenched internationally, formal peace "came to Guatemala hand in hand with open markets" (McAllister and Nelson 2013, 17). Much of the international funding to support the implementation of the accords came as loans with conditions attached. The International Monetary Fund (IMF), the Consultative Group of Experts, the Inter-American Development Bank (IDB), and the World Bank, among others, pressured the Guatemalan government to eliminate state subsidies, liberalize trade policies, privatize national

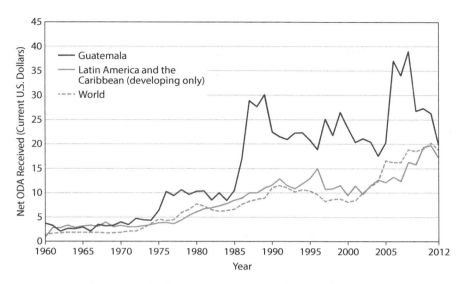

FIGURE 2.2. Net official development assistance (ODA) received per capita
(World Bank 1960–2012).

enterprises, and improve public sector capacity.[3] In the mid-1990s, they found
an especially receptive audience in President Álvaro Arzú Irigoyen and his
National Action Party (PAN), which hastened and deepened the process of
neoliberal transformation that had been initiated half-heartedly in the mid-
1980s. Arzú privatized a number of state agencies and eliminated government-
sponsored programs in the face of austerity cuts, enlisting instead private corporations, NGOs, and market-oriented development projects.

Influenced by USAID's aggressive promotion of an export-led development
strategy, the Guatemalan government welcomed maquiladoras[4] and extractive
industries as part of the country's liberalization and industrialization efforts.
The results were dramatic. In under a decade (between 1985 and 1993), the
maquiladora industry expanded more than twenty-five times (Petersen 1994).
By the early years of the next century, the number of people—around 80 percent women—working in the mostly Korean-owned maquiladoras was nearly
three times what it had been just a decade earlier (Way 2012, 191–2). Similarly,
after the implementation of a 1996 mining law[5] that opened Guatemala to
foreign investment in extraction on very favorable terms, foreign investment
in natural resource exploitation (at times financed by World Bank loans) increased dramatically, leading to sometimes violent clashes with local populations that continue to this day.

Economic growth through regional integration and free trade was aggres-

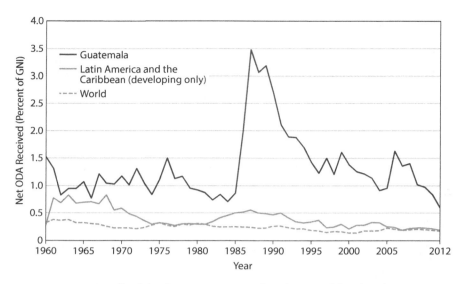

FIGURE 2.3. Net official development assistance (ODA) received (% of GNI) (World Bank 1960–2012).

sively pursued with the Mexico–Northern Triangle Free Trade Agreement (2000–1), the Plan Puebla-Panama (PPP, 2004), and the Central American Free Trade Agreement (DR-CAFTA, signed in 2004 and put in effect in 2006). As part of trade liberalization, President Arzú reduced tariffs for agricultural goods including yellow corn, exacerbating the precarious nature of *campesinos*' livelihoods and contributing to the corn crisis. The PAN government also reversed a congressional approval of a progressive generic drugs law in order to ensure membership in CAFTA and avoid cuts in U.S. aid. As a result, despite being the largest maquiladora drug producer in Central America and committed to expanding health care by the peace accords, Guatemala continued to have some of the highest prices for medicine in the region. The Guatemalan government, drawing on foreign support, also began the process of privatization by selling the national telephone company, inviting in private energy firms, and freeing up land for privatization to increase efficiency and production, with negative effects for Guatemala's poor and working class.

Support for agricultural extension and investigation declined following the democratic opening and eventual peace process, and the agricultural programs that remained often recycled previous strategies, tying them even more explicitly to market-based solutions. In Chimaltenango, for example, USAID funded horticulture projects in the 1980s that privatized land, introduced nontraditional crops that were more labor-intensive but less land-intensive, and focused on providing access to the technology and credit needed to purchase chemical fertilizers, fungicides, and pesticides that new crops required (Smith 1990, 23–4). By the late 1990s, the earlier focus on training was abandoned in the most significant agricultural projects funded by international organizations. World Bank loans sponsored market-assisted land reform, which aimed at regularizing and formalizing existing property rights and promoting a "willing-buyer, willing-seller model" for land redistribution, facilitated by subsidized loans (World Bank Independent Evaluation Group 2010, ix). Again, credit was a fundamental aspect of this project. As part of the program, beneficiaries could receive financing through a government agency, Fontierras, to use toward the purchase of land. The assumption was that requiring beneficiaries to take on debt would screen out applicants with limited commitment to make productive use out of the land (in contrast to outright redistribution). Subsequent evaluations, however, found that the terms of loans were not explained or understood and families were often left indebted. A decade after the program's start, roughly 60 percent of the Fontierras loan portfolio was classified as at risk (World Bank Independent Evaluation Group 2010, 19).

In many ways, the results of these interventions echoed earlier patterns during the Green Revolution. As before, development programs resulted only in the further concentration of land ownership and exacerbation of existing inequalities (Ybarra 2008; Milian and Grandia 2013). Many areas became more dependent on agriculture, but most of those employed in this sector were now working land that was not their own. Those who maintained their own plots increasingly needed cash to do so, given the rising prices of synthetic fertilizers, fungicides, and pesticides, upon which they had become dependent. Unemployment increased as residents migrated from the countryside to cities seeking work and as the armed forces (once a significant employer) reduced in size. The growing supply of unemployed Guatemalans and the "desperateness of their situation" drove wages down (Smith 1990, 32).

Despite assumptions about the empowerment and productivity gains that would come with private property rights, there was little evidence that tenure security or productivity had increased as a result of market-assisted agrarian reform. In fact, regularization of land tenure actually facilitated land speculation and land grabs on the part of more powerful cattle ranchers and agroexporters eager to expand the production of export crops such as African palm. This pattern vividly demonstrated "how the latest tools of the transnational corporate economy, such as World Bank land administration programs, inadvertently reinforce[d] traditional landed elites . . . whose tactics and operations [had] changed remarkably little since the colonial period" (Grandia 2012, 170; see also Ybarra 2008).

Despite the failure of previous programs based on Green Revolution technology and nontraditional crops to address inequality, as late as 2007 the World Bank continued to hold up the country's macro-successes in growing nontraditional crops such as broccoli and raspberries as evidence that countries dependent on agriculture, "with its attendant poverty and inequalities," are still capable of sustaining "spectacular growth" (McAllister and Nelson 2013, 27).

CASTING NGOS AS THE MAGIC BULLET FOR DEVELOPMENT IN THE 1980S AND 1990S

Although they have a much longer history (see Lissner 1977; Lewis 2009), development NGOs rose to international prominence during this neoliberal era, quickly becoming the "new sweethearts of the development sector" (Banks and Hulme 2012, 5). For different reasons, incorporating NGOs into development agendas appealed to a wide variety of stakeholders (Korten 1990; Lewis 2009). Neoliberal proponents argued that NGOs would be better able to carry out social projects than national governments because they were small, flexible, and innovative; they were therefore better equipped to identify and address local needs (Clark 1991; Paul and Israel 1991). They were also thought to be more efficient and less corrupt than governments in developing countries and capable of filling the gaps that the retreating state had left behind. Ideally, NGOs could act as a safety net for women and children, who were overrepresented among the economic losers of structural adjustment programs (Alvarez 1999). Thus, NGOs were seen as allowing for structural adjustment with a "human face" (Cornia, Jolly, and Stewart 1987) and were depicted as the "*preferred channel* for service provision, in *deliberate substitution* for the state" (Edwards and Hulme 1996, 4).

Others, reflecting the hopes of alternative development, thought that because of their grassroots connections and participatory nature, NGOs could promote a more empowering, sustainable development (Sen and Grown 1987; Carroll 1992; Fisher 1993; Bebbington 2004). Those who saw development as a radical project of empowering the poor thought NGOs could act as counter-publics, where members of the subaltern could "invent and circulate counter-discourses" and "formulate oppositional interpretations of their identities, interests, and needs" (Fraser 1990, 67; see Korten 1990). Leftist thinkers saw NGOs as potential embodiments of new politics that avoided "the capture of state power and the centralizing tendencies of the Marxist-Leninist movements" while still maintaining a "commitment to a structural transformation of society" (Clarke 1998, 40). Feminists hoped that NGOs could provide women spaces of legitimate mobility and the reflexive vantage point from which they could question their given relationships and imagine different realities (Kabeer 2011).

Across much of the developing world, NGOs increased rapidly. The number of NGOs working in more than one country increased tenfold between the mid-1980s and the mid-1990s alone. The NGOs in the Philippines increased by 148 percent in roughly a decade (between 1984 and 1993), more than doubling the growth rate of private sector organizations. In Kenya, the number of NGOs increased by 229 percent between the mid-1970s and the late 1980s, and by the mid-1990s, 40 to 50 percent of education in Kenya was provided by NGOs (Hofer 2003; Hulme and Edwards 1997; Agg 2006). By the early 1990s, Brazil and India were each home to more than 100,000 NGOs (Clarke 1998). These organizations became key actors in development, receiving funds that rivaled, and in some cases surpassed, that of their government counterparts (Banks and Hulme 2012). And with women and development increasingly linked, NGOs focusing on women became one of the fastest growing groups within the NGO sector (Silliman 1999, 25).

By the late 1990s, international development discourse had coalesced around the new policy agenda based on the twin goals of neoliberalism and good governance (Lewis 1998; Lewis and Kanji 2009). Increasingly, NGOs were seen not only as agents of development and efficient providers of goods and services, but also as "vehicles for democratization and as essential components of a thriving civil society" (Hulme and Edwards quoted in Murdock 2008, 31; see also Alvarez 1999; Banks and Hulme 2012). Between 1995 and 2000, 35 percent of U.S. aid and 40 percent of the World Bank's sponsored projects involved NGOs (the latter up from 10 percent just a decade earlier) (Hofer 2003, 383–4). While in the mid-1990s, more than $1 billion of aid worldwide was being channeled through NGOs, by 2004, that number had risen to $23 billion, representing 30 percent of overseas development assistance (Rooy 1998; Riddell 2007). Still, despite the rhetoric of building civil societies and spreading democratic institutions and values, the vast majority of NGOs and NGO funding remained squarely focused on the delivery of goods and services (Werker and Ahmed 2008, 76). Increases in funding for NGOs fundamentally changed the way that people in developing countries interfaced with development; by 2002 NGOs were thought to affect the lives of roughly 250 million people in the global south (Haque 2002, 412).

Following the signing of the 1996 peace accords in Guatemala, private actors such as NGOs were cast as central to expanding social services (as required by the accords) and to combating the inequality and marginalization that had contributed to the armed conflict. Guatemalan NGOs were also promoted in hopes of rebuilding a civil society damaged by decades of violence and of improving democratic quality and consolidation after years of authoritarian rule (Ruthrauff 1998, Beck 2014). The NGOs were seen as particularly attractive and gained considerable influence in the Guatemalan context, which was characterized by a weak state with limited territorial reach. Additionally, a focus on NGOs fit well with the peace accords, which emphasized citizen participation, civil society, and decentralization in response to local social mobilization and global ideas. In response to the accords' foci on inequality, women's rights, and indigenous rights—and to the broader trends in the field of international development—poverty alleviation and human resource development was emphasized and development programs targeted poor communities, indigenous people, and women.[6]

By this point, the Guatemalan development terrain was already populated by NGOs, public and private training institutes, trade associations, and development organizations (Way 2012, 125). But the NGOization of development became further entrenched following the signing of the peace accords, when there seemed to be a "magical abundance" in which upon submitting the proper paperwork, "you too could start a Mayan women's organization or turn a struggling coffee plantation into an organic fair trade cooperative" (McAllister and Nelson 2013, 34). The Guatemalan landscape became densely populated by foreign as well as locally led *proyectos* (projects), creating a marketplace that rewarded "Pedro Proyectos": those who were "adept at *gestionando*, or maneuvering through the complex paperwork, new languages, and bookkeeping requirements necessary to bring projects and money to their locales" (McAllister and Nelson 2013, 35).

Much of this NGOization was driven by attempts to expand social services, as required by internationally backed peace accords, at the same time the size of the government was shrinking, as required by international financial institutions.[7] For example, committed by accords to increase spending on health and encourage social participation in health care reform, in 1997 the Guatemalan government implemented a national health sector reform, largely financed by IDB. The new Comprehensive Health Care System (Sistema Integral de Atención de Salud, SIAS) provided the foundation for the partial privatization of health care by allowing the health ministry to contract private organizations—largely NGOs—in the administration of health care. The

Ministry of Health's "outsourcing" of its activities "moved small NGOs into the business of filling gaps in areas of the country where the state's activities have been suspended or attenuated" (Rohloff, Díaz, and Dasgupta 2011, 429). The privatization of health, alongside other social services and development projects, contributed to a "proliferating patchwork of small and foreign NGOs" (Rohloff, Díaz, and Dasgupta 2011, 428) such that NGOs, for good or for bad, became the face of development for many poor Guatemalans.

The new policy agenda emerging at the end of the 1990s also encouraged NGOs to change their very nature. The twin goals of neoliberalism and good governance put pressure on NGOs to act as efficient subcontractors for states and surrogates for civil society. The demands of these roles, as well as those of new public management, meant that donors and government agencies favored NGOs that were professionalized, technically adept, specialized, and focused on policy or goods/services provision rather than popular education, mobilization, or advocacy (Alvarez 1999). These organizations were pressured to demonstrate measureable results in the short term, comply with donor requirements for evaluation and reporting, and interact with government officials and international donors as experts. As a result, some NGOs looked for staff with formal educations, converted their goals into quantifiable targets, focused on demonstrating efficiency and effectiveness, and incorporated new forms of paperwork alongside new processes of monitoring and reporting. But pressures for professionalization and measurement did not yield uniform reactions. In Guatemala, some NGOs shifted their attention to measureable goals that would align with international pressures for evaluation and international buzzwords, others were able to ignore these pressures because they enjoyed alternative sources of support, and still others found ways to assign quantitative figures to their existing practices without altering them (see figure 2.4 for an example of the last).

NEW SOURCES OF FUNDING FOR DEVELOPMENT EFFORTS: SOCIAL ENTREPRENEURS AND RELIGIOUS ORGANIZATIONS

Toward the end of the 1990s and in the first few years of the 2000s, a new aid regime emerged that promised to "move beyond growth-focused neoliberalism" toward increased consultation with recipients, focus on poverty, and "responsibility for the nation-state" (Banks and Hulme 2012, 5). While scholars and practitioners alike had started bringing the state back into development and questioning the assumptions about NGOs' benefits, still popular discourses of empowerment, participation, and rights-based, people-focused

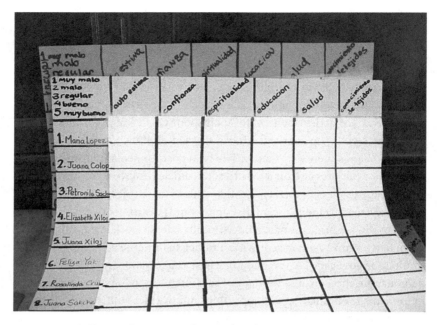

FIGURE 2.4. A Guatemalan NGO working with indigenous women attempts to quantify its goals, including self-esteem (*auto-estima*), confidence (*confianza*), spirituality (*espiritualidad*), education (*educación*), health (*salud*), and weaving expertise (*conocimiento de tejido*). Photograph by the author.

approaches ensured that NGOs, as "representatives" of the grassroots and government partners, enjoyed a continued role (Banks and Hulme 2012). Indeed, official development assistance (ODA) going to NGOs actually increased during this period, from roughly $7.3 billion in 2001 to somewhere between $15 billion and $27 billion by the end of the decade (Ronalds in Lewis 2014, 25).

These organizations also benefited from other sources of support beyond ODA. Some NGOs looked to social entrepreneurs, who were successful businessmen and women who leveraged market forces for social ends, deployed the techniques of venture capital investing in philanthropic decisions, or drew on business techniques to advance social missions. Business mentalities, characterized by "an entrepreneurial result-oriented framework, leverage, personal engagement, and impatience," entered into the field of development. This increased the availability of funding for development efforts and contributed to an increased focus on specialization, efficiency, measurement, accountability, and results-driven action (Foster in Edwards 2010, 25). This model of the entrepreneurial individual contributing to development attracted backing from foundations such as Ashoka, the Skoll Foundation, and the Schwab

Foundation (Thekaekara 2013). Many social entrepreneurs, like Namaste's founder and funders, found microfinance intuitively appealing as a form of social investing that leveraged both the market and women's innate entrepreneurial spirit in order to eradicate poverty. In 2010, public and private investors, including social investors, committed $3.6 billion to microfinance (Roodman 2012).

Those promoting development projects could also look to religious networks for support. With the increasing prominence of NGOs in development and democratization in the 1990s and beyond, a space was opened for the incorporation of religious NGOs (RNGOS),[8] like the Fraternity, in the field of development. Of course, religious missionary and charity work had a much longer history in the global south. But for much of that time, religious work stood separate from the broader field of international development, which was itself influenced by secularization theory (Ver Beek 2000). This led development institutions to ignore the role of faith in the lives of the poor and to limit their partnerships with missionaries, churches, and RNGOs. However, this began to change by the end of the 1990s in response to the growing political influence of evangelicals in the United States,[9] the call to include civil society in development, and the mobilization on the part of religious communities as exemplified by the Jubilee 2000 campaign to forgive developing countries' debts (Clarke 2007).

Religious NGOs have since become important partners in international development efforts, with government and international agencies enlisting them in service provision. While there is no reliable estimate on the number of RNGOs, "observers increasingly [recognize] that their numbers are huge and in all likelihood growing rapidly" (Lynch 2011, 22). Those RNGOs influenced by Christian churches, most dramatically evangelical denominations, have become especially influential in Africa and Latin America (Bornstein 2005). In Africa, it has been estimated that between 30 and 70 percent of health care is provided by religious NGOs, depending on the community (Lynch 2011, 22). In Central America, many Christian NGOs began working with microenterprise development starting in the mid-1990s, either focusing exclusively on such programs or adding them to their existing programming (Hoksbergen and Madrid 2000).

Religious NGOs are influential because of the resources they command, their territorial reach, and their long-standing relationships with remote, rural communities (Hearn 2002). Despite the growing field of NGO studies and recognition of RNGOs' increased influence, however, religiously driven NGOs have been largely understudied (but see Clarke 2010; Bornstein 2005; Hearn

2002; Occhipinti 2005). This lacuna limits our understanding of "what exactly 'faith-based' development is and how the [religious] orientation of an organization affects its mission and programming" (Haffernan 2007, 888).

THE CONVERGENCE OF INTERNATIONAL AND GUATEMALAN HISTORIES AROUND MICROFINANCE AND CULTURALLY APPROPRIATE DEVELOPMENT

During the "golden age" of NGOs, donors often judged NGOs based on their levels of professionalization and compliance with results-based action, as well as the degree to which NGOs' target populations and methods fit with the latest international trends. In Guatemala, international and national realities converged to promote NGOs that worked with indigenous groups and women and, especially among groups working with women, those that offered loans or microenterprise development. Yet even in the face of such international pressures, the institutional and development legacies of particular communities and organizations, as well as the agency of NGOs and other development actors, ensured continued diversity of such NGOs. International trends influenced, but did not determine, development initiative in Guatemala because they entered a field already populated with development legacies and actors with agency. I illustrate this point by drawing on histories that are particularly relevant for understanding the origins and trajectories of Namaste and the Fraternity: the histories of targeting women with microcredit and of religious groups and social movements targeting indigenous populations for development outreach.

Linking Women and Microcredit

By the 1980s and 1990s, women's empowerment had been well established as an important development issue. Because it fit well with the overall shift to neoliberal policies popular at the time, microcredit in particular was increasingly seen as a particularly attractive development tool for women. Microcredit, the provision of small loans to those who typically lack collateral, was a development technology pioneered and popularized by NGOs in South Asia such as the Grameen Bank, BRAC, and the Association for Social Advancement (ASA) and in Latin America by the Foundation for International Community Assistance (FINCA) and the Bolivian NGO PRODEM. Although the programs varied, they generally provided small loans at subsidized interest rates to undercapitalized entrepreneurs—mostly women working in the informal sector who might otherwise be beholden to usurious loan sharks. Depending on the program, these loans may have been accompanied by group payment meetings and other services such as consciousness raising or leadership training. Eventually, organizations started offering other financial services to the poor, such as flood insurance or savings accounts, and thus the term microfinance, rather than microcredit, came to be used. Microfinance institutions eventually included a variety of institutions including banks, credit unions, foundations, and NGOs.

Microfinance institutions (MFIs) often targeted women because they faced discrimination in accessing commercial loans, in part because they were less likely to be literate, have a credit history, and own collateral in their names. Women were also targeted because they were seen as more responsible clients. They were said to repay their loans more reliably and be more willing to form loan groups, which decreased the costs of delivering many small loans (Mayoux and Hartl 2009). It was also assumed that women would spend their increased incomes in ways that would spill over into other areas—on health care, nutrition, and education for their children. Providing loans to women was therefore seen as both inherently positive and instrumentally so, as women were assumed to channel the benefits of their productive labor into their reproductive labor. In this sense, microfinance sought to challenge traditional gender roles by providing women access to income, but it also relied on women maintaining their traditional gender roles as caretakers and living up to essentialist notions about women being more responsible and altruistic.

Some feminists hoped that microfinance would have the added benefit of empowering women and promoting gender equity. Increasing women's earning potential and giving them access to their own incomes was thought to generate virtuous spirals that would extend beyond the economic sphere, as illustrated in figure 2.5 (Mayoux and Hartl 2009; Hashemi, Schuler, and Riley 1996; Pitt and Khandker 1998).

Access to income was said to increase women's self-esteem and their bargaining power in the household (Kabeer 2001; Rahman 1986; Pitt, Khandker, and World Bank 1996). Participating in meetings with their loan groups was thought to increase women's mobility, expand and strengthen their social networks, enhance their capacity for collective action, and encourage them to question their given relationships (Sanyal 2009; Kabeer 2011). Thus microfinance was seen as a development intervention that would simultaneously meet women's practical needs to provide for themselves and their families and their strategic interests in challenging traditional gender relations. Women would become empowered as they became enriched (Kabeer 2001; Rahman 1986; Pitt and Khandker 1998; Sanyal 2009; Duffy-Tumasz 2009).

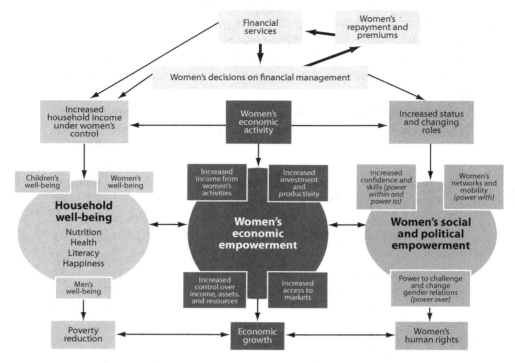

FIGURE 2.5. Microfinance and virtuous spirals for women's empowerment (Mayoux and Hartl 2009, 9).

Donors were particularly attracted to MFIs because they responded to demands to include women in development efforts and to compensate for the gendered effects of structural adjustment plans, while simultaneously encouraging market-led rather than state-led development. In the late 1980s, international trends that focused on microfinance as an important development tool reached Guatemala. International organizations channeled funds and technical support to microfinance projects in the country, repackaging the historical foci on credit and training (*capacitación*) and discourses of entrepreneurialism and self-help—this time applying them to women's long-standing survival strategies and networks in the informal sector.

Responding to the new international interest in microenterprises, USAID began to finance small and microenterprise projects in the 1980s, initially as part of broader strategies of agro-industrial and women's development. By the end of that decade, CARE, the Peace Corps, the International Institute for Development, and Catholic Relief Services, among others, had also turned their attention to supporting microenterprises, and some had begun to focus explicitly on microfinance as a development strategy (Canellas and McKean 1989). In 1988, USAID and Boston-based Accion International helped to establish Guatemala's most successful MFI, Fundación Genesis Empresarial (Genesis). Within two years the institution was autonomous and self-sustaining; today the MFI loans to roughly 170,000 clients, 64 percent of whom are women. They also supported other organizations such as the Foundation for the Development of Socio-Economic Programs (FUNDAP) in their provision of small loans and technical assistance to develop small-scale producers' "latent business skills" (Gutierrez 1990, 259).

Nationally, the Microenterprise Multiplier System (SIMME), a special project of the office of the vice president, Roberto Carpio Nicolle, "became identified as the government's centerpiece vis-à-vis the informal sector" (Otero 1994, 191). With the help of USAID, the Inter-American Development Bank (IDB), and the UN Development Program (UNDP), as well as funding from the European Economic Community (among others), SIMME contracted six NGOs to distribute subsidized loans and training to microenterprises in hopes of improving employment in urban areas (Canellas and McKean 1989; Blumberg 1995). The program was largely seen as a failure because it was too costly, inefficient, overly bureaucratic, plagued by problems of loan delinquency, and used for political purposes in the lead-up to the 1990 presidential elections (Almeyda and Branch 1998; Blumberg 2001).

Ironically, microfinance's rapid spread worldwide was also accompanied by foundational changes that arguably limited its ability to achieve the many goals that had been assigned to it. In microfinance's early years, the focus had been squarely on poverty alleviation, and MFIs had often targeted the poorest of the poor. They maintained low interest rates for their beneficiaries, many of whom lived in remote areas and were seen as high risk, by drawing on government subsidies or international donor funds. By the 1990s, however, international trends promoted the commercialization of microfinance, encouraging MFIs to generate sufficient profits from their loans to sustain themselves, with the aim of ensuring large-scale outreach and sustainability without the need for subsidies.

In the 1990s, the World Bank joined the microfinance "movement" and pushed for a new wave microfinance model that prioritized financial sustainability and commercialization. The core principles of this model included phasing out subsidies, offering small loans to income-generating activities that yielded quick returns to reduce the risk of default; initiating regular repayments soon after loans were distributed to "instill financial discipline";

setting interest rates high enough to cover costs; mobilizing women's savings; and implementing group delivery to reduce costs (Mayoux and Hartl 2009, 23; CGAP 2006). The emphasis was on offering a minimal package of financial services to the bankable poor and seeking cost recovery in the process (Kabeer and United Nations 2009). The push toward financial sustainability led to increasing specialization on the part of many newly established and long-standing MFIs, and discouraged offering costly education, training, health, or other services.

Many of the most famous MFIs worldwide answered the call, introducing commercializing changes including raising interest rates, expanding reach, and establishing joint ventures with private companies (Karim 2011). But "nowhere [did] the commercialization of microfinance [proceed] more rapidly than in Latin America" (Christen 2001, 1). The MFIs in Latin America became more financially self-sustaining and more profitable more quickly than their counterparts in Southeast Asia, and regulated financial institutions played a much larger role in the MFI sector. By the end of the century, commercial banks provided 29 percent of microcredit and licensed financial institutions (including those that had previously operated as NGOs) provided another 45 percent in the region (Christen 2001, 1). Since that time, the region's growth in the microfinance sector can be attributed largely to private investment, with microfinance capital from private sources growing at a rate of more than 50 percent a year in the early part of the twenty-first century (Micro Capital Institute 2004). Private investors have been attracted to Latin American MFIs, which are on average the most profitable in the world, earning returns that in many cases exceed those of commercial banks.

The commercialization of microfinance pushed by the new wave model was accompanied by its rapid spread. The number of people worldwide receiving small loans from MFIs increased consistently and dramatically in the 1990s and the following decade, as did the number of MFIs. Between 1997 and 2010, the number of borrowers (most of them women) increased more than fifteen-fold, from 13 million in 1997 to 205 million in 2010 (Maes and Reed 2012; Daley-Harris 2009; Hermes and Lensink 2007). In that same period, the number of MFIs reporting to the Microfinance Information Exchange Market (Mix Market) alone increased twenty-one-fold, from 72 in 1997 to 1,514 in 2010 (Mix Market 2013).[10] Microfinance's central place in development was highlighted when the United Nations declared 2005 the Year of Microcredit and Muhammad Yunus and the Grameen Bank jointly won the Nobel Peace Prize the following year. This created an environment in places like Guatemala in which MFIs, dependent on profits and expanding reach, competed against each other for the chance to offer women small loans. Today, microfinance in Latin America accounts for 45 percent of all lending and reaches eighteen million clients, the vast majority of whom are women (Bateman 2013, 14).

This new wave of microfinance entered a Guatemalan context that already had an established network of credit unions that distributed small loans to mostly men. International and national efforts aimed not just at establishing and partnering with microfinance NGOs like Genesis, but also at modernizing the approach of credit unions, which were popular lending institutions among the rural and urban poor. The USAID-funded World Council of Credit Unions (WOCCU) Cooperative Strengthening project (1987–94), for example, encouraged Guatemalan credit unions to decrease their reliance on external funding and to establish higher interest rates that were closer to market rates for private banks. The project rejected the traditional model of credit unions, which was "based on a theory that the rural poor lacked the resources necessary to save and fuel their development potential" (Richardson, Lennon, and Branch 1993, 3). In order to avoid a "'bail out' attitude," USAID conditioned continued assistance on adopting a new model that included a shift to "market-based, results-oriented business planning" (Richardson, Lennon, and Branch 1993, 4) and a commitment to managing credit unions as businesses. The National Credit Union Federation (FENACOAC) labeled new interest rates (based on credit unions' business, rather than social, orientation) the "entrepreneurial rate" (Almeyda and Branch 1998, 21).

In the decade following the signing of the peace accords, and in the face of the growing international enthusiasm for microfinance, the increase in the size, activity, and number of MFIs in Guatemala was "astounding" (McIntosh and Wydick 2005, 275). Commercial banks made forays into the microfinance market in the mid-1990s and quickly realized that lending to poor Guatemalans could be profitable. By 2009, fourteen out of eighteen commercial banks were providing microfinance loans, distributing $200,250,000 to 187,115 borrowers (Khavul, Chavez, and Bruton 2013). Credit unions, commercial banks, and NGOs increasingly found themselves competing for borrowers and undertook aggressive marketing and outreach strategies.

The international pressure to transition to the new wave of microfinance, which included expanded outreach, drove the thirst for more, and better-off, borrowers. For example, between 1988 and 1993, FUNDAP offered an average initial loan size of US$135 for businesses with an average of US$291 in monthly sales. By 1999, these figures had increased to US$543 in average initial loans and US$672 in average monthly sales, indicating that the MFI was lending to better-off clients with larger businesses (McIntosh and Wydick 2005). Soon, loan delinquency became a concern across the microfinance sector, sparking the formation of a credit bureau for MFIS (CREDIREF).[11] Within a few years, close to four hundred MFIs had joined the system.

While microfinance sectors in other regions (most notably South Asia) are dominated largely by NGOs, in Guatemala (as in many other Latin American countries), NGOs represent just one type of MFI. According to the most commonly cited estimates, Guatemala is now home to roughly two thousand formal and informal institutions that provide microcredit, including credit unions, nonprofit NGOs, private foundations, and commercial banks (Herrera Castillo 2003). The majority of microloans come from credit unions, commercial banks, or NGOs like Genesis that are concerned with financial sustainability, and thus most women encounter MFIs that are concerned with profits and hungry to expand. Today, women in many communities shop around among MFIs and have become increasingly knowledgeable about the intricacies of loan cycles, interest rates, and hidden fees. While some NGOs, such as the Fraternity, Fe y Alegría (Faith and Joy), and CARE, have tacked microfinance programs onto their existing (faith-based) activities with diverse results, others, like Namaste and Genesis, were founded with the explicit purpose of offering small loans to the poor. Among those, some have bought into the new wave microfinance model, others have accepted only some of its tenets, and still others have rejected it altogether.

In the microfinance sector, discourses about self-help and entrepreneurship that have a long history in Guatemala are repackaged. Many MFIs leverage images of smiling women in colorful *trajes* and emphasize that "entrepreneurial women" are "much more likely to focus on long-term generational impacts such as children's education, family health-care needs, and improvements to housing stock."[12] They celebrate the entrepreneurial spirit of Guatemala's population on their websites and in their pamphlets, stating that Guatemalans are "hard-working, enthusiastic people," and that microfinance works because "with a little, they can do a lot."[13] Similar discourses about "[overcoming] poverty through entrepreneurship," "helping to lift the poor to become self-reliant," and "helping aspiring entrepreneurs" to "work with dignity to support their families" are mirrored in a wide variety of MFIs, including commercial banks (BanCafé, Compartamos), international NGOs (FINCA, CARE, Mentors International, Social and Healthy Action for Rural Empowerment (SHARE), Friendship Bridge), and Guatemalan NGOs (FUNDAP, FONDESOL).[14]

Guatemala is "a country of small and informal businesses," with informal businesses representing 98.9 percent of firms (Khavul, Chavez, and Bruton

2013, 31) and employing three-quarters of the economically active population (Way 2012). Women remain overrepresented among managers of these unregistered, unlicensed, and often very small businesses. Formal lending practices and networks emanating out of MFIs complement rather than replace informal practices and networks (Khavul, Chavez, and Bruton 2013). Women often borrow from friends and family to repay loans to MFIs, or combine personal and MFI loans in order to meet their expenses. In rural areas, for example, roughly the same percentage of small farming businesses reported receiving loans from family or friends as did those borrowing from formal banks despite the fact that commercial banks have rapidly turned their attention to lending to the rural poor (Armendáriz et al. 2013, 110).

Women laboring in the informal sector had formerly been illegible to development actors who focused on women in their reproductive roles, but today national and international actors have recast these same women as "entrepreneurs" and their survival strategies as "microenterprises."[15] As with previous government or internationally led development interventions, many of the Guatemalan MFIs targeting women and the informal sector often leverage discourses of entrepreneurialism and self-help, and couple credit with mentorship (asesoría) and/or training (capacitación). In these programs, survival strategies of the poor, relabeled microenterprises, are seen as potential engines of employment and growth, and women's informal networks are often leveraged to improve efficiency and repayment. Images of women as possessing the willingness and "natural" ability to dedicate themselves to both their productive and reproductive roles are often central to these programs.

Missionaries and Movements Targeting Guatemala's Indigenous Populations

Starting in the 1980s, post-development theorists called the concept of development itself into question. They argued that development comprised discourses and practices that reproduced inequality and Western hegemony. Post-development scholars were especially influential in their call for the revaluation and regeneration of indigenous, local knowledge and values and alternative conceptions of the good life (Escobar 1995; Ferguson 1994; Sachs 1992). Despite their radical critiques, and as with alternative development ideas before them, post-development ideals were easily incorporated into the mainstream, where talk of culturally appropriate projects fit well with the push for state decentralization and privatization. By the 1990s, the idea of drawing on local cultural traditions to support grassroots development interventions was supported by the World Bank, the Inter-American Foundation, the Ford

Foundation, and the United Nations Research Institute for Social Development (UNRISD), resulting in 1988–97 being declared the World Decade for Cultural Development (Fischer 1996). The result was a "convergence between neoliberal political economic values and indigenous cultural difference" (De-Hart 2009, 69; see also Hale 2006).

Guatemala, a country in which roughly half of the population was indigenous (including twenty-three distinct ethnolinguistic groups), represented an attractive location in which to pursue such projects. But international actors and ideas promoting indigenous communities' involvement in Guatemalan development did not enter a vacuum. Indeed, there had been a long history of Protestant[16] involvement in indigenous communities and a more recent history of pan-Mayan activism, both of which are relevant to readers' understanding of the Fraternity's trajectory as an indigenous, religious NGO.

Protestants' involvement in Guatemalan development has taken both conservative and progressive forms. In the early twentieth century, Protestant missions began formal work among indigenous populations, eventually creating a "vast network of Protestant-run development projects" targeted at both ladino and indigenous rural populations and tying religious messages with "a whole body of secular values, standards, and models for living" (Garrard-Burnett 1989, 130). Although they initially encountered little success among indigenous populations, they were encouraged by Liberal administrations who appreciated the goods and services they provided and the "modern," capitalist values they promoted. After a period of disappointing conversion rates and stagnation in the 1920s and 1930s, Protestant missionaries aligned themselves with the leftist government of Arévalo over a shared opposition to the Catholic Church and a concern with literacy. They established Protestant-run schools that operated in close collaboration with government-sponsored literacy programs, founded institutes for the study of indigenous languages (to help integrate indigenous populations into the national school system), helped to strengthen labor unions, and supplied schoolbooks and teacher training to indigenous areas (Garrard-Burnett 1989; Fischer 1996).

In the following administration, President Árbenz's nationalism led to conflicts between the Guatemalan government and foreign Protestant missionaries, as most U.S. mission boards were staunchly anticommunist and opposed to Árbenz. Yet Guatemalan Protestants, especially those in indigenous communities in the western highlands, were actively involved in Árbenz's leftist policies—helping to administer land reform and leading peasant leagues (Garrard-Burnett 1989; Martin 1990). The diversity of Protestants' responses to Árbenz was facilitated by the fact that they lacked the direction of a single authority, such that churches in essence became "microcosms of their communities at large" (Garrard-Burnett 1998, 94). During the ten years of democratic spring, political controversies led to rifts between congregations, and many Guatemalan Protestants broke with their foreign missionary mentors. Indigenous Protestants in particular often cultivated a "new brand of indigenous, native Protestantism that rejected old foreign missionary forms but completely embraced the fundamental theology of Protestant Christianity" (Garrard-Burnett 1989, 138). In the years that followed, autonomous churches were established in the Mayan highlands, Protestant denominations splintered, and Bibles were translated into Mayan languages—all of which contributed to the growth of Protestantism among indigenous populations (Martin 1990).

The 1976 earthquake also accelerated the spread and influence of Protestantism (especially Pentecostalism), as Protestants distributed supplies, provided temporary housing, and helped to rebuild homes and churches. At the same time, new missionaries and religiously affiliated organizations, like World Vision, arrived to aid in relief efforts. In the months following the earthquake, membership in Protestant churches increased from 8 to 14 percent of the population (Garrard-Burnett 1998, 121).

During the armed conflict, the Guatemalan government favored pro-American, conservative Protestant organizations. These organizations, especially those with ties to North American fundamentalist churches, were allowed into former conflict zones by government leaders like Efraín Ríos Montt (1982–3), himself a member of Iglesia el Verbo (Church of the Word),[17] and Óscar Humberto Mejía Victores (1983–6). They were seen as modern imports and counterweights to the liberation theology–inspired elements of the Catholic Church. This further contributed to Protestant organizations' presence and influence in many communities. Whereas Protestants represented just over 2 percent of the population in the early 1970s, two decades later, between 30 and 35 percent of Guatemalans belonged to one or more Pentecostal congregations (Philpot-Munson 2009, 45).

Because of this history, it is often assumed that Protestants were overwhelmingly conservative and supported military governments in Guatemala. In reality, ordinary Protestants were divided among those who tried to stay out of politics altogether, those who supported the military government (acting as informants and undertaking development projects in the context of the government's pacification program), and those who were sympathetic to and supported guerrillas (Martin 1990; Garrard-Burnett 1998). In the context of the armed conflict, progressive Protestants, notably those from the autonomous indigenous Presbyterian Church, shifted their attention from evangelizing to social services in indigenous communities, emphasizing the goal of justice in this world and lifetime and eschewing their traditional apolitical stance (Schäfer 1991; Samson 2007; Adkins 2009). While most ordinary Protestants viewed their churches as a "spiritual refuge from the turmoil of their world" (Garrard-Burnett in Martin 1990, 254), others participated in churches influenced by pro-guerrilla forces. By the end of the conflict, for example, indigenous presbyteries of the Presbyterian Church had cultivated both an oppositional stance to the military government and significant ties with the pan-Mayan movement, in stark contrast to their much more conservative, ladino counterparts.

Thus, long before the international development community discovered indigenous populations, religious missionaries targeted development efforts at them, and indigenous populations themselves mobilized around religious identity in diverse ways, crafting syncretic ideas about development by drawing on religious and ethnic identities. This legacy is reflected in organizations like the Fraternity, which grew out of religiously motivated social service provision and progressive Mayans organizing through religious networks for social justice and cultural recognition.

The pan-Mayan movement also preceded (and helped contribute to) the international focus on indigenous populations. Since the early 1980s, the pan-Mayan movement had been organizing at the national level around issues of cultural and language rights and pushing for the recognition of Guatemala as a multiethnic, multicultural, and multilingual nation. The movement involved itself in cultural revitalization through the creation of Mayan schools and informal education programs, and actively took part in discussions around the peace accords (K. B. Warren 2001). In part as a result of their activism, indigenous rights were explicitly mentioned in the peace accords, which set the development agenda for many international donors and national and local NGOs, thus complicating depictions of international priorities running roughshod over national and local interests.

At the local level, Mayan organizations had been cultivating programs that pursued culturally appropriate development. Some of these programs challenged mainstream views that mistook development to be "simply an augmentation in consumption" and ignored the "unity of spiritual and material development" (Raxche' 1996, 76). They challenged neoliberalism's emphasis on individuals and markets by arguing that cultures were "groups of people with human dignity" rather than "masses of consumers and producers of profit for industry and commerce" (Raxche' 1996, 76). Many groups, for example, promoted the use of natural pesticides and fertilizers—a backlash against the chemical inputs long promoted by foreign and government-backed development initiatives. This impulse was also part of their broader tendency to "exalt all that is 'traditional'" and desire to eliminate their dependence on the market that, in their view, caused the demise of their traditional culture (Fischer 1996, 65).

Responding to alternative development and post-development critiques and the activities and demands of indigenous movements and organizations, international actors looked to indigenous NGOs that could pursue development at the local level in ways that were both culturally appropriate and consistent with neoliberal reforms. Looking to Guatemala, for example, IDB publicly held up the Cooperation for the Rural Development of the West (CDRO) as an international model of culturally appropriate development. This organization sought development through the *pop* (woven mat) methodology, a methodology based on a vision of development that was "universal, inclusive, democratic and egalitarian" and strategies that mobilized various members of the community as agents of change (DeHart 2009, 66). While this type of approach differed from top-down modernization efforts of previous decades, it was also entirely compatible with "the market-oriented, locally managed development policies" that were heralded by international development industry at the time (DeHart 2009, 69).

Thus, historical developments, grassroots mobilization around indigenous demands, and international trends that made indigenous organizations attractive allowed for a variety of indigenous organizations in Guatemala. Some, like the Fraternity, grew out of indigenous people's mobilization or represented outgrowths of religious or social missions that had a long history in Guatemala and were either enlisted or ignored by international actors. Others were developed by outsiders or local brokers in response to increased funding for projects that targeted indigenous populations. In both cases, international trends influenced but did not dictate the form that development interventions targeted at indigenous groups would take on the ground.

CONCLUSION

Despite shifting international trends, development efforts in Guatemala (as elsewhere) have often served to repackage past mentalities and practices under the guise of new buzzwords. As a result, patterns, inequalities, and contradictions have resurfaced again and again. Throughout Guatemalan history, macroeconomic policies favored the long-standing agricultural-industrial-financial elites while projects targeting technology, credit, and training to the urban and rural poor aimed to encourage self-help strategies in place of re-distribution. These strategies—from the promotion of the Green Revolution to diversify agriculture, to the maquiladora industries to employ the urban poor, to microfinance to empower and enrich women—have failed to make a meaningful dent in poverty, and in some cases, they have served to further concentrate wealth and distract from structural solutions. Yet, as seen in the chapters that follow, even when development projects have failed to achieve their stated goals of combating poverty, they have continued to influence, and be influenced by, the vibrant social landscapes that they encountered. Thus, these projects' multiple, often contradictory realities and effects are not adequately captured by traditional forms of evaluation that continue to weigh the value of development projects against a relatively narrow list of stated objectives.

A historical overview of development in Guatemala also demonstrates that international forces have been transformed to a greater or lesser extent by the peculiarities of the Guatemalan context and by Guatemalan actors with their own goals and meanings. Modernization-inspired efforts took on militarized and racialized forms in Guatemala, bottom-up alternatives were politicized and constrained, and neoliberal strategies intertwined with existing institutional landscapes and social actors, prompting mixed reactions on the ground. This created an environment in which NGOs as different as Namaste and the Fraternity were able to develop, survive, and exercise agency even in the face of powerful international pressures.

The number of NGOs in Guatemala multiplied dramatically in the post-conflict period, with some estimating that their numbers increased fivefold in less than a decade—from two thousand in the year 2000 to ten thousand in 2007 (Sridhar 2007, 205), making NGOs "one of the most prevalent features of the late capitalist landscape in Guatemala (Way 2012, 186).[18] The proliferation of NGOs in post-conflict Guatemala has at times inspired a sense of competition within the NGO sector and opportunism among community members, who attempt to secure immediate gains from NGO projects that are often short-lived (Rohloff, Díaz, and Dasgupta 2011; Aviva 1999; Sundberg 1998). Although changing development trends have clearly influenced the contours of Guatemala's NGO sector, there continues to be considerable diversity (in terms of origins, forms, and foci), even among NGOs working with similar populations, toward similar ends, and with similar technologies (Beck 2014). There are NGOs that are professionalized and partner with large international organizations and others that are informal and driven by grassroots action.

Some are secular but others are influenced by progressive or conservative religious faiths.

While Guatemalan advocacy NGOs have received a good deal of attention (see, for example, Berger 2006), the majority of the NGOs in the country today are development NGOs; they focus on the provision of goods and services rather than advocacy. And though better-studied, mega-NGOs such as SHARE, Caritas, and World Vision control vast sums of money, they are "vastly outnumbered by small NGOs and rarely engage in sustained direct action" (Rohloff, Díaz, and Dasgupta 2011, 428). Many Guatemalans are accustomed to interacting with small NGOs, about which we know relatively less. The following chapters focus on these understudied spheres of development by highlighting how organizations and women navigate this new landscape, variously influenced by local contexts, international and national histories, and trends in development thinking and practice.

CHAPTER THREE

NAMASTE'S
BOOTSTRAP MODEL

Wary of nonprofits operated in an unbusinesslike manner, I wanted to be in an organizational culture that integrated accountability, cost effectiveness and recognition of
the economic laws of supply and demand into its programs. And whomever I worked
with—be they poor, sick or uneducated—I thought should participate in the cost of the
work. In other words, they should pay something, for I saw the goal as being to increase
their self-reliance. It seemed to me that just giving them something would be counter-
productive toward that goal. —ROBERT GRAHAM (1997, 71)

Robert Graham, founder and chief financial officer of Fundación Namaste
Guatemaya/NamasteDirect (Namaste), made the statement above when reflecting on his initial forays into philanthropy. Graham and his colleagues
drew on their habitus to apply business techniques and mentalities to nonprofit work, driven by a model of bootstrap development. Rooted in resource-
based definitions of poverty, bootstrap development is based on the expectation that, given the opportunity, the poor can lift themselves out of poverty
through their own entrepreneurship. Namaste's policymakers targeted women
because they assumed doing so would give them more bang for their buck.
Because of simplified conceptions of third world women promoted in media,
academic studies, personal conversations, and promotional material to which
early policymakers were exposed, women were assumed to have less access to

resources, paid employment, or loans and have limited business knowledge, yet be more likely to channel resources toward their children and community's well-being.

Early on, Namaste's policymakers hoped to promote development by raising women's incomes, teaching them business skills, and strengthening their microenterprises. They decided to specialize in credit and business education based on what they saw as their comparative advantage in inculcating women with the skills and habits required to become good businesswomen, fully incorporated into the market. In so doing, they leveraged their interactions with workers, beneficiaries, and materials such as databases and paperwork to institutionalize their values and mentalities.

Although the importance of founders' values, ideologies, and actions is often overlooked (but see Selznick 1984; Child 1987; Kimberly 1979; Kimberly and Bouchikhi 1995), this chapter demonstrates that NGOs' interactional origins can have long-lasting consequences for organizational logics, values, networks, and structures. Influenced by their personal dispositions and previous experiences, and embedded in philanthropic and international microfinance networks in the global north, Graham and early policymakers incorporated northern business practices into Namaste's design and operations and adopted a bureaucratic structure. Like many social entrepreneurs, they applied the dispositions and strategies of action (Swidler 1986) developed in the private sector—strategies that incorporated the language of efficiency, measurability, and market calculations—to development. They set goals amenable to their well-honed strategies of action, demonstrating that "people come to value ends for which their cultural equipment is well suited" (Swidler 1986, 277). They based their operations around a faith in the market and the entrepreneurial spirit of poor Guatemalan women.

Subsequently, the organizational habitus developed in Namaste's prehistory and founding continued to be expressed and reinforced through the NGO's programs, paperwork, internal conversations, trainings, and processes of organizational change. By tracing these origins and expressions of Namaste's development model, alongside other organizational characteristics, this chapter answers a question central to development: namely, where do development models and organizational characteristics come from? It additionally establishes the foundation for the chapter that follows, which focuses on the interactions between developers and beneficiaries in Namaste's interfaces, where development models and organizational characteristics are experienced and transformed by diverse actors.

NAMASTE'S PREHISTORY: APPLYING BUSINESS NETWORKS
AND MENTALITIES TO PHILANTHROPY

The preface to Robert Graham's autobiography prepares readers for the "true story of a highly successful, conservative accountant/businessman" who was "increasingly drawn from the world of logic and linear thinking into the world of the spirit." And yet, it continues, "in this brave new world, symbols, ritual and ancient wisdom do not replace the 'bottom line' but become a complementary part of it" (Graham 1997, iii). A businessman, certified public accountant (CPA), and cofounder of a California farming and food processing company, Graham was drawn into social networks that inspired him to give back. Thereafter he became both a product and a driver of the microfinance wave that spread across the developing world in the 1980s. The backgrounds, values, and experiences during Namaste's prehistory of Graham and other early policymakers, alongside broader developments in the field of microfinance, shaped the organization's characteristics and trajectory in ways that continue to impact the practices, experiences, and interactions of Namaste's workers and beneficiaries to this day.

In the early 1970s, Graham participated in the California Agricultural Leadership Program (CALP), through which he and thirty other "potential leaders" participated in leadership seminars, traveled to Washington, D.C., to meet with politicians, and undertook lengthy international trips to Central America, the Middle East, and Russia. During these international trips, Graham had two epiphanies: one social and one spiritual. In Guatemala, Graham was struck by the poverty and exclusion faced by indigenous populations. He explained in a 2011 interview, "that's where the original idea came about to do *something*." The widespread poverty in the Guatemalan countryside disrupted his "cozy middle-class world, where progress and prosperity seemed open to everyone":

> [Many Guatemalans] lived lives of extreme difficulty and quiet desperation, farming small plots of poor land, or as virtually indentured laborers on the huge plantations of the oligarchy. There were millions of them, clearly the vast majority of the population. . . . As I rode through Guatemala and talked with my buddies about what we were seeing, I determined that someday I would reach out and try to help people to whom little seemed possible. (Graham 1997, 42)

In Israel, Graham experienced a spiritual awakening upon visiting locations mentioned in the Bible, challenging his assumption that "the Bible was pretty much fabrication from beginning to end" (Graham 1997, 47). He began to explore various belief systems and eventually pursued a master's degree in philosophy, cosmology, and consciousness, all of which further strengthened his commitment to philanthropy.

Through CALP and other business contacts, Graham connected with networks that would shape his trajectory, including the Social Venture Network, which "connects, supports and inspires business leaders and social entrepreneurs in expanding practices that build a just and sustainable economy" (Social Venture Network 2010), and the Threshold Foundation, an organization for wealthy individuals interested in philanthropic work. Through these networks Graham became immersed in the world of social entrepreneurship, which developed into a source of inspiration, information, ideas, and partnerships for his future work.

The seeds planted during early international trips bore fruit ten years later, when Graham decided to live his life by his philosophy of "50-50 at 50": after turning fifty, Graham would dedicate half of his time and resources to social service. Yet his background as a CPA and businessman led him to reject traditional development and charity models and to instead pursue the goal of social entrepreneurship, which entailed "taking the spirit and skill set of the entrepreneur into the not-for-profit or [socially responsible business] sector" as Graham explained in a 2011 interview. In 1983, Graham got an early start on his 50-50 plan, cofounding a U.S.-based NGO, the Katalysis Partnership, which funded projects in rural development in Belize and the Eastern Caribbean. Although he had relatively little experience with nonprofits and philanthropy, Graham held strong beliefs about how development-oriented NGOs should operate. As he highlighted in his autobiography and in a 2011 interview with me, Graham wanted them to leverage the market and integrate business mentalities that focused on accountability and cost effectiveness. The ultimate goal was to encourage self-reliance, allowing the poor to lift themselves out of poverty.

Katalysis quickly took off, spurred forward by Graham's connections in North America to wealthy businesspeople and the support of larger agencies, such as USAID. Graham, the quintessential businessman, was adept at transforming chance encounters into funding opportunities. At the end of the 1980s, Graham and a colleague at Katalysis found themselves departing Belize on the same plane as an official of USAID and an inmate being transported to the United States. The inmate caused a commotion by scrambling out of the plane to reunite with his girlfriend, who was running down the tarmac. In the commotion, Graham and his colleague finagled seats next to the USAID representative; as Graham wrote in his autobiography, "as I remember it, there were a lot of free drinks on the way to Miami. By then the three of us were 'bonded' pretty good, and the USAID grant was on fast-forward" (Graham 1997, 75). By 1990, USAID had awarded Katalysis its first matching grant of $600,000.

Funders found Graham's approach especially appealing because it fit well with the demands of the neoliberal consensus and new public management, which sought to reform social service delivery by leveraging markets, incentives, and targets and by requiring beneficiaries to share in the costs. Not long after he founded Katalysis, Graham read a *Wall Street Journal* article about the work of Muhammad Yunus and the Grameen Bank, and to the businessman and CPA, "it just clicked." Graham explained the intuitive appeal of the Grameen model to me in a 2011 interview: "Here was this business guy . . . and he was doing better than other development projects. Better than [US]AID projects, all that stuff. *Because it was being run as a business.*"

Soon thereafter, Graham met Jonathan Hatch, who had been working with microcredit in Bolivia, applying the "village banking" model of FINCA based on the motto "give poor communities the opportunity [loans], and then get out of the way!"[1] At a leadership conference, Hatch convinced Graham that they should conduct a pilot project of the village banking model in Central America. Graham was so enthusiastic that when Katalysis's board of directors voted against funding the pilot project, he wrote a personal check for $4,000, sending Hatch and a Honduran partner (himself a former USAID employee) to administer the pilot project.

"So was the pilot a success?" I asked Graham in 2011 as we sipped after-lunch coffee and tea, looking over Lake Merritt in Oakland, California. Graham's eyebrows shot up and his blue eyes widened as he laughed: "No! It was terrible!" Each month, fewer and fewer women came to the payment meetings, until no one arrived at all. Rather than seeing the pilot's failure as a condemnation of microcredit, however, Graham learned from the experience that implementation was central to success. "I said John [Hatch] is Johnny Appleseed. He goes hilltop-to-hilltop handing out money and expecting the market to work. But what we need is to find an existing structure—local organizations [to partner with]." Graham and his partners at Katalysis therefore sent a board member on a scouting mission to Honduras to find potential partners through which they could channel funds, eventually selecting the Women's Business Development Organization (Organización de Desarrollo Empresarial Femenino, ODEF). At the time, ODEF was a relatively small organization that provided business training and individual loans to roughly three hundred women. Today, ODEF is the largest microfinance organization in northeastern Honduras, with thirty agencies in nine departments and more than 28,000 active borrowers.

From there, Katalysis branched out, looking for more partners first in Honduras, and then in other Central American countries, including Guatemala. In 1990, USAID connections introduced Graham and his colleagues to two Guatemalan partner organizations—the Women's Development Association (Asociación de Mujeres de Desarrollo, MUDE) and the Cooperation for the Rural Development of the West (Asociación Cooperación para el Desarollo Rural de Occidente, CDRO). Although MUDE is still a member of the Katalysis Network, Katalysis eventually abandoned its partnership with CDRO. As noted in chapter 2, CDRO was held up internationally as a model of culturally appropriate development; thus, partnering with CDRO had initially fulfilled the Katalysis board of directors' desire to work with indigenous populations. However, Katalysis eventually severed the partnership, in part because CDRO refused to charge market interest rates and therefore, in Graham and the board's view, failed to respect the economic laws of supply and demand and increase their beneficiaries' self-reliance.

Katalysis came to specialize in raising funds for local microcredit projects in El Salvador, Guatemala, Honduras, and Nicaragua. Their local partners agreed to apply modified versions of the Grameen model of solidarity groups or the FINCA model of village banks. Loans were distributed with market interest rates because Katalysis's policymakers strove for "sustainability for all participants" (Graham 1997, 214). Graham and his colleagues also insisted that they target very poor women who did not have access to credit. They publicly championed the spillover effects of group-based microcredit targeted toward women, which included group solidarity, increased self-esteem, and a sense of self-efficacy among participants. Graham went as far to write in his autobiography that microcredit was "destined to be one of the most powerful, world-wide concepts of the 21st century" (Graham 1997, 215).

Katalysis was so successful that it eventually grew into the Katalysis Network—a regional nonprofit linking microcredit organizations across Central America. By the mid-1990s, the organization's original four partners had formed over three hundred village banks and made thousands of individual loans for small businesses. By 2003 the network had reached over 160,000 individuals, mostly women, and had a loan portfolio of $50 million. Today, the Katalysis Network links twenty-three microcredit organizations in Guatemala, Nicaragua, Honduras, and El Salvador. After twenty years, Graham and his associates turned the operation and management of Katalysis over to the regional nonprofit. He explained, "in other words, we accomplished our mission and went out of business." Graham emphasized in a 2011 interview that he saw the transfer of power to his local partners as part of an overall strategy, claiming it was the "guiding logic all along." He aimed to transfer "money, expertise, knowledge, goods," and in the case of Katalysis, he succeeded in "the final transfer, which is the transfer of power."

APPLYING EXISTING VALUES AND STRATEGIES OF ACTION
TO SHIFTING TARGET POPULATIONS

Graham's personal history as a businessman and social entrepreneur working in the field of microcredit allowed him to develop clear goals and strong opinions about the best way to go about doing development. He stressed targeting poor women because they had the highest level of need, they were more likely to be undercapitalized, and their successes were more likely to have positive spillover effects for families and communities. But he also insisted that nonprofits apply business models to their work—placing a premium on measurement, efficiency, and accountability, respecting market forces, and ensuring that beneficiaries share in the costs of interventions.

These principles, along with Graham and his colleagues' focus on women, fit well with broader changes in the field internationally, which increasingly wed women to development and strove for financial sustainability of development projects. By the 1990s, Graham recalled, increased funding came alongside a change in mentality among NGOs, a change that, by the time of our 2011 interview, he recognized, "taken to the extreme can be damaging." Graham "[pled] guilty to the charge" of contributing and responding to "new talk about accountability, results, and running a NGO like a business."

Still, Graham and other policymakers on Namaste's board of directors did not wholeheartedly accept *all* of the resulting changes in the field of microcredit. They found themselves wary of the shift from what they saw as the microcredit movement, rooted in a desire for social and economic justice, to what they considered the microfinance industry, under the new wave of microfinance, which placed inordinate focus on financial sustainability and profit to the detriment of social aims. Graham noted that in their search for financial sustainability and profits, MFIs were targeting better-off clients in urban areas rather than the rural poor. Once he left Katalysis, Graham founded Namaste in 2004 with the explicit goal of bucking this trend by focusing on first-time women borrowers in the rural areas of Guatemala.

Namaste's Guatemalan office was originally located in Panajachel on the volcano- and mountain-ringed Lake Atitlán, where it applied Graham's well-tested strategy of partnering with local MFIs to provide funding and business training. Namaste provided interest-free loans to its partners and employed local workers, known in Namaste as advisers, to provide business training to the women receiving those loans. In turn, its local partners agreed to distribute Namaste-funded loans to women in rural areas who were first-time borrowers. Namaste's local partners were given the autonomy to set loan conditions, including interest rates, loan cycles, and methods of delivery (solidarity groups or individual loans).

Namaste's program consisted of three key components: loans, education, and mentorship. Not only did the organization provide poor women with a small loan (usually between $225 and $400) through a local MFI intermediary; it also required that women attend monthly group classes that covered business management and financial literacy. Most uniquely, it assigned a business adviser to each woman. Advisers visited women each month in their homes or places of business to record their costs and sales, help them calculate their profits/losses, and provide customized business advice. Advisers were required to have at least two years of experience managing their own businesses and were expected to establish close relationships with beneficiaries based on trust and respect such that beneficiaries would provide them more accurate data on their sales and expenses and would be more likely to carry out advisers' recommendations.

By 2007, Namaste's policymakers (Graham and the board of directors) began to doubt their original strategy of partnering with local MFIs for a number of reasons. First, with the entry of commercial banks and new NGOs into the microfinance sector in Guatemala (described in chapter 2), they found it increasingly difficult to find first-time borrowers. Second, they became concerned that the local MFIs with which they were working did not value their partnership. Across the region, local MFIs began to argue that accepting interest-free money from organizations like Kiva and Namaste came with too many conditions in terms of target population and requirements for loan administration and reporting. As a result, some had begun turning down interest-free loans from these types of organizations. Finally, Namaste's policymakers, NGO leaders, and workers were frustrated with their MFI partners, who in practice set low, or no, conditions for women receiving loans. This meant that the local MFIs were lending to women who were already in debt or who lacked viable businesses. They additionally noted that their partners at times used questionable tactics to ensure that women paid higher-than-advertised interest rates. Namaste's policymakers felt that if they were to contribute to development, small loans needed to be targeted to the "right" kind of women and managed differently.

The following year, Namaste's Guatemalan headquarters moved to a gated community in Antigua, a small city featuring colorful buildings, colonial architecture, language schools, and expensive restaurants. Over email and Skype and in the apartment-turned-office in Antigua, Namaste's policymakers, leaders, and workers underwent a period of internal analysis and self-evaluation, all the while opening up these conversations and their day-to-day practices to me.[2] As a result of these conversations, Namaste begun to shift away from partnering with local intermediaries toward providing loans, education, and one-on-one mentorship directly to women in 2010. This decision was supposed to allow Namaste to streamline its approach and simultaneously correct for many of the mistakes that characterized the new microfinance "industry."

To avoid contributing to "microdebt" and dependence among its borrowers, Namaste established a limit to the amount of outstanding debt an incoming beneficiary could have. The organization additionally required women to undergo an initial evaluation with workers (business advisers) to ensure that Namaste selected ideal borrowers: ones that had significant levels of need, managed preexisting businesses with the potential for growth, agreed not to use their loans for personal consumption, and had a clear plan for using their loans in their businesses.

These qualifications reflected the importance that policymakers placed on business as key to development and responded to their growing criticisms of microfinance's new face. In contrast to other MFIs, Namaste regularly turned away women deemed unfit for their program; Namaste's internal communications and field reports from NGO leaders often included updates such as "these women are not in our target group," "[only six] women received the loan ([we] ended up weeding out [four] potential borrowers)," and "there were [six] women who already have bad credit and reputation with the other organizations."

The organization also shifted its target population when it became clear that first-time borrowers were difficult to find and that the very poorest women were more likely to use their loans for consumption rather than business investment. Because Namaste's leadership saw business as the engine of growth, it decided to target women who would actually use the loans in small enterprises. As a result, it moved away from targeting the most impoverished women and first-time borrowers, their initial target populations. Employees explained to me that while in the past they had been trained to focus on women who lived on less than $2 a day, after this transitional period, the organization began to target women who already had their basic food needs met, who had some literacy skills, and whose businesses had a viable chance of success in the given marketplace, which implied targeting better-off women than they had in the past.

The strategies of action that Namaste had developed as an organization—based in measurement, accountability, and a focus on providing women resources to better integrate them into the market—were therefore more persistent than the ends to which they were applied. Namaste had been founded with the explicit goal of helping the poorest women who were being overlooked by other MFIs in the new development climate. When they discovered that the very poorest would simply "eat the loan," rather than invest it in businesses, Namaste's policymakers concluded that microcredit "[was not] a solution in really poor areas," as Graham himself explained in a 2011 interview. Rather than looking for a different solution, the leadership adjusted its target population to one it felt it could help with its existing services and strengths. Namaste's shift in target population was therefore driven by its skill set and vision of development, which focused on individual entrepreneurship as a solution to poverty and business as an engine of growth.

Still, the organization's management was hesitant to follow the lead of other MFIs that were targeting urban, better-off populations to expand their base and reduce their risk. Namaste's workers perpetually felt conflicted and confused by policymakers' and NGOs' dictates to focus on the underserved *and* to target women whom they could best help—women whose businesses had the real possibility for growth, who tended to be slightly better off and live closer to urban markets. To avoid ambiguity, policymakers attempted to articulate clearer targets. In an email to field staff and me, Graham outlined in 2010 that "women *must* have the capacity and the environment to *successfully* make use of Namaste's services," meaning there was room for their businesses to grow. Once this condition was met, he claimed, they preferred that women live in rural areas and were poor, earning less than $2.50 a day. By the end of 2013, the income ceiling had been raised to $6 a day. As a result, beneficiaries were not the poorest of the poor. Most had electricity (96.6 percent) and access to potable water (94.8 percent), compared to the national averages of 78.5 percent and 93 percent, respectively (World Bank 2012a, 2012b). Incoming women's annual average household income was $1,276 per person, which was roughly at the level of the national poverty line of $1,277 per person (World Bank 2009), but well below the average per capita income of $3,590 (World Bank 2015).

By bringing all elements of programming under its central control, policymakers were able to standardize their loan conditions and were forced to more clearly articulate their image of a model client. In the face of growing skepticism surrounding microfinance, Namaste also undertook changes with potential donors in mind, undergoing a period of rebranding. Because they relied on ties to northern agencies and donors, Namaste's policymakers could not afford to ignore other MFIs' bad reputations. In the midst of my time studying Namaste, the *New York Times* published an article revealing that MFIs were making enormous profits off of microcredit, "with some charging interest rates of 100 percent or more" (Macfarquhar 2010). The article questioned the beneficial effects of microcredit and criticized the lack of transparency in the industry. Namaste was quick to respond. An email chain began the following day between policymakers and NGO leaders, drafting a response to be posted on their website and conveyed to current and potential funders that emphasized their comparatively low interest rates, focus on education, high levels of transparency, ability to measure outcomes, and focus on women's incomes, rather than repayment rates, as their marker of success.

A year later, Namaste's policymakers decided to separate themselves further from the rest of the industry, emphasizing what they saw as the organization's unique strengths—business education and mentorship—and abandoning their earlier marketing strategy, which emphasized microcredit. Graham explained the decision to me in a 2011 email, "Our tagline MMW [Making Microcredit Work], is under water. It features microcredit, which is in the process of being discredited in the press, and is stated in the negative by implicitly saying what we lead with, small loans, typically [does not] work." Namaste's policymakers and leaders began to emphasize Namaste's focus on business mentorship and education to potential donors and northern partners, depicting loans as one of the relatively less important services that they offered. Today, Namaste's mission statement contains no mention of loans at all, even though the organization continues to distribute them. Instead of highlighting loans, Namaste's public mission is "to directly contribute to women's economic empowerment by providing business development programs and analytics that increase the business profits of low-income entrepreneurs."[3]

This rebranding process was so complete that some policymakers—including Graham himself—no longer consider Namaste to be a microcredit NGO. This shift occurred despite the fact that the mix of services the organization provides to women on the ground has not changed significantly. The organization continues to provide small loans to women, and women themselves see these loans as central to Namaste's program. Yet Graham explained to me in a 2013 interview, "I'm for what works. That's why we left the microcredit business. It wasn't making a meaningful dent in poverty." Namaste's developers attribute their success in raising women's business incomes largely to the one-on-one mentorship that they provide and to a lesser extent to group classes on business education and financial literacy. While Namaste's donors, policymakers, and leaders have accepted this rebranding, the women whom the NGO targets have not, as seen in the following chapter. They continue to view Namaste as roughly equivalent to other MFIs operating in the area.

More recently, Namaste has attempted to expand its impact by training other MFIs and NGOs in its approach, which incorporates mentorship, business education, and quantitative analysis of women's business data alongside loans. Namaste hopes that other MFIs and NGOs will consider paying for their "Train the Trainers" program, which will provide them with the knowledge and tools to implement this "business development approach." The promotional material for this program argues that Namaste can provide MFIs comparative advantages over competitors that only offer credit. It additionally claims that it can help NGOs offering social benefits respond to the broader pressure for financial sustainability, claiming that these NGOs "will find that clients [receiving] the Namaste Business Development training and mentoring will have increased income from business that *will allow them to purchase on their own the benefits previously given to them at no or little cost.*" The result is that those NGOs will be able to integrate "income generation and job creation into the NGO services" as a "direct answer to the question of sustainability."[4] Although Namaste was founded with the goal of bucking the trend toward full commercialization, it has, in some sense, gone commercial.

What has remained constant despite these shifts is the organization's commitment to bootstrap development, as well as the application of a business mentality to its operations. These characteristics, alongside the organization's values, bureaucratic structure, and network connections (described later), shape Namaste's daily practices—allowing the organization to efficiently increase women's incomes in the short term, monitor its own performance, achieve sustainability, and secure funding. But as we will see in the next chapter, women are not merely passive recipients of Namaste's services. They assign their own meanings and goals to the NGO. While women's perceptions of Namaste are in part shaped by the NGO's organizational characteristics, they often diverge from those of Namaste's policymakers and leaders.

NAMASTE'S DEVELOPMENT MODEL AND
ORGANIZATIONAL CHARACTERISTICS

Bootstrap Development and Faith in the Market

Despite incremental organizational changes, Namaste's prehistory, its found-ers' values and beliefs, and the broader international networks in which its policymakers have historically been embedded have imbued the organization with an enduring model of development. The NGO focuses on income-based definitions of poverty and impact, with the idea that enhancing women's in-comes and businesses are key to development. In this view, although gov-ernments have a role to play in development, "if combating poverty entails raising incomes and growing the economic base, business is effective at that," as Graham explained in a 2013 interview.

Namaste therefore specializes in increasing women's access to resources in the short term rather than tackling long-term structural change. In personal conversations and interactions with funders, Graham and other policymakers and NGO leaders feel comfortable discussing the assumed spillover effects of microcredit, such as increased self-esteem, improved child education and nu-trition, and community development. In a presentation designed to convince potential partners to replicate their approach, for example, Namaste outlines its vision that "low-income entrepreneurs in the developing world will have the tools and access to business information necessary to attain higher busi-ness cash flow and thereby move from semi-poverty toward middle class." This, they claim, "will promote the well being of each entrepreneur and their family, healthy community economics and participatory democracy."[5] The spillover effects described are, in part, "feel good" statements for marketing purposes, but they also reflect a belief that if enough women in a community increase their business incomes, the local economy will benefit. Graham made a connection between these economic goals and broader political goals in a 2013 interview. Because in his view a strong middle class is key to democracy, he believes helping women enter the middle class will lead to more democratic societies. In this view, one can target the dual goals of development and de-mocracy through a single intervention into women's incomes.

Namaste therefore confronts the contradiction between its ambitious goals and the lack of technology with known links between inputs and outputs by focusing on a measurable, short-term goal that it assumes will have spillover effects. Despite personal conversations and publicity material, the day-to-day operations are focused on one goal alone—increasing business income as effi-ciently as possible. I was struck when, in my first observation of a staff meeting in 2009, Graham stated bluntly, "I know all about the spillovers, but we are not concerned about [claiming or measuring] that. We specialize in increasing women's incomes. That's it." The emphasis on economic success, which contrasts with other Guatemalan NGOs' emphases on holistic development, pervaded all aspects of the organization. Classes were devoted to financial literacy and business education and avoided topics that many other women's NGOs incorporated, such as women's leadership or self-esteem. Although it eventually became a regular component of its annual conference for beneficiaries, some visiting members of the advisory board initially complained about a workshop on women's rights, as they saw the topic as outside of Namaste's focus on business training and financial literacy.

The organization not only tracked each woman's monthly cash flow using data collected from one-on-one meetings with business advisers, but it also developed sophisticated systems for data management and analysis. Namaste used this information to determine how women's incomes had changed throughout the course of their participation and which characteristics correlated with business success. It did not make similar efforts to measure or track assumed spillover effects. When the NGO moved toward commercializing their data management system, representatives explained to prospective partners that they focused on answering two questions: Was there an increase in beneficiaries' income, and was the cost justified? As such, policymakers developed a single indicator that took both of these into account: return on investment (ROI), defined as how much women's incomes increased in relation to the costs of serving them. At least one of the funders that Namaste approached expressed relief that Namaste's ROI did not incorporate an increasingly popular measure—*social* return on investment—because it was so hard to measure. Graham explained in 2013, "[We are] not in the business nor do we have the [expertise] on increasing self-esteem."

By specializing in increasing women's incomes, Namaste's policymakers drew on their existing cultural repertoires and habitus. Historically most board members had been successful businesspeople and current or former representatives of other northern NGOs. Through their experiences, they had come to value entrepreneurship, self-reliance, and individualism—traits that had served them well. Many already possessed the cultural tools needed to focus on narrow economic goals because of their business backgrounds. These tools included the language of accountability and efficiency and a familiarity with quantifiable goals. They therefore felt more comfortable focusing on incomes and profits, which were measurable in ways that self-esteem and empowerment were not. By leveraging forms, databases, and evaluation techniques that centered on quantifiable measures, they shaped the organizational habitus for years to come.

Policymakers' backgrounds not only afforded them the networks and skills needed to access financial support; it also gave them the sense that they understood what businesses of any size needed to succeed, because they could look to their own experiences as guides—reflecting the tendency for developers to assume a commensurability of needs and desires between themselves and beneficiaries. For example, because they had benefited from business conferences in the United States, which had given them opportunities to forge networks and access new ideas, the board sponsored an annual business conference for their beneficiaries, replicating an elite practice for the benefit of the poor. Beneficiaries traveled from their homes to spend two days at a hotel in the touristy town of Panajachel to attend workshops and classes and to network with other businesswomen. Because Namaste's policymakers wanted women to see themselves as businesspeople rather than mothers, and to avoid distractions, they banned children from attending with their mothers. By focusing on women's singular identities as entrepreneurs, they were able to draw connections between their own and women's experiences despite the many differences in their identities, skills, goals, and contexts.

Namaste's narrow focus was also based on the economic rationale of comparative advantage and specialization, which informed policymakers' worldview. Graham explained that while multiservice organizations at times have a role to play, they often fail to do any one thing well. He argued that if others think, for example, that the goal of increasing women's self-esteem is worthwhile, then those with the comparative advantage in doing so would establish NGOs to meet those objectives. That is, he believed that if the demand existed for a project focused on self-esteem, the market of nonprofits would meet it. Still, he added, suppliers would have to struggle with ways to measure outcomes related to self-esteem.

Namaste's bootstrap model of development is based on a faith in individual entrepreneurship. Based on this faith, Namaste encourage women to achieve empowerment through the market, rather than inspiring them to question its underlying structures, and to act as individuals rather than collectives. This model is reflected in the organization's explanation of how its activities reduce poverty. The NGO's 2009–10 website stated, for example, that "conventional wisdom" identified four barriers to escaping poverty: lack of capital, lack of education, poor health conditions, and natural and man-made disasters. Rather than highlight the structural forces that produced these barriers or the ways that they intersected, Namaste focused on overcoming the first by providing "hard-working, determined women with the means to lead their families out of poverty" and measuring its effectiveness on an individual, "woman-by-woman" basis.[6]

Namaste's internal process of setting loan conditions also reflects this underlying faith in the possibility of bootstrap development and the moralizing work that it entails. The organization charges market interest rates and small fees for mentorship and education for both symbolic and practical reasons. Symbolically, Namaste's administration believes it is important for women to share in the costs of loans and education. They argue that people tend to value that which they pay for more than that which is given to them for free. What is more, they argue, women are more likely to complain about sub-par services if they are paying for them. In past internal communications, Namaste's policymakers floated the idea of mimicking the business strategy of a money-back guarantee, in which women could ask for a refund for an educational services fee if they were unsatisfied, although I never witnessed this guarantee being explained to women in practice.

Practically, Namaste's policymakers are concerned that highly subsidized interest rates are in fact detrimental to users because they protect them too much from market forces. Before shifting to microcredit, Graham and his colleagues had focused on rural development programs in Belize and the Eastern Caribbean. During this time, they observed that when organizations like the World Bank provided cheap loans to farmers, farmers became dependent on these artificially low interest rates. Once lending sources dried up, farmers found that their production did not generate sufficient margins to absorb higher interest rates. This led Graham and his colleagues to value market interest rates because they put businesses to an "outside reality test"—one that would determine if they were indeed viable ventures in the "real" world in which market forces dominated.

When Namaste began directly administering loans (rather than working with local partners), the leadership surveyed banks' interest rates for small commercial loans and strove to set comparable rates, rather than basing them on its internal costs, profit margins, or women's capacities and desires.[7] Policymakers hoped that some of the women with whom Namaste worked would make the leap from microenterprise to small or medium-sized businesses, and they therefore wanted to prepare women for the terms they would confront in the commercial sector. Today the NGO remains committed to maintaining interest rates that compare with those of commercial banks, even though its leaders and workers recognize that women working in the informal economy often lack the paperwork and stability that banks desire and policymakers acknowledge that they have no clear evidence that women's businesses continue to grow after leaving Namaste.

The strategy of charging education fees and market interest rates also communicates Namaste's long-term goal of inspiring self-reliance, which is additionally enforced by limiting the number of loans women can receive from Namaste. For much of its history, women have been limited to two nine-month loan cycles, restricting women's interactions with Namaste to eighteen months.[8] By charging market interest rates and education fees, limiting loans, and providing education about the proper way to manage one's business, Namaste attempts to create entrepreneurial subjects that are self-reliant and market-oriented.

Of course, not all developers involved in Namaste universally and wholeheartedly support the narrow focus on women's incomes and its model of bootstrap development. All NGOs are made up of real people who arrive with their own worldviews and goals. Some of Namaste's leaders and workers think that the potential non-economic effects of the NGO's programming are being ignored because they are difficult to measure and they depart from the organization's specialized approach. This group successfully pushed for the continued inclusion of a workshop on women's rights and self-esteem in Namaste's annual business conference, even though members of the board originally questioned its inclusion. Others privately question if they can effect real change in just eighteen months. They wonder if increasing women's incomes is enough to improve communities' economies and contribute to development, given that many women in any given loan group operate similar, competing businesses and there is limited empirical evidence that they are able to scale up.

The guiding model of development and strategies of action that were institutionalized in Namaste's founding created organizational logics, values, structures, and networks that have been surprisingly sticky over time, profoundly shaping its day-to-day operations. But, as we will see, they do not wholly determine practices and experiences on the ground, because NGOs comprise diverse people with their own experiences, meanings, and goals; encounter workers and beneficiaries who act with agency; and enter complex environments over which they have limited control.

Namaste's Bureaucratic Structure

Reflecting its interactional origins, Namaste is organized internally according to a bureaucratic structure, one that is hierarchical and is arranged and managed according to impersonal rules and established criteria. Bureaucratic organizations like Namaste value and encourage "precision, speed, unambiguity, knowledge of files, continuity, discretion, unity, strict subordination, reduction of friction and of material and personal costs" (Weber 1958, 214). As a result, they have often been seen as the most efficient types of organizations.

Namaste's internal hierarchy has ensured that workers in the field have historically had little direct communication with the NGO's policymakers in California. The northern policymakers visit Antigua from time to time but, to my knowledge, have never visited Suchitepéquez, where many of Namaste's employees work and roughly half of its beneficiaries live. Personnel decisions are made centrally, such that workers are often unaware of changes until they occur and rarely are informed of the reasons for their colleagues' promotion or dismissal. When I asked Namaste's workers about how changes were made in the organization, I was told, "Up there [in California] they do everything"; "they send instructions and we carry them out." At least one worker explained that he did not mind the system because he assumed that "if they are ordering something, it is because they have studied it," indicating that there was a perceived gap in expertise that prevented workers who interacted with women daily from shaping policies.[9]

Namaste is also highly institutionalized, with meticulous files and detailed records of internal conversations and program outcomes. Policymakers, leaders, and workers leverage relationships with each other and with these materials to negotiate expectations and reinforce organizational structure. The organization incorporates formal feedback mechanisms that rely on written notes, forms, and databases to monitor performance and reduce the gaps between formal institutions and daily practices. The NGO's leaders are often in the field monitoring everything from group classes and one-on-one advising to data entry. According to field updates, in a typical field visit in May 2009, for example, the program manager met with Namaste's MFI partner, attended operational meetings with business advisers, "spent all day . . . reviewing the client files for both business advisers," and observed the process of data entry. In a description of another visit, under the heading "quality control," the program manager reviewed a business adviser's paperwork and made surprisingly detailed comments: "Incurred Sales are different from Projected sales [and] should be applied per the change to a monthly reporting style. Changes still need to be made based on comments from beginning of April, especially points from the Baseline. She has a higher [percentage] of clients that do not know [their] costs. She needs to write the name of the person on the outside of the folder. Her evaluation of the business since the change to the monthly reporting scheme appears to be general [and] not based on the [numbers]."

Leaders' supervisory visits often focused on business advisers' roles as data collectors and educators. When, for example, the regional director observed business advisers meeting with women without asking for specific numbers on costs and sales, she became concerned. In a 2008 field update that she emailed to policymakers in California, the regional director claimed, "I believe this is just a cultural difference, and it will be difficult to change in the [business advisers] but it is something that we will need to work through. We should consider adding a topic like 'The importance of mathematical analysis to an adviser' to the [business advisers'] training." The NGO's leadership also consistently monitored and critiqued business advisers' performances in group educational sessions and one-on-one meetings. The field updates generated by the managers included detailed comments such as "went [fifteen] minutes over time allotted," "read stories well," "lost attention of group by the end," and "her reading was 'choppy' during the stories." This regular monitoring meant that inconsistencies in the field rarely went unnoticed.

For example, as a result of monitoring, Namaste's leaders realized that in practice, business advisers were so focused on completing the required forms during their one-on-one meetings with women that they did not provide concrete advice. Rather, they might tell a woman borrower to "keep working hard" or "invest the loan in the business and buy other products." Namaste's policymakers' and leaders' assumptions about workers' goals led them to overlook the fact that many workers saw their position in Namaste as a job; as such they prioritized completing paperwork so as not to risk their employment and at times sought to minimize the time and effort that meetings with beneficiaries required. When combined with workers' varying goals, Namaste's emphasis on measurement and paperwork often made forms, rather than concrete advice, the center of workers' interactions with beneficiaries, even though one-on-one advice was supposed to be the heart of Namaste's operations (its comparative advantage). A volunteer observing business advisers' interactions with women reported in 2010 that they were affected by "too many forms and processes . . . to complete on a monthly basis" and explained that they were "tied down with paper work and administrative reporting, which does not give them the time to do research/follow up on client's needs." The volunteer went on to write that despite policymakers' intentions, "it is my belief that the Business Adviser feels that the main role of the in-field monthly visits is to accurately record cash flow."

This finding led to an internal study and a pilot project to improve training for business advisers and new forms that included visual reminders to provide advice that was specific, action-oriented, measureable, achievable, and related to a set timeframe—reflecting a tendency to enroll paperwork, databases, and other materials to manage workers and beneficiaries' actions.[10] This pattern of evaluation, piloting, transformation, and paperwork is common. Namaste's policymakers and leaders regularly solicit internal and external evaluations of its work and are constantly innovating. While I was observing the NGO, the organization was in the process of revamping and piloting new forms, testing out new methodologies for group classes and individual visits, and developing new ways to enter client data into an online database. Worried that the figures that beneficiaries provided their advisers were estimates rather than exact recordings of expenses and sales, Namaste considered methodologies for measuring income that had been described in academic studies and experimented with having a few groups of women record their daily expenses in notebooks before implementing financial journals across all of their groups.

I began observing Namaste during a transitional phase, when the organization was moving from partnering with local MFIs to working on its own. This contributed to the fervor for evaluation and improvement. But it also became clear that these projects were the result of an overall organizational culture that promoted constant evaluation and feedback. Organizational documents going back years reflected nonstop internal conversations reporting quantitative outcomes, piloting projects, adjusting programming, and setting clear targets for improvement. Years later, the organization continues to adjust its programming and employ more and more sophisticated techniques for data collection, management, and evaluation. This is in contrast to many other NGOs, where problems or informal practices arising in the field often go unnoticed or unaddressed, and changes are either rare or implemented much more haphazardly.

Valuing technical knowledge, measurement, and evaluation, Namaste's policymakers and leaders base personnel decisions on expertise, training, and preestablished criteria rather than personal loyalties and relationships. These same values also affect the ways that they interact with beneficiaries. The NGO's policymakers essentially turn women into numbers. They ask workers to assign women borrower and loan identification numbers, collect demographic and socioeconomic data on each woman, and track their monthly cash flow and the number of hours they spend in their businesses. It also asks them to track women's monthly performance in terms of their attendance, use of financial journals, and application of business advice, turning these evaluations into quantitative measurements.

Although it also comes with costs, this bureaucratic structure yields a number of benefits. Tied to its emphasis on evaluation is an impressive level of transparency. Not only did organizational members share the results of internal and external evaluations openly with me, but they also provided me with access to archives of email exchanges and field updates, their database, staff meetings, and trainings, as well as their day-to-day operations. This openness to external review and potential criticism is unique not just within the Guatemalan context but among nonprofits more generally.

The organization's institutionalized, impersonal rules and extensive monitoring also ensure that women are treated similarly, regardless of their ethnicity or geographic location. Deviations from standard operating procedures do not go unnoticed, leaving less room for workers' personal biases to affect their interactions with participants.[11] None of Namaste's participants complained of unequal treatment, and ladina (nonindigenous) and indigenous participants appear to have had similar participatory experiences. Namaste's expectations for its beneficiaries, and what beneficiaries can expect from Namaste, are clearly established and generally fulfilled. As a result, women who join Namaste subsequently have less reason to use their voice in the organization to protest unmet expectations or unequal treatment.

Over time, Namaste has only become more bureaucratic. Within the organization, task differentiation, specialization, and monitoring have increased. Policymakers have added specialized positions to the top management of operations in Guatemala, including a finance manager, operations manager, and information technology manager to the regional office in Guatemala. The NGO's new data management system allows the operations manager to disaggregate women's profits according to business adviser, giving her the capacity to catch underperforming employees or those reporting results that appear too good to be true. The new data management system automatically flags outliers for the operations manager—women whose cash flow decreased or increased dramatically from one month to the next. In this way, she can ensure that the data is indeed correct and investigate the causes of any anomalies. The result is criteria for decision-making that is clearer, more explicit, and seemingly more objective and scientific.

Namaste's policymakers are currently attempting to market their strategy to other MFIs and NGOs in order to determine if their results are replicable and to "massify" their impact without expanding their own client base. In the process, they have described Namaste to potential partners as a "poverty alleviation test laboratory," stating their goal is to "continually test new ways to increase the monthly business cash flow of low income women, which will accelerate their rate of achieving financial stability and fund betterments in their families."[12] Recognizing that the NGO has had limited effect in scaling up women's businesses, the organization has recently launched a new STARZ program, which gives larger loans to fewer women on more flexible terms, in the hopes of transitioning them from microenterprises to small or medium-sized businesses.

Worried that their business advisers were unable to successfully lead one-on-one mentorship as well as group classes, the NGO tasked specific workers (internally called educators) with taking over all group classes, leaving remaining workers (business advisers) to specialize in one-on-one mentorship. Rather than continuing with monthly group classes, the organization's policymakers have also decided it is more efficient to pursue three separate two-hour education sessions, one to be provided before women receive the loan, one at the time of loan disbursement, and one at the time of women's first monthly payment. The result may be more efficient for the organization, but it further limits women's regular interactions with each other and with their business advisers. Today, women joining Namaste participate in their respective loan groups only at the very beginning of their loan cycle; thereafter they interact with Namaste on a one-on-one basis, further emphasizing the organization's focus on individuals rather than groups. A number of Namaste's longtime workers expressed concern about this transition because they believed that women were not able to absorb two hours of information in one sitting and that women could benefit from meeting in groups more regularly. The organization's hierarchical structure and emphasis on efficiency, however, prevented these voices from being heard, and the more efficient model for business education won out.

Organizational Networks:
Strong Northern Ties, Weak Southern Ties

The bureaucratic characteristics just described appeal to the northern agencies, NGOs, and social entrepreneurs with whom Namaste strives to connect. Like a business, Namaste is highly attuned to issues of marketing. It attempts to solidify its identity as an NGO focused on business mentorship and education in order to avoid being lumped together with profit-driven MFIs, which are increasingly common in the global south. As a result of its successful rebranding, and its policymakers and leaders' skills in grant-writing and networking, Namaste has cultivated relationships with northern agencies such as USAID, World Vision, Freedom from Hunger, Catholic Relief Services, IDB, and Kiva. As of 2013, IDB was considering granting Namaste $250,000 over the course of three years to develop its Train the Trainers Program. Namaste was also preparing to partner with Oxfam's Women in Small Enterprise (WISE) program, which gives much larger loans to women running small businesses. Originally the program was to be implemented in Guatemala, Haiti, and Colombia, but Oxfam could not find NGOs in Haiti and Colombia with a focus on and capacity for measurement similar to that of Namaste. Additionally, WISE was considering buying the rights to use Namaste's data management system, itself designed by a northern software engineer who volunteered his time and expertise. Tenmast software developed a customized online database to manage Namaste's loan and educational data, and Qlik donated software, services, and training to further hone their online tracking system.

Through Namaste's relationship with members of Kiva, a U.S.-based non-profit, Graham was recently introduced to another retired CPA based in Canada who, like Graham, was interested in raising money for microcredit programs in the global south. The Canadian has since founded his own NGO to raise money to fund Namaste's loans, in many ways following in Graham's footsteps. All told, 37 percent of Namaste's funding comes from foundations and institutions such as the Canadian NGO or the Bank of America Charitable Foundation, 25 percent from board members, 25 percent from individual donations, and 13 percent from service fees and interest paid by beneficiaries. Namaste's leadership successfully leveraged northern networks to access funding and support and transferred to Namaste a management culture that incorporated transparency and eschewed personalism, allowing it to escape tendencies common to Guatemalan organizations, which were often highly personalistic and rarely transparent.

That said, Namaste's foreign nature and its policymakers' limited connections to the communities in which it operates means that Namaste's work is not imbued with a local identity. Even its name marks it as foreign, as Namaste is neither a Spanish nor a Mayan word. As we will see in chapter 4, women actively assign meaning to Namaste by comparing it to other institutions in their communities, seeing it as "the gringo bank," more or less comparable to other MFIs. Although Namaste now employs Guatemalans to manage its operations in the country, the organization's ties to the communities in which women live are relatively weak. The most important decision-makers have historically been located in California or the regional offices in the tourist city of Antigua. This means that those making organizational and programming decisions are less connected with the reality of women's daily lives, contexts, and businesses and more able to make simplifying assumptions about beneficiaries and their contexts than they would be if they were deeply embedded in local communities and familiar with women's quotidian realities.

Among Namaste's simplifying assumptions is that women have stable businesses in which they are going to invest. In reality, poor women often engage in informal, small businesses as survival strategies, switching businesses often and becoming more or less engaged in them depending on the time of year, familial demands, and other sources of income. It is not uncommon for women to switch businesses mid-loan cycle, or they claim the loan is for one business and then tell me they used it for another. Other women do not seem very interested in significant business growth if it means taking time away from their other responsibilities. This reality, which can only be gleaned from in-depth knowledge of local communities, complicates Namaste's approach to data collection and tracking, which is based on assumptions of continuity, linearity, and women's thirst for business expansion.

Business advisers are the workers on the front lines but have relatively little influence over major decisions. They are often from the region in which they work, but rarely do they live in, or close to, the semirural communities in which women live. A 2010 report by a Namaste volunteer found that of the eight business advisers observed, "zero [lived] in the actual community of the clients and [all] only [visited] the communities for client visits and business education sessions." As a result, business advisers "do not know the 'ins and outs' of the community, i.e. best practices[,] nor the business market." Field visits with women are not frequent enough for advisers to build strong relationships with women, to "find specific client needs and act on them," or for women "to go to the [business adviser] outside of the field-visit and education session if they want mentorship." Namaste's weak connections to local communities therefore narrows and limits women's relationships with the organization and decreases the likelihood that women will come to identify with the NGO in any meaningful way, especially because their participation is limited to designated activities and curtailed by temporal limits. As we will see in the next chapter, women see themselves as customers, not members.

Because it is a foreign-founded NGO that lacks strong local ties and seeks a very specific type of beneficiary, Namaste must invest more resources in recruitment than other local NGOs with broader target audiences or local connections. Business advisers canvass their assigned regions on foot, talking with women who operate small businesses and distributing flyers highlighting the economic benefits of the program. Flyers depict a woman meeting with a business adviser, participating in group educational sessions, and finally with more money in her hands. After an informational meeting, a visit to women's businesses, and a completed credit history search, business plan, and incoming assessment, advisers present the information, woman by woman, to the regional leadership, who have final say over decisions about loan disbursement and size. Thus Namaste compensates for its lack of local ties through a rather technical recruitment process that enrolls flyers, applications, business plans, and other forms. We will see in the following chapter that women actively interpret this recruitment process by comparing it with that of other MFIS operating in their communities, assigning it a meaning that Namaste's policymakers do not intend.

Women who participate in Namaste sense its foreignness. Many become accustomed to the presence of foreigners because the NGO often accepts foreign volunteers, has employed foreign staff, and regularly arranges visits for donors who delight in traveling down dusty roads to women's humble homes. The presence of foreigners is so common that after I asked one of Namaste's participants if she had any questions for me following an interview, she hesitated before blurting out with a smile, "Why are there so many gringos in Namaste?" Another woman in the same loan group explained that she joined Namaste rather than another MFI because she enjoyed that it was associated with gringos, demonstrating that for at least some women, the organization's foreignness made it more, rather than less, appealing. As we will see in the next chapter, the fact that Namaste is not embedded in local communities and is largely seen by women as relatively similar to other MFIS affects women's expectations in ways that limit their participation and Namaste's potential spillover effects.

CONCLUSIONS

This chapter focuses on the interactional sources and expressions of Namaste's central organizational characteristics. It demonstrates how the organization's prehistory and its policymakers' personal experiences and values informed the NGO's model of bootstrap development and its values, which led to a narrow focus on individual women's incomes and simplified views of women and their contexts. Using their backgrounds, Namaste's policymakers successfully institutionalized an audit culture by leveraging hiring procedures and requirements, training programs, paperwork, databases, and evaluation techniques that focused on quantitative measurements. They also drew on their existing ties and ability to speak the language of results-based management to successfully enroll donors and volunteers. They institutionalized networks to their favor by replicating organizational structures with which they were familiar and that would give them disproportionate influence in the future, cultivating a bureaucratic organizational structure. In turn, these characteristics allowed policymakers to develop and strengthen networks with foreign institutions, despite Namaste's relatively small size. Although Namaste reflected broader international trends that valued microfinance, incorporating women in development, and results-based management, seeing Namaste's characteristics as directly caused by those trends would overlook the contingent, interactional processes of translation that produced them.

The following chapter focuses on how these characteristics shape the interactions between workers and beneficiaries and the everyday practices and experiences of bootstrap development. It also demonstrates that the organizational characteristics described in this chapter interacted with beneficiaries' distinct meanings, goals, and actions to co-constitute practices and experiences on the ground. That is, while policymakers' values, structures, and models affected what unfolded in the context of Namaste, they did not determine it. Even though policymakers exercised disproportionate power, the tensions inherent in development projects ensured significant room for maneuver and negotiation. The result was mixed development outcomes. While Namaste was able to achieve some of its intended goals in the short term, the potential for spillover effects for women's identities and empowerment was limited. This was because in Namaste, developers and beneficiaries together created development sites akin to hallways, moving women efficiently from "before" to "after" but limiting the space for other, unplanned activities and meanings in between.

CHAPTER FOUR

WOMEN AND WORKERS
RESPONDING TO
BOOTSTRAP DEVELOPMENT

Adriana, a young woman wearing a *corte* (Mayan skirt) and a dark maroon blouse, moved the chipped, blue-painted gate blocking the lower half of her doorway to let Raúl, one of Namaste's business advisers, and me enter. We took our seats on the worn stuffed chair and couch that were pushed along one wall, facing six women sitting in a semicircle of plastic chairs. The recent rains had turned the dirt floor slightly muddy. As he set up his easel and roll paper, Raúl joked, "Look, I brought you a surprise. I brought you a gringa!" The women covered their mouths and giggled. He asked the women to introduce themselves, and one by one they covered their faces or looked down in embarrassment before standing up to state their names and describe their businesses. Four of the women acted essentially as middlemen—buying cortes in bulk and selling them in the surrounding communities. One woman bought meat, butchered, and sold it; another sold bread and pastries.

Most of the women's husbands, like almost 90 percent of the economically active population in Minalapa, were agricultural workers—harvesting coffee, bananas, and corn. The two exceptions were Adriana, whose husband was a retired soldier and was then working as a mechanic, and Isabella, whose husband migrated to the capital eight months prior to work as a security guard. So many people migrated from rural communities like this one to Guatemala City that at the time I was conducting research, the government had recently granted private contracts to a Taiwanese company to develop model communities in areas from which many migrated to the capital. These communities were meant for *personas de escasos recursos* (literally, people with limited resources—the politically correct way of saying "poor"). It was hoped that these communities, complete with housing, offices, shopping, even universities and hospitals, would stem the tide of migration to Guatemala City.[1]

Being *personas de escasos recursos* themselves, few of the women in this group had the opportunity to attend school. Aurora's father was killed during the armed conflict, when "everything was very delicate" because "people would get kidnapped and show up dead" (Aurora, 2010). Left alone to support her family, her mother relied on Aurora's earnings. Aurora therefore only attended first grade and then went to work in her neighbors' homes, before moving to Minalapa when she married her husband at the young age of fifteen. Isabella, who recruited a few other women in this loan group to join Namaste, never attended school. Her mother claimed that she would only go there to play so it was better for her to stay home to help with the housework. Liliana was raised by her grandparents. She was grateful that they never sent her to school because she "would just be surrounded by other children who had things" that she did not (Liliana, 2010). Instead she went with her grandparents to plant coffee and collect bananas. Despite their lack of experience with formal education, through their interactions with each other, Raúl, and materials (chairs in a semicircle, poster board hung on the wall, a "textbook" in Raúl's hand), they help generate a makeshift "classroom" in Adriana's one-room house—a concrete site of "bootstrap development."[2]

Despite—or more likely, because of—the geographic and experiential distance between these women in Minalapa and Namaste's policymakers and leadership in California and Antigua, the organization is driven by clear ideas about the knowledge and resources that Guatemalan women possess and what these beneficiaries require to improve their lives. Based on the idea that women lack access to capital and their own sources of income, the organization provides women small loans. Based on the assumption that women lack business knowledge and struggle to keep track of their finances, the NGO designs classes and mentorship around the themes of business education and financial literacy. But observations on the ground reveal that in reality, women display varying levels of access to loans and income, existing knowledge, and interest in educational material.

Back in Minalapa, before delving into the day's topic, "Selling to Clients the Right Way," Raúl reviewed the previous month's lessons. Pointing to a picture of a hand, he read off words written on each finger—promotion, price, place, product, and person. "There is always competition, but remembering to think about these things is what is going to force us to improve customer service," he said. That day, he explained, women were going to learn to better serve the client and to classify them. Reading from the book in his hand provided to him by Namaste, based on material from Freedom from Hunger, he told a story about a woman who was trying to sell vegetables to a variety of clients. The women sat patiently, some with their chins resting on their hands, others picking at loose threads in their cortes or looking at their fingernails. Raúl turned the book around to briefly show women an illustration of a woman selling vegetables to a line of customers with a smile. "This is how we should sell to the client." He then pointed to a handmade poster outlining the different types of clients that someone selling vegetables might encounter and discussed the obstacles that might come with selling to each type.

Eventually, Raúl asked women to pair off to discuss the ways that they had attempted to identify and attract new clients. After a minute or two the women reported that they were done, and Raúl collected their responses. One woman said, "Before anything else, you have to know your client." Two other women repeated different variants of this same response before Adriana chimed in: "If someone orders meat and does not pay, I do not take their order again." Raúl nodded. "Yes, but is it not sometimes the case that someone will pay the first and second time but maybe not the third? This is why it is important to know your client. Does he have a good job? Is he from here? If not, deal in cash." Satisfied with the day's lesson, Raúl began packing up, turning his head toward the still-seated women, asking how the loan payments were going. "Good," one responded, "my husband went to pay."

This chapter focuses on the quotidian practices like the ones described in Minalapa that Namaste's developers (policymakers, NGO leaders, and workers) undertake in their attempt to help women like Adriana, Aurora, Isabella, and Liliana, as well as the perceptions, strategies, and goals that these same women develop and pursue in relation to Namaste.[3] Embedding oneself in these interfaces in which Namaste's workers and beneficiaries interact provides unique insights into how models of bootstrap development, Namaste's organizational characteristics, and the demands of social entrepreneurship play out on the ground, as well as how they are assigned meaning, leveraged, and transformed by employees and beneficiaries alike. The chapter reveals that Namaste's practices shape and are shaped by women's expectations, meanings, goals, and environments, ensuring that policymakers' predictions are never fully fulfilled and contributing to Namaste's mixed outcomes.

This chapter first focuses on how Namaste's workers recruit beneficiaries in ways that mirror other microfinance institutions. Yet women are not passive in this process. They challenge or accommodate workers. They actively assign the organization meaning and craft expectations of the NGO based on their initial interactions with Namaste's employees, previous experiences, and knowledge of other institutions. And they strategically engage with MFIS for their own purposes, taking advantage of MFIS' simplified perceptions of them and their communities. Although policymakers intend otherwise, these initial interactions encourage women to see Namaste as just another MFI and to value their potential participation in the organization instrumentally, as a means to the end of receiving a loan, rather than seeing it as valuable in its own right. Thus, while the previous chapter highlighted how policymakers identify solutions and form expectations about beneficiaries by drawing on their prior experiences, existing strategies of action, and dispositions, this chapter explores the other side of that analysis. It addresses how beneficiaries form expectations about development interventions and NGOs, as well as what happens when developers and beneficiaries' expectations and simplified views of the other converge in the context of development interventions.

The chapter then highlights the various ways that Namaste's developers attempt to create concrete sites of bootstrap development by creating classrooms, where targeted skills are taught, and by providing one-on-one business mentorship that allows Namaste to monitor and shape women's businesses and practices. In so doing, Namaste reinforces women's expectations of the organization and demonstrates that, like women themselves, it values women's participation instrumentally, as a means to an end of increasing women's incomes, rather than valuable in its own right. The result is that women, workers, NGO leaders, and policymakers, pursuing their diverse goals, co-constitute development hallways—narrow spaces that promote efficiency but limit creativity. In these spaces, Namaste's developers attempt to turn poor women into entrepreneurial subjects by refusing to work with certain women, teaching its beneficiaries new business practices, monitoring their activity, conditioning future loans on their behavior, and compartmentalizing women's identities as businesswomen. In the face of these attempts at governmentality, women (sometimes in collaboration with NGO workers themselves) display strategies of accommodation, guile, and, less regularly, resistance.

Finally, the chapter concludes by connecting the interactional practices and experiences of bootstrap development with outcomes for women's daily lives. Through the stories of three women, it demonstrates that Namaste appears to succeed on its own terms by raising many women's business incomes in the short term. Similarly, women, for their own reasons, often see their participation in the organization as a success. Yet these women's stories also demonstrate that Namaste's worldview overlooks the significant structural inequalities that affect women's daily lives, and that developers and beneficiaries thus unintentionally collude in limiting the organization's broader spillover effects.

HOW WOMEN COME TO VIEW NAMASTE AS JUST ANOTHER MFI

MIRAVERDE

In Miraverde, John, a tall American with a broad smile then serving as Namaste's program manager, met with two representatives from Fundación de Asistencia para la Pequeña Empresa (FAPE). This was a Christian organization that provided both solidarity group loans and individual credit. Alessandra was FAPE's promoter—she traveled to communities like Miraverde to knock on doors and inquire if residents were interested in loans. When she believed she had enough interested women gathered, she notified Eva, her administrator, who arranged an informational session to explain the program in more detail. In the car ride here, John had explained that in the future, Namaste would not be partnering with local MFIs like FAPE but would instead recruit and screen women and administer the loans itself.

The four of us walked up the slight hill leading away from the town's center, past metal-roofed houses—some made of concrete blocks, others made of sticks and mud or wood—and knocked on a black metal door. Flor answered and led us past a table piled with fabric to the dirt patch in front of her house, where four other women were seated. Eva stood in front of the women, who formed a semicircle on long wooden benches and plastic chairs, and introduced herself. She explained that they were there to explain how the loans worked, what solidary groups were, and what business education entailed. She asked the women to introduce themselves, and they stood up one by one to say their name and business. One woman ran a *tortillería* (making and selling corn tortillas), two embroidered, one bought and sold used shoes, and one grew and sold vegetables.

Eva quickly explained the terms of the loan.

We are offering loans between 800 or 1,000 and 2,000 quetzal [roughly $100/$125 to $250] but we are only giving them to women

who really have a business in which to invest. If you were just participating with FAPE alone, you would be charged 4 percent interest monthly. But with Namaste, we are charging 2 percent, which
means on a loan of 2,000 quetzal, one would spend about 40 quetzal [$5] each month. You have to pay every fourteen days. We're
operating on a six-month cycles. For a loan of 1,000 quetzal, one
would pay 115 quetzal [$14.40] each month—83.25 quetzal [$10.42]
in capital, 11.75 quetzal [$1.47] in savings, and the rest in interest.

I frantically scribbled down the numbers while the women nodded
patiently.

After John briefly described the key features of their educational
program, the women turned to Eva to ask more questions about the
loans: "Are there fees for late payments or early cancellations?" "How
much do we pay back each month?" "What happens when someone is
sick and cannot pay? Does the rest of the group pay for her?" "No," Eva
replied, "we work differently than Genesis [another MFI in the area].
There, the [group's] president goes to the bank to pay for the whole group
each time," so if someone misses a payment, the others have to make it up.

It was striking that the women were so well versed in the conditions
of loans and were able to ask about small fees that Eva had not originally
mentioned. It was clear that at least a few of the women had taken out
loans before. Finally, one woman spoke up: "To me, everything sounded
good. I was in another group and what I learned is that what is important is that the women actually want to work. That they show up on time
and invest in a business." Eva nodded and stated, "Good, then what
you need to do is gather five more women, because we cannot work
with this many. There needs to be at least ten." John and Eva packed up
their posters and we all headed back toward the town's center. When
we parted ways with Eva and Alessandra, John told me that Namaste
did not have any say about how much each woman would get, but once
Namaste took over distributing the loans, this would change. "Then, it
will be based on their businesses."

A few weeks later, although the women had successfully recruited
five others, John reported that Namaste decided not to work with them
because the women had already taken on too much debt: "Most already
had a loan. Some had two."

This vignette demonstrates that because NGOs and banks targeting poor women with small loans are increasingly common in Guatemala, many of the women who apply to enter Namaste's program have previously received a loan from another MFI.[4] As a result, women are becoming increasingly familiar with the process of accessing and managing loans and the language and practice of microcredit—they are forming expectations of MFIs, feel comfortable interrogating them, and have started to use MFIs strategically for their own purposes.

The scene in Miraverde took place while Namaste was still partnering with local MFIs; at that time Namaste's MFI partners largely shaped recruitment practices. However, as we will see, even after Namaste began working independently, its recruitment tactics remained relatively consistent. In addition to mirroring the recruitment practices of other MFIs, Namaste's workers often emphasized the loan during their first interactions with women, based on their views of women's priorities and women's own demands. The result was that the core programs that distinguished Namaste from other MFIs (group education and one-on-one mentorship) were underemphasized. These first impressions shaped the nature of women's initial interactions with Namaste's workers. In environments with a number of NGOs, MFIs, and businesses targeting women, women made comparisons between institutions that they perceived to be of the same type. Their initial interactions with Namaste led them to view Namaste and other MFIs as comparable institutions, thus shaping both their expectations of participation and their goals and demands in relation to Namaste.

TAMACURÚ

Walking down a dirt road in Tamacurú, José Miguel paused in front of a small store next to a tortillería with a metal sheet as a makeshift roof. Through the open doorway of the house located behind these small businesses, two women sat in plastic chairs and one sat up in a hammock strung up inside. José Miguel waved to them and we headed inside. The one-room cement-block house had been divided in two by curtains and a rickety wooden divider. In addition to a number of plastic chairs and the hammock, this side of the house had two plush chairs and a couch facing a boxy television and stereo in the front, with a small wooden table pushed into a corner in the back.

The owner of the house, Mita, sat down next to us and began to chat while we waited for the other women to arrive to the informational meeting. "There are seven of us, altogether," she explained. José Miguel asked about her business and she replied that she sold eggs, coffee, and tortillas to her neighbors and restaurants in the surrounding areas. "Before I had a business selling sheets but my mother died and I gave it up. Now I am starting again." Later, she explained that she knew that it was important to treat her clients well. "For example, if they complain about me showing up [with tortillas] later than they want them, I will go earlier the next day." The other two women had been listening and started talking about their businesses. Jimena, sitting up in the hammock, explained that she collected and sold kindling; Noa harvested corn.

"How long has this organization been around?" Noa asked. José Miguel pointed to the paper he had taped to the cement wall that detailed the history of the organization. "It has been in [this area] for a couple of years but it was partnered with Raíz before." Noa turned to Jimena: "Raíz?" Jimena nodded. "I have heard of them but I did not get involved because there were high interest rates. . . . I cannot remember how much exactly, but they were high." Noa turned back to José Miguel: "And can you get a loan even if you already have one with another organization?" José Miguel explained that yes, you could, but your debt could not be more than 30 percent of your income. Noa nodded and looked down at the paperwork she brought with her—a copy of her *cédula* (identification card) and an electricity bill.

Two more women, Silvia and Carmen, arrived. Satisfied with the number of women there, José Miguel stood up next to the paper on the wall. He explained the history of the organization and the meaning of the word "Namaste," and he began to detail the three components of Namaste's program—the one-on-one advising, educational sessions (group classes), and the loan. "Another Namaste employee and I visited another group with which we have been working. One woman, Adriana, approached us. She said she did not want to continue on with Namaste. When we asked why she said that she had her savings and now she wanted to work on her own. This, for us, is good."

During the story, another woman entered, lowering her head as she walked past José Miguel. As he paused and looked around the room, the tardy woman asked loudly, "And how long is the loan for?" José Miguel pointed to another sheet of paper taped to the wall and outlined the loan cycle and the monthly rate. The woman seemed quite pleased, nodding enthusiastically.

Silvia, the woman that was sitting to my left, asked, "And what happens if someone does not pay?" José Miguel smiled. "I get the sense that this will not happen in this group because you all know each other; but yes, you have to pay." He again pointed to the paper, but before he got out more than a few words, Silvia insisted, "But what if someone does not?" José Miguel avoided answering the woman directly, stating, "Well, you have to choose people to enter your group that you trust. Now once you get your group together—" Silvia interrupted him a second time: "Excuse me, you have not answered my question. What happens if we do not pay?"

Mita jumped in. "I suppose that is why there is a guarantee"—referring to a small fee women paid at the beginning of the loan cycle that was returned after repayment. "I have been in other groups where this has not happened. They all paid. If they were late it was only because of a sickness in the family or something, but [they missed their payment] with a lot of shame. Because one does not want others to pay for her. I heard of another group that ended badly. I was working with BanTrab [Banco Trabajador] but I have already finished with them." Another woman added, "I am working with FINCA."

As the women started to talk among themselves, José Miguel moved to the back of the room to the small table in the corner and began to complete women's paperwork one at a time. Silvia scowled and walked out the door and across the street to her house, having decided against joining.

Some of the women did not have the required paperwork, so José Miguel agreed to return in the afternoon to finish collecting their information. In the meantime, he walked up the nearby hill to do some more promotion. He stopped at roadside stores and small businesses. One woman said that she received a 10,000 quetzal (roughly $1,250) loan from Fe y Alegría to open her store and tortillería. Fe y Alegría (Faith and Joy) was a Christian international NGO that described itself as a movement dedicated to popular education and social development. They, like many other NGOs, had started providing loans as an element of their work.

Most of the women José Miguel approached took a flyer and thanked him for explaining the program. At the top of the small hill, José Miguel approached a woman who had chips and other snacks hanging from a rope outside of her small house, which was situated next to a schoolyard swarming with children. Before José Miguel could finish explaining the program, the woman cut him off, saying she was not interested: "We do not have much, but I always thought it was better to work with what we have than borrow." José Miguel looked surprised at the woman's response and the firmness and confidence with which she gave it.

Later in the afternoon, José Miguel returned to Mita's house to finish collecting the women's documents. While he was filling out Noa's paperwork, a *tuk tuk* (a small three-wheeled taxi, with a metal frame and canvas bench seats) rattled up the dirt road, stopping in front of the store by Mita's home. A neatly dressed woman in her thirties climbed out and began talking with a number of the women waiting to meet with José Miguel. When she pulled a clipboard out of her bag with the logo of Promerica Bank on it, it became clear to me that she was here as a representative of the bank to collect women's monthly loan payments.

The final meeting of the day took place outside the town's gymnasium. By 3:30, seven women had arrived, but they insisted that more were coming. Five more arrived, one with her husband, who interrupted José Miguel as he described the program with questions about the monthly payments. Toward the end of José Miguel's presentation, by now well rehearsed, a tall man approached the group. He explained that he was a representative of Omnilife, a company that relied on women to sell their dietary supplements. He claimed that he "had" twenty-five women for José Miguel that needed loans. The two men exchanged information and arranged to meet the following week before José Miguel packed up his belongings and we headed to the center of town to wait for the bus.

These vignettes depict the new landscape that many poor women are now navigating—populated by the increasing number and spread of NGOs, banks, and companies seeking to "help" them. But they also demonstrate that women are not mere dupes. Neither victims nor heroines of bootstrap development, some are eager aid recipients; knowing the right things to say and how to accommodate MFIs, some women strategically engage multiple NGOs at once, while others reject them altogether. The reality of women's environments, which they adeptly navigate, and the diversity of women's goals complicate Namaste's policymakers' expectations and assumptions about women, their communities, and the centrality of the development intervention that they are offering.

The vignette from Tamacurú also demonstrates that Namaste's recruitment practices in many ways replicate those of other MFIs, like the one I observed in Miraverde, FAPE. This affects who joins as well and their expectations upon doing so, because beneficiaries' perceptions of any given development project or NGO are in part informed by their prior experiences of development and the existing landscape of projects and organizations. That is, "the *memory* that people have of previous interventions tends to shape the way they imagine development relations, and to shape their present demands accordingly" (Hilhorst 2003, 108).

In this case, Namaste's strategy combines with an organizational environment heavily populated by MFIs, NGOs, banks, and businesses targeting women such that women's decisions to join or not to join Namaste are often based on their previous (or ongoing) experiences with development projects, or their knowledge of other organizations that women perceive as similar. Clearly, some women have become comfortable interacting with MFIs as customers who have multiple options. They have established opinions about these types of organizations and often ask surprisingly informed questions about payment cycles, interest rates, and hidden fees. Women interested in joining Namaste seem most concerned with the conditions of the loan, and their questions show that many have become adept at comparing MFI programs and are prepared to interrogate organizations up front rather than seeing the loans as gifts for which they should feel grateful. Thus, the agency that many women exercise while considering Namaste is akin to that of customers—they are interested in Namaste's product but know they have other options. Although Namaste often imagines an exclusive relationship with women, in reality women view the organization in relation to other institutions and look to Namaste to achieve their own ends, which are sometimes at odds with those of Namaste's policymakers.

Comparing Namaste to other MFIs that do not incorporate classes into their programs, many women see Namaste's educational components as an added cost to the loan. Field updates from 2009, for example, often included notes about women turning down the loan and education: "Mauricio promoted to [three] groups . . . all with bad responses—one group 'is a possibility with half the group accepting (but the other half firmly no)'; one said yes if there is no added cost to them [they did not want to pay the small fee for education], and the last group 'simply said no they did not like the program.'" Others mentioned that women who had already joined Namaste were "grumbling about so many meetings." Workers explain that even when they try emphasizing the educational components to women, "the first questions they have are 'do you give credit?,' and 'how much do you give?'" As a result, Namaste's workers tend to emphasize the loan over the other services offered in their interactions with women. Employees argue that if they did not provide loans, "no one would join."

Most of the women I met who were uninterested in loans cited fear of debt as their main reason for their reticence, a fear rooted in women's experiences with other MFIs or rumors that they had heard. They shared stories of neighbors defaulting on their payments or debt collectors seizing property. Namaste's recruitment strategies and programming therefore interact with women's experiences and environment such that Guatemalan women, both those who want to join the organization and those who are reluctant to do so, are likely to view Namaste as just one among many MFIs, NGOs, and businesses focusing on poor women and they judge it accordingly.

As we will see, these expectations, based on women's initial interactions with Namaste and their knowledge of other MFIs and NGOs, lead most of the women who join Namaste to value their participation instrumentally, as a means to an end of accessing a loan. Their subsequent interactions in Namaste do little to change these views, as Namaste's policymakers, leaders, and (to varying degrees) workers also value women's participation instrumentally. Pursuing their own goals, developers involved in Namaste's projects help to create hierarchal spaces in which women are seen as relatively passive recipients of knowledge, which in turn reduces the likelihood of engaging with or even recognizing the full complexity of women's lives.

WORKERS' DIVERSE INTERPRETATIONS OF BOOTSTRAP DEVELOPMENT AND WOMEN'S CREATIVE REACTIONS

Developers Cultivating Hierarchical Classrooms

The educational session in Minalapa depicted in this chapter's opening is representative of many of Namaste's activities. Group educational sessions, which at the time of this research were held monthly, were relatively brief classes focusing on women's businesses and financial literacy. These classes are often based on material from Freedom from Hunger, an international NGO with the tagline "Self-help for a Hungry World." Group classes cover topics under three general themes: managing your money, increasing your sales, and planning for a better business. Namaste's policymakers and leaders hope to make these classes as efficient as possible so as to avoid taking up too much of beneficiaries' time and taking them away from their businesses. The organization therefore emphasizes punctuality (with limited success) and concrete, targeted lessons and, at times unintentionally, encourages hierarchical interactional spaces.

On the ground, workers and beneficiaries create classrooms out of homes by adjusting physical spaces—lining up chairs or placing them in semicircles and taping pieces of flimsy gray roll paper to concrete or wooden walls. Advisers also position themselves as teachers—standing in front of the seated women, directing the time they spend together, teaching them the correct answers, even occasionally giving women homework (rarely completed). In his observation of an educational session, the program manager indicated his discomfort with some aspects of this environment, noting in a 2009 field update that the business adviser he observed "chastised the women for talking in [K'iche':] '*Por favor en español*'" (in Spanish please) and treated them "like children in a school: '*atención, silencio por favor*'" (attention, silence please).

Although the program manager critiqued it, this behavior is in fact unsurprising given that both Namaste's programming and structure position business advisers as providers, and women as recipients, of expertise that is deemed important by Namaste's policymakers. The business advisers, themselves influenced by their desire for job security and status, at times internalize and interpret this role of teacher in ways that cause them to position themselves as authority figures, rather than advisers. The following scene depicts one such situation and reveals that Namaste's approach to group education, like its recruitment practices, mirrors that of other MFIs that offer education, further shaping women's expectations about participation.

ORAZUL

By the time David and Rodrigo, two of Namaste's business advisers in this region, and I stepped down from the colorfully painted, repurposed school bus, it was pouring rain. With our hoods pulled over our heads, we waited for a momentary lull in the traffic before bolting across the highway and settling into a walk up the one-lane road leading to Orazul. When we arrived at the designated house for the informational session, there were only two women present. While David and Rodrigo waited for the others to arrive, the owner of the house showed them a poster hanging on her wall, explaining, "This is how we work." The poster featured a number of pictures, including a clock and money above an image of a Bible. These two women were members of a group receiving loans from Grameen Bank, which partnered in Guatemala with the microfinancial arm of a commercial bank, Banrural. "The clock means that we are supposed to arrive ten minutes early with everything in order," the woman explained. "And the money and the Bible?" asked David. "That means that we should be thankful to God for the money we earn."

David saw an opportunity to learn more about the "competition" and began to ask questions about Grameen's program, which operated, according to the woman, on a one-year loan cycle with payments every two weeks. Like Namaste, it included classes alongside every payment meeting, but the women added, "They are given by people who do not speak Spanish very well," presumably foreigners. The women were paying 74 quetzal (roughly $9) every two weeks on a loan of 1,500 quetzal ($190)—an effective interest rate between 18 and 19 percent—one of the lowest in the country. The two women showed David the small booklets that they were given to keep records of when they made payments. Payments were made individually, "but the group's president collects the books from everyone each meeting to make sure that they are in order," the other woman explained. "There are fines for being late—you have to pay three quetzal for arriving late to meetings. Two quetzal for forgetting to bring your stool. And five quetzal for not attending [class]." Rodrigo looked surprised and laughed: "And I bet the adviser pays fines too [if he is late]!" "Actually," one of the women interjected, "he does."

As other women began to arrive, Rodrigo sat on one of the beds in the one-room house and placed his wet backpack on the neatly arranged comforter before leaning back against the wall in a semireclined position. He took a towel that had been laid over the pillow, rolled it up and placed it behind his head. David sat down in the wooden chair next to the bed and gently moved Rodrigo's dripping bag to the floor.

As the women took their seats, they talked with each other and with David about other MFIs. A few of the women were complaining about FINCA and explaining the problems that a group working with FINCA was having with repayment. Another woman explained that she took a loan out with a different institution and had to pay 25 quetzal ($3.17) a day for twenty-three days, which ended up being 15 percent interest, according to her calculations. She pulled out a few notebooks to show David where she kept records of her payments. All the while, Rodrigo looked disinterested and bored. When everyone had arrived, ten women total, he finally stood to begin the informational session.

Rodrigo asked two different women why they arrived, and when the women began to say that they came to learn about the program, he cut them off, saying, "That is good. The Bible says, those who have ears, listen." The women nodded as Rodrigo continued to explain the details of the loan conditions, educational sessions, and business mentorship. Throughout, after he explained an aspect of the program, he paused and walked up to one of the women, leaned forward, pointed at her, and asked her to repeat what he had just said.

At the end, he quizzed the women to see if they remembered what they covered, and he looked disappointed when women could not answer questions like "what is the interest rate," "what is the guarantee," and "how much do you pay for education?" He then went around the semicircle, standing in front of each woman, leaning forward, and pointing at them: "Are you interested? Are you interested? And you, are you interested?" Each of the women nodded. "Good," he said. "I will be the professor and you will be the students. But I will also be your employee." He arranged for women to drop off their paperwork—copies of their identification cards and electricity bills—as a next step in the process.

This scene demonstrates the ways that Namaste's employees interact with women, material, and space to create hierarchical social relations. Because business advisers are cast in the role of teachers and take pleasure in the status this brings, some begin to treat women as schoolchildren, although few do so as explicitly as Rodrigo did. Policymakers do not intend for condescending and disrespectful behavior; indeed, when the NGO's leaders observe it, they correct advisers. But policies become transformed when real people with their own diverse goals, biases, and personalities put them into practice. Rodrigo, for example, was known among his colleagues as a *fanfarrón* (a show-off or loudmouth), and his self-aggrandizing behavior was expressed in both his personal and professional lives. He saw his position at Namaste only as a job, privately explaining to me that Namaste's focus on women was flawed because, in fact, women "are not the engines of growth." Reflecting his machismo, in the previous vignette, he treats women as ignorant students even though moments before they had demonstrated that they had considerable experience with other MFIs, had already received business education from Grameen, and were well versed in the requirements that borrowing entailed.

Eventually, the regional director let Rodrigo go. Yet I have decided to include the scene here for two reasons. First, it demonstrates how development models do not translate predictably into practice. Even in highly institutionalized organizations with extensive monitoring systems like Namaste, the actual practices and experiences of development models and policies are shaped by the agency—the goals, beliefs, and personalities—of real people, including people like Rodrigo, who do not necessarily accept or internalize the development models and policies they are enacting.

Second, this vignette is included because it demonstrates both explicit and implicit ways that MFIs, including Namaste, establish hierarchical relationships with women. The women depicted with Rodrigo have experience with an MFI, Grameen, which establishes a system of fines to enforce rules that Grameen has set without consultation with women themselves. Rather than asking women about their needs and desires, Grameen's policymakers designed scripted educational sessions, given by "experts" who are not entirely fluent in Spanish. Women are therefore accustomed to complying with MFIs' rules and sitting through educational sessions that are of limited use in order to gain access to a loan.

Similarly, Namaste's informational sessions are spaces in which Namaste's workers are cast as the experts. By the time Namaste's workers interact with women, the terms of the loans have already been set, the content of the educational sessions has already been planned, and the goals have already been established. Women are essentially asked if they want to take it or leave it, rather than having any meaningful say over loan conditions or programming. Business advisers are seen and see themselves as teachers and experts in these spaces, leading to the natural conclusion that women are students and novices. One employee, for example, critiqued Namaste's decision to limit women's participation to two loan cycles by claiming in an interview in 2013, "It is like you are giving them first and second grade, but not third, fourth, or fifth."

In the past, women were given *some* say over educational content. As an additional educational element that accompanied loans, Namaste provided groups with one vocational training session per loan cycle on a topic that women requested. Women could ask Namaste to send them someone to teach them how to sew pants, to raise chickens, or to plant a new kind of vegetable. However, the organization eventually abandoned vocational training sessions because Namaste's policymakers deemed them too expensive and thought that they produced limited measureable results, as women often selected trainings that did not apply to their businesses. In so doing, they eliminated the one element of Namaste's services in which women were allowed to participate in decision-making and planning. The remainder of Namaste's services were selected and designed by Namaste's policymakers in consultation with NGO leaders, and women simply became consumers of the final product. In essence, they became customers instead of members; indeed Namaste's policymakers, leaders, and workers referred to women as clients.

DEVELOPERS' VIEWS OF WOMEN AND THEIR PARTICIPATION TRANSLATING INTO ON-THE-GROUND PRACTICES

As already described, based on their initial interactions with Namaste, women establish a simplified view of Namaste as "just another MFI" and thus expect their participation in the organization to be minimal. They often see this participation as a necessary cost to receive a loan—valuing it instrumentally and often seeking to minimize the time and effort it requires. Their subsequent interactions with Namaste confirm and reinforce, rather than challenge, this view.

Like beneficiaries themselves, Namaste's policymakers value women's participation instrumentally—as a means to an altruistic end of increasing women's incomes more efficiently and effectively. In group classes, Namaste's policymakers and leaders encourage business advisers to selectively solicit women's participation to keep women focused. Business advisers ask for examples from women, pose questions that can be answered relatively quickly (but do not require lengthy discussion), or break them into small groups from time to time. Still, the bulk of any given class entails business advisers standing in front of women, reading them stories or outlining lessons—teaching and reinforcing the correct answers. This means that women are expected to be relatively passive recipients of information; in practice, advisers do not expect women to lead discussions nor do they consistently put them in a position to teach their peers.

In one-on-one meetings, women's participation is seen as important in part because women can provide the data that Namaste needs to evaluate women's businesses and its own effectiveness as an organization. Business advisers arrive at women's homes or places of business with standardized forms to guide their interactions. They sit with pen or pencil in hand, asking women how much they spent on various business inputs and how much they sold in the previous month. Once the information is gathered and numbers are punched into a calculator, business advisers hand women forms detailing their total expenditure, income, and profits or losses, using pictures to illustrate. All told, one-on-one meetings last between ten and twenty minutes and mostly involve business advisers dealing with forms while women watch.

In the past, advisers were instructed to ask about women's businesses and offer advice on how to improve in the following month. Yet because they worried about keeping their jobs and knew that leaders consistently monitored their paperwork, advisers often became so focused on filling out the forms that advice was often vague or given as an afterthought. Since then, Namaste has retrained business advisers and provided them with new forms to make one-on-one meetings more useful for women—demonstrating the ways in which the policymakers and leaders rely on paperwork to meet their goals. The new forms include spaces for expenses, sales, and profits, as before, but also prompt business advisers to detail any emergencies that interfered with women's businesses in the previous month, to note the number of hours women have spent in their businesses, and to calculate women's hourly "wage." The new forms remind advisers to summarize the previous month's advice and note whether it has been initiated, is in progress, was completed, failed, or was not accepted. Business advisers are then prompted to discuss the latest educational session, to ask if it was applicable to women's businesses and if women had applied and understood the session's lessons. Finally, advisers are directed to give women business advice for the following month. Using words and pictures, the forms remind them to give advice that is "specific, actionable, measurable, and achievable in the given time duration."

Thus, one-on-one mentorship activities, like group classes, place Namaste workers in the role of providers, and women in the role of as recipients, of knowledge and expertise. This type of relationship may help women's businesses, but it hinders women's desire and ability to direct their interactions with business advisers, as does the fact that business advisers are often focused on completing the forms and following the dictated steps. There is, of course, room for maneuver. Some women reveal worries or gossip with business advisers. But just as often, advisers (attempting to perform their assigned tasks quickly) and women (anxious to get back to their businesses or chores) collude to limit the interaction and hasten the process of data collection by relying on estimates or the previous months' figures and keeping questions and answers short.

Namaste's bureaucratic nature reinforces its tendency to value women's participation instrumentally and to create narrow, hierarchical interactional spaces. The hierarchy, specialization, speed, uniformity, and technical knowledge valued in bureaucratic organizations like Namaste often discourage dynamic, substantive, creative, and engaged participation on the part of their members. Instead, members are seen as parts in a machine that runs most effectively when each part performs its assigned functions as expected, without deviations.

The previous chapter revealed how Namaste's policymakers often develop simplified views of women, their needs, and their environments, based on their own habitus. These simplified views are enacted and reinforced in the everyday practices of bootstrap development, and in many ways, they make the complexity of women's lives illegible to the organization. In their attempts to help women effectively and efficiently, Namaste focuses narrowly on women's compartmentalized identities as entrepreneurs, even if this compartmentalization does not make sense in women's daily lives. For example, women are asked how many hours they spend in their businesses each month so advisers can calculate women's "hourly wage." Many women run their businesses out of their homes, intertwining housework and childcare with their business activities such that separating their reproductive and productive labor in this way is at best an artificial endeavor. Namaste's employees themselves do not understand the emphasis on an hourly wage, a relatively foreign concept in Guatemala, where the poor and working class (when employed in the formal sector) are generally paid by task rather than by hour. Still, because it is legible to Namaste's northern policymakers and donors, the hourly wage remains one of the organization's measures of success, even if it is not necessarily a measure that is meaningful to women's everyday lives.

Further evidence of compartmentalization is that women's roles in their families are rarely discussed in the spaces that Namaste creates, even though they are central to women's lives outside of the organization. When they are mentioned, women are often taught that families make demands that impede business success. They are warned that husbands or children will try to eat the food they prepare for sale or take items from their stores. When women are invited to Namaste's annual business conference, they are explicitly told to leave their children at home to avoid distractions. Compartmentalizing women's identities in this way invites women to focus on their identities as businesswomen and to take this role seriously. But it also decreases the chances that women will reexamine and critically assess their relationships, the reality in their communities, or their own identities as women in Namaste.

The ways that Namaste's instrumental view of participation, bureaucracy, and simplified views of women are enacted on the ground interact with women's expectations and goals and generate narrow interactional spaces. These spaces resemble hallways: they encourage relatively uniform forms of participation, efficiently move women from "before" to "after," but often fail to inspire much creativity in between.

WOMEN MAKING STRATEGIC CALCULATIONS IN THE FACE OF TOP-DOWN PROGRAMMING

Even in the most bureaucratic organizations, life overflows rules and standard operating procedures (Berk 2009). Namaste emphasizes punctuality but women often arrive late; business advisers assign homework but women often claim to have forgotten about it; Namaste values accurate data but women collude with business advisers to provide estimates rather than exact figures to save time and energy. And even though Namaste emphasizes short, targeted educational sessions, there have been cases in which women have put the spaces Namaste creates for bootstrap development to different uses. On rare occasions, activities lead to discussions about illnesses or other problems affecting women's families, and group classes provide a space for women to share their worries, as can be seen in the next vignette.

COLOMTEPEQUE

Having finished the day's educational session, David took down the paper he had taped to Alison's wall and walked toward the patio's outer door. Alison and Isidora walked with David and me and as we paused at the door to say goodbye, Alison's face looked worried as she told David, "I made a mistake." Soon she was talking lowly and quickly, explaining that a woman she knew came to her recently because she needed money to repay a loan she had taken out with another MFI. "It is one where you pay the whole amount at the end, not month by month," she explained. "She said that she only needed to pay back the loan and they would give her a new one." Alison explained that she did not have any money, but she lent the woman some necklaces that she could pawn, with the understanding that the woman would get them back when she received the next loan. "But the institution did not give her another loan!" Alison said, now with her voice raised. "I got the necklaces back from the person she pawned them to, but now he is insisting that I pay the debt, even though it is not my debt!"

David nodded but did not interject. "Now I am worried," Alison added, "because I did not tell my husband about all of this. He has never hit me but maybe now he will." After a big sigh, David looked down at his dusty shoes and back up at Alison. "My advice is to tell your husband. Because imagine if he finds out from someone else." Alison nodded but looked unconvinced as David opened the door to leave.

This type of encounter, while rare, demonstrates that women can use Namaste's spaces to discuss their worries, problems, and lives outside of their businesses. In this case, Alison looks to David for advice, perhaps hoping that he can provide financial support as a representative of Namaste. David, however, has not been trained to deal with these types of encounters. He supports Alison by listening carefully to her and by providing what he sees as sound advice, but his ability to do more is limited by the fact that he has to hurry off to his next meeting and will not return until the following month.

The fact that these types of interactions between workers and women do not occur regularly does not imply that there is no room for their agency. Agency, after all, does not necessarily imply that actors will always and everywhere take advantage of and expand their room for maneuver; it may well imply that actors imagine constraints that "are made effective only because actors devise patterns of practice according to them" (Hilhorst 2003, 107). Scenarios like the one described here, in which women use Namaste's participatory spaces creatively, are relatively rare. Yet this is in part because women themselves view their own participation in the organization instrumentally; thus, they seek to reduce the time and energy expended in these spheres and have limited desire to use Namaste's space in unintended ways. The reasons women give for joining or not joining Namaste reflect their assessments of the potential material and temporal costs and benefits of participation. They often see group classes and one-on-one mentorship as a requirement to access the loan. When asked her opinion of Namaste's classes, for example, Raquel replied simply, "I signed up. I signed the paper, so I have to attend classes" (Raquel, 2010).

Women entering Namaste who have already received loans from or been exposed to minimalist MFIs enter Namaste with an expectation of what participation will entail, gleaned from experiences with institutions in which participation involves little more than showing up to payment meetings on time. The program manager noted as much in a 2009 email to policymakers when he reported that women who had previously received loans from FAPE were accustomed to a system in which "each women just [dropped] off her deposit slip and skedaddle[d] off," and as a result, these women were "not used to sitting down as a group." One Namaste worker explained in a 2013 interview, "The program is working but the environment is the challenge" because the presence of so many other MFIs without social missions was "robbing [Namaste] of [women's] drive." Women's participation in Namaste clearly demonstrates that people perceive development projects based in part on their previous experiences and respond to organizations in relation to one another, and in this sense Namaste's beneficiaries exercise agency even while they limit their own participation.

Participation in Namaste aligns closely with Sarah White's depiction of instrumental participation, in which participation is valued from the top down for its ability to enhance efficiency and seen from the bottom up as a cost in a rational cost-benefit calculation (White 1996).[5] That is, developers and beneficiaries *jointly* construct Namaste's narrow "development hallways." Thus, although women participate minimally and make little effort to expand their room for maneuver, women's agency remains key to understanding the practice, experience, and outcomes of bootstrap development.

Despite Namaste's focus on education, many women continue to see the loan as central to its programming and as the main benefit of participation. When asked what they would change about Namaste, most are reluctant to voice any criticisms. But the few who offer suggestions focus on loan conditions, arguing for longer loan cycles and larger loans, comparing the organization to other MFIs in the area or to previous MFIs in which they have participated. Beyond the loan, women participating in Namaste generally have very little to say about their participation in the organization. They see it as a relatively unimportant part of their lives and have few strong feelings about the NGO. Namaste's identity as a loan-granting institution, and a foreign one at that, makes women less likely to identify with it or see themselves as active members.

With the exception of its annual conference, Namaste does not provide women with opportunities to participate above the targeted and scripted activities required to receive a loan. This approach combines with women's expectations and goals to channel women who join Namaste into relatively limited and uniform forms and levels of participation. Although some women are more talkative than others or have slightly higher attendance rates, the differences between the most active participants and the least active participants are small. Because women often decide to participate minimally and Namaste itself limits the length of time women can participate and streamlines activities, participation in Namaste entails far fewer small encounters than participation in many other NGOs, and it is therefore less likely to transform women's power within (internal sense of self-worth and self-efficacy), identities, or interests (Snow et al. 1986; Wood 2003; Munson 2008; Blee 1991, 2003).

NAMASTE'S ATTEMPTS AT CULTIVATING ENTREPRENEURIAL SUBJECTS AND WOMEN'S CREATIVE REACTIONS

In order to realize its vision of bootstrap development, Namaste aims to recruit the ideal beneficiaries, internally referred to as clients, and subsequently to shape their behavior to transform them into successful entrepreneurs. The first phase of this process is creating an image of the model beneficiary—one who is poor but has her basic needs met, some literacy skills, and an established business with access to a market and room to grow. Namaste's ideal client is also not overly indebted, and she either has a history of successful repayment or is a new borrower. Namaste communicates this image to potential partners in their description of the Train the Trainers program. The NGO recommends that women "carry no more than one simultaneous loan" and prefers that clients have at least a year of experience running a business and are not in the business of large animal production or medium- to long-term crop cycle farming. The informational material Namaste provides notes that women with these types of businesses are less suitable for this program because they face a "shortage of short-term business feedback loops that promote change and improvements" and are influenced by "change resistant agricultural traditions" (Fundación Namaste Guatemaya n.d.).

The second phase of cultivating entrepreneurial subjects entails recruitment and screening. Business advisers and beneficiaries jointly take on the tasks of recruitment, monitoring, and enforcement, performing unpaid or undercompensated labor that is often profoundly gendered (Beck and Radhakrishnan forthcoming). Advisers travel to their assigned communities distributing flyers and informing women operating businesses about the program. Women then take on the task of gathering together loan groups, drawing on their kin and non-kin networks and leveraging emotional ties, essentially providing unpaid labor in doing so. When interested women have gathered a group of at least five businesswomen together, the adviser returns to provide an informational session. The adviser then collects information about women's incomes, business, and backgrounds, examines their repayment histories using a national credit bureau for MFIs, visits and photographs their businesses, and discusses women on a case-by-case basis to determine their eligibility.

Those who pass through this screening process then meet with the business adviser, who collects more detailed information regarding their businesses and women's plans for loan use, often visiting women's businesses to verify the accuracy of their reports. Advisers present women's applications to the NGO's regional leaders for approval of the loan and final determination of the amount. More recently, Namaste has decided to require women to attend two two-hour educational sessions before they gain access to their loan, in place of monthly group classes. This method is seen as more efficient and comes with the added benefit of testing women's commitment to education and communicating that education is central to their program.

The third phase entails the active cultivation of good entrepreneurs through daily practices and interactions with beneficiaries. Women are required to keep financial journals that document their daily business expenses and sales, and business advisers verify and report the degree to which women are using journals in their one-on-one meetings. Business advisers counsel women to prioritize their businesses. Alongside counsel about products, prices, and locations, advice is given during one-on-one meetings that places pressure on women to take responsibility for their businesses' success or failure. Examples of the latter type of advice are "take your business seriously because only you can be detrimental to it," "you have to be careful to not take rests in your production because your interest payments depend on this," "dedicate more time to your business," and "weave more" (Namaste Volunteer 2010).

Advisers use one-on-one meetings with women not only to monitor their businesses and the implementation of their advice, but also to ensure that women are spending at least 80 percent of the loan on their businesses. If women do not comply, advisers recommend that women not be granted a second loan. In contrast, those that invest their money in their businesses, follow Namaste's business advice, keep financial journals, and attend the required activities are eligible for a second loan. The most successful women who have completed two loan cycles are now eligible for Namaste's new STARZ program, which provides very few women with larger loans granted on more flexible conditions.

Alongside its loan conditions and one-on-one mentorship sessions, Namaste's educational components contain explicit messages encouraging women to regulate their own behavior and that of their peers. In the following scene, Namaste and its partner MFI at the time ignore women's concerns about obstacles to business success and respond instead with explicit and implicit messages about the responsibilities of borrowers and businesswomen.

I traveled with Milagro, Namaste's regional manager, a petite woman with long wavy hair, to a vocational training session for a group in Cuixal. Namaste had recently decided to discontinue vocational training sessions because of the costs involved and because women often chose trainings they did not apply in their business. But this particular group, as Milagro explained, was "really calling for training in how to make new products" because "they were sick of all the posters; they wanted to learn how to do practical things." As a response, Milagro decided to schedule one last vocational training session for this particular group.

On the way, Milagro stopped at a luxurious gated community on the edge of Antigua to pick up Sharon, an American woman who had lived in Guatemala for many years. Sharon owned a large souvenir and furniture store in Antigua that sold overpriced handmade goods to tourists and expatriates. Milagro had recruited her to lead the vocational training session. After a quick trip to Sharon's store to pick up some sample products, we merged onto the Pan-American Highway. We stopped at a gas station to pick up Diego, Namaste's representative in this area, and Maribel, the representative of Namaste's partner institution, FAPE. We continued to Cuixal, a town largely populated by Maya Kaqchikel people and known for its handicrafts.

When we arrived in Cuixal, Maribel was told that "there is bad news." Someone in the community had recently died of old age, so some women would not attend the day's activity because they were at the funeral services. Milagro looked annoyed but insisted that they continue anyway, even though many of those who had asked for the activity would not be present. There were seven women waiting inside, sitting in the plastic chairs and on the beds in the one-room house. There were two back-strap looms resting on the floor, and the women eagerly showed them to Sharon and explained with large gestures how they used them to make their textiles. A number of women had brought examples of their work. Some women wove, some embroidered, and others did both. One woman laughed and said that she wove and her brother embroidered: "I do not know how he learned to do it. He just taught himself because he likes it." All the while the women spoke a mixture of Spanish and Kaqchikel, while Diego translated for Sharon, Milagro, and me.

As the women settled into their seats, Maribel stood up and began to talk as Diego translated. "Some of you are late with your payments," she stated, looking around the room, "and we cannot continue working with you if this happens." This prompted murmuring in Kaqchikel among the women. One woman said something in Kaqchikel to Diego, who translated: "She says many of them are on time so that it is not fair." Maribel responded firmly, "This loan, with us, it's based on the group. So it does not matter [if some of them are on time]."

Milagro was eager to begin the day's training on time. She interjected and the matter of late payments was left unresolved. She introduced Sharon, explaining that she was an example of a successful businesswoman and was there because they had asked Namaste to help them learn how to make new products. Sharon stepped forward and began by explaining the concept of a "family of products," showing examples from her store of coordinating purses and makeup bags and matching dishware. "If a customer likes one of these products, they are more likely to buy the other product in the 'family' because they go well together. This way you can sell more." The women seemed very excited about the products that Sharon displayed, passing them around and talking in Kaqchikel among themselves.

One woman held up a purse and said, using Diego as her translator, that they wanted to learn how to make such things, but they did not have sewing machines so they could not make similar products. Sharon smiled brightly and stated confidently, "Well, there are always problems. But that is what a businesswoman is, someone who overcomes obstacles." The woman furrowed her eyebrows as Diego translated Sharon's response.

Before further discussion, she passed out magazines to women and asked them to find families of products. The women looked through the magazines, fascinated but too embarrassed to share what they found. When Sharon singled out women to see their examples, they covered their faces with their hands or reluctantly pointed to a page without showing the group. Not that the other women were paying much attention — they seemed more interested in combing through the Pottery Barn magazines.

After more discussion, Sharon told the women that she needed women to embroider for her. She held up the purses she had brought with her. "The next step is to bring me samples. But I cannot work with just anyone. It needs to be quality work, and women need to have good communication skills; they have to be dedicated and responsible." By this time, however, some of the women appeared to have lost interest and a few were leaving, as it was around the time for them to start preparing lunch. They slowly filtered out, and by the time we packed up Sharon's magazines and samples, there were only three women left.

In this scene, we see evidence of multiple ways in which MFIs regulate women's behavior. The most obvious is the fact that FAPE puts poor women in charge of enforcing repayment. When someone protests this policy, the topic is quickly changed because Milagro is eager to start the day's lesson promptly. Women have requested an activity by successfully leveraging Namaste's promises. Yet when an unexpected event makes it difficult for many of them to participate, the organization moves ahead nonetheless. The women who are able to attend identify an important obstacle that they confront as businesswomen: their inability to produce certain products without sewing machines. Rather than brainstorming solutions with women or, for example, suggesting that women pool their resources to purchase one together, the training leader says only that good businesswomen are able to overcome obstacles. Later, they are told that in order to work with this foreigner, they need to produce quality products, and as an example, Sharon inadvertently holds up the very purses that the women explained they could not make without sewing machines. Finally, these women, who by and large are illiterate and do not speak Spanish, are told they need "good communication skills."

Of course, women do not wholly accept the roles assigned to them. The fact that Namaste provided vocational training for this group even though the NGO had recently decided to stop offering these trainings demonstrates women's ability to resist top-down decisions. They not only pushed for the training to take place, they also talked back and left the activity before it was concluded, revealing that they were able to maneuver even within these narrow spaces, though with limited effect.

Namaste's focus on individual women's businesses and the creation of good entrepreneurial subjects means that the NGO also attempts to change practices that are common within women's communities, the most notable of which is the practice of selling on credit. In the past, it was very common for women to provide goods to neighbors who did not have money at the time of purchase with the understanding that they would eventually be paid back. This practice has a long history in the country, and even in the early to mid-twentieth century, "bank credit did not define the Guatemalan landscape; personal credit did" (Way 2012, 82). This reality understandably led to local-level disputes, but it also tied Guatemalans together in complicated webs of debt, relations, and underground commerce. Namaste teaches women that this practice should be universally avoided.

In one class, for example, the business adviser asked women what they thought of selling on credit. One woman responded that she thought it was better to deal in cash. The adviser, reading from his Freedom from Hunger book, replied that she was correct because people might not pay them back and they could have used that money to buy more products to sell in the meantime. He then read stories about three women, asking if they would sell to each on credit. Another woman responded that she would not sell to any of them on credit because she needed the money to repay her loan. After further discussion, the adviser inquired again about the dangers of selling on credit, asking, "What would you do if a woman has a sick child; would you sell to her on credit?" The women looked uncomfortable, but as it was clear that the desired answer was no, they shook their heads, perhaps hiding their true reactions. While it is likely that adhering to this advice, common among MFIs who provide training, will lead to higher business profits, it might also come at the expense of community dynamics that have long served an important purpose in very poor communities. Women accommodate advisers in the context of classes, but outside of these public transcripts, the degree to which they actually adhere to this advice varies.

In other cases, group solidarity is strained when women fall behind in their payments, because MFIs often look to beneficiaries to enforce desired behavior. This was especially the case when Namaste was partnering with local MFIs, who had their own rules for disciplining women: FAPE charged women $5 fines for late payments, and Raíz required the group to pay for defaulting members. When Namaste was still partnering with Raíz, Namaste's program manager reported in a field update to policymakers that Raíz was threatening to remove goods from women's businesses if payment was not made for a group member who had gone missing. A employee explained in a 2009 field update, "The clients say that they do not need to pay for the missing person, they understood nothing about the terms (specifically the solidarity group) because it was explained in Spanish, not in [K'iche'] and so have no responsibility." These threats of punishment for defaults call on women themselves to enforce desired behavior, yet women also leverage stereotypes (as they did when they played into the stereotype of the "ignorant" indigenous women by

FIGURE 4.1. Women participating in Namaste wait while their repayments are verified. Photograph by the author.

claiming they did not understand the terms of the loan) or practice a combination of accommodation and resistance in the face of these demands, as can further be seen in the next vignette, which took place when Namaste was still partnering with local MFIs.

XOCOLAJ

Up a hill and down a narrow alley that led to the covered patio with long wooden benches on a dirt floor, Namaste's monthly educational session was off to a bad start. Only two women had arrived. Agustina was seated one of the benches, her legs stretched out and her back against a concrete wall, while Paz sat at a wooden table marking down the payments and fines for absent women. Eduardo (Namaste's adviser) and the FAPE representative, Lesli, were standing and talking quietly, waiting to see if any of the other women were going to show up, though it looks doubtful. A number of women sent their payments along with Agustina, indicating that they were not planning on attending.

After some time, Carmen arrived sweating and breathing heavily. "I fell asleep. I am sorry, I overslept," she explained, and Agustina, Paz, and I laughed at her honesty. Eduardo decided there were not enough women to warrant moving forward with the day's educational session, but Lesli interjected; they needed to discuss what to do with a woman in the group who had not paid in some time. "She keeps asking for one more month, one more month," Lesli complained. "What we can do is bring the contract [that she signed] and go and collect things from her home." The three women seemed nervous about this possibility; they remained silent and looked at each other. Lesli continued: "If you all want to pay for her, that is fine, but if not, this is the other option. The good thing with this [option] is that her debt will not affect your credit, only hers."

After another moment of silence, Carmen spoke up. "I have worked with other organizations—with FAFI [FAFIDESS] and Genesis—and in these groups there was a board of directors [selected from the group of borrowers] that was in charge of making sure that all the women came and paid. Why is it different here?" Lesli replied that in these other programs there had been many complaints, "because what they do is send the money with the directive to pay off the loan. And if for some reason the directive is late or does not turn the money in, everyone in the group is affected. So if the head [the directive] is not right, then the body fails too." Looking at the women, she added, "In this group, one of the directive members does not even participate. We are having the same problems with [the president of the women's loan group]; she is behind on payments."

After some more discussion, Carmen announced that she would confront the woman but would not talk. "Why not try to resolve this in a nice way?" she asked. The women discussed further and decided that they would approach those who were not paying in order to convince them to make their payments nicely. Lesli agreed but warned, "Do not tell them about the possibility of FAPE confiscating their possessions because then they will just hide their valuables."

Here, women are asked to act as loan collectors or risk their reputation and credit. They are able to resist on the margins—agreeing to have uncomfortable conversations with their neighbors rather than seizing their property right away—and in this way FAPE succeeds in enlisting the women in debt collection but not on its own terms.

Namaste eventually stopped partnering with local MFIs like FAPE in order to administer the loan on its own. At this point, the NGO decided that it would not seize defaulting clients' property, although this decision was not clearly announced to women. Today, the organization applies pressure in different ways. It requires each woman to deposit a small fee (a guarantee) from which Namaste can draw in case a member of the group defaults, and advisers encourage group members to help defaulting members repay their loans out of their own pockets, even beyond these guarantees. Women are reminded in educational sessions of the importance of repayment, with workers emphasizing that women have made commitments and if they do not fulfill them, others will have to pay in their stead. An employee explained to me in 2013 that if a woman fails to repay a loan and her group members refuse to cover her debt above that covered by their guarantees, Namaste's workers visit the defaulting member on various occasions to pressure her to repay, require her to sign an acknowledgment of the debt, and eventually enter her default into the National Credit Bureau system—thus limiting her ability to access loans in the future.

Women's experiences with MFIs like FAPE and Raíz, and to a lesser extent Namaste, reveal the degree to which these types of organizations often encourage women to discipline each other's "bad" behavior and how this has affected women's expectations of Namaste. Enforcement strategies have influenced women's willingness to join organizations like Namaste and have forced them to become more selective about the women with whom they choose to associate. I often heard from potential and current Namaste beneficiaries that one "has to choose her group members very carefully." This decreases the likelihood that women will form groups with others whom they do not already know and shapes the dynamics of microfinance and women's interactions thereafter.

Thus Namaste and other MFIs deploy multiple strategies to cultivate their ideal beneficiary, through recruitment, screening, and subtle and not-so-subtle practices thereafter. Women respond to these attempts at governmentality with a mixture of strategies—by accommodating or openly resisting organizational demands, adjusting which organizations they join and with whom, leveraging stereotypes, or maintaining distinct public and hidden transcripts.

THE MIXED OUTCOMES OF BOOTSTRAP DEVELOPMENT: SHORT-TERM ECONOMIC GAINS WITH LIMITED SPILLOVER EFFECTS

In women's eyes, Namaste might appear to be quite similar to other MFIS in the region, but its operations diverge from surrounding institutions in a number of important ways that are at times difficult for women to perceive. In its management of loans, Namaste has resisted external pressures, sometimes from its own funders, to continually raise interest rates. Instead, the leadership remains committed to setting rates that are comparable to those of banks, which are often lower than those of most MFIS. In its educational programming, Namaste's commitment to one-on-one mentorship is, to my knowledge, unique. Former Namaste beneficiaries frequently cited Namaste's mentorship and education as something that set the organization apart from other MFIS that did not follow up after distributing loans and failed to "ask you how you are doing" (2013 survey respondent). Other MFIS have expressed interest in replicating this strategy of coupling loans with education and one-on-one mentorship, only to reconsider upon realizing that interest rates and fees cannot feasibly cover program costs.

The prevailing microfinance model's strict commitment to financial self-sustainability precludes such costly services. In many ways, the goals of the new-wave model of microfinance—which focus on increasing access to financial systems rather than reducing poverty—appear to have been fulfilled. In Guatemala at least, it appears that poor women in many communities have ample access to small loans from multiple institutions, although these loans are rarely accompanied by other services. While a significant number of Namaste's former beneficiaries surveyed in 2013 reported having had a loan either before entering Namaste (49 percent) or after (60 percent), far fewer reported receiving any form of business education (13 percent before Namaste, 9 percent after), suggesting that Namaste's approach is indeed unique.

Also unlike MFIS in the developing world that measure success according to repayment rates, Namaste focuses on women's incomes as its markers of success. While other MFIS in practice do not seem concerned with how women repay their loans (even if they are borrowing from other sources to do so), Namaste's policymakers and leaders have a sincere desire for women to repay out of their business profits.

What effects does Namaste actually achieve in the area of development and in women's daily lives? In many ways, Namaste succeeds on its own terms. According to Namaste's data, 60 percent of women who receive a loan from Namaste increase their business incomes during their first loan cycle. On average, women's monthly business incomes at the end of their first loan cycle are $45 higher than when they began the program,[6] although these aggregate figures obscure substantial variation across beneficiaries (Beck, Aguilera, and Schintz, forthcoming).

While preliminary follow-up research and surveys raise questions about the degree to which increased business incomes are sustained after women leave the organization, they also indicate that Namaste may have a positive impact on business survival: two years after leaving the organization, women whose businesses have survived had participated in Namaste for longer and implemented their advisers' advice more frequently than those who have closed their businesses (Beck, Aguilera, and Schintz, forthcoming). This suggests that the education women receive in Namaste may lead to longer-lasting businesses, even if they do not guarantee continued increases in profits. One cannot deny that on a daily basis, most poor people worry about money. In that sense, Namaste's ability to increase the income of the poor in the short term should not be dismissed. And its ability to increase the survival rate of businesses that allow women to smooth out their consumption patterns may have long-lasting consequences that are not adequately captured in monthly profits.

Yet because Namaste tends to see women as individuals, compartmentalizes their identities, and values quantitative measures of success, its developers are often blinded to the long-standing structural problems that contribute to women's poverty, insecurity, and subordination. The experiences of a few women help illustrate both the structural violence that Namaste's focus on bootstrap development necessarily ignores and the concrete ways that it helps poor women in the short term. The focus on individual women's lives here is instructive because it reminds us that while issues of gender inequality and poverty are often the topic of abstract discussion and international policy, they are experienced as an everyday reality among actual women. It is therefore useful for illuminating the possibilities and limitations of Namaste's brand of bootstrap development. I have intentionally selected stories that are, in my judgment, representative of the average experience of women who have participated in Namaste with some short-term success, although there are of course some women who do not even benefit from their participation in the short term (roughly 40% do not experience an increase in their monthly business profits while participating in Namaste).

Mariana, the women depicted in the introduction, was a typical case. Mariana was a seventy-four-year-old woman who was born on Agualinda, a community that had since been, for all intents and purposes, abandoned. Her father worked as a laborer on the plantation, planting corn, cotton, and beans. Her parents sent her and her siblings to the *monte* (the uncultivated land) to gather weeds that they would cook for lunches and dinners. She never attended school because "at that time, there was not a school nor a clinic on the farm. If you needed to get medicine, you had to cross the river to buy it in the town over." During this period in her life, "there was very little food. We ate *yerbas* (grasses and weeds). We would go to the river to get fish and shrimp. The river used to be abundant with them, but not now . . . because they have poisoned the river" with litter and runoff from chemical fertilizers and pesticides, which became popular during the Green Revolution in Guatemala (see chapter 2).

When the owners of the plantation rented it out for the cultivation of sugarcane in the late 1960s, Mariana's family moved north to Santana. Guatemala's production of sugar expanded during this time as a result of the United States' decision to reallocate Cuba's sugar quotas to Central America in 1960. Large-scale production of sugarcane, along with other products such as cotton and later African palm, only served to exacerbate land inequality. Small-scale farmers, like those in Mariana's family, lacked the capital and resources needed to compete and were forced onto infertile land or dispossessed of their land altogether, following the national level patterns described in chapter 2.

The process continued as Western governments subsidized biofuel programs and looked to countries like Guatemala for the raw materials needed, including sugarcane and African palm. In the area where Mariana lived, large sugarcane and African palm companies were quickly buying up smaller plots that were previously dedicated to small-scale farming. They were affecting the environment, the economy, and communities' livelihoods by polluting and diverting rivers and streams to their ever-expanding farms. When Guatemalans protested or refused to vacate land, events turned violent (Brodzinsky 2013). As a result of these historical and present-day forces playing out across the Guatemalan countryside, today more than two-thirds of the fertile land belongs to less than 3 percent of the population.

When she was eighteen, Mariana married an agricultural worker who was "a good man, responsible in everything [he did]." They, like the majority of Guatemalans, did not own any fertile land of their own. Their six children went with their father to work in the fields as laborers rather than attending school. "I did not have enough to support my children," explained Mariana. At the time of my interview with her, three of Mariana's children lived in Santana while the others had traveled to larger cities looking for work.

"I have had my *ventaditas* [meager sales] for a long time, but I do not earn very much with them," explained Mariana. At the time of our discussion, she had participated in Namaste for almost two full cycles, receiving loans for the small store she operated out of the front of her home. When I asked if she had any doubts about getting involved with Namaste, she nodded: "Yes. It shames me to borrow money. I was worried because maybe I would not be able to pay. Then I would cause problems for my children." But, with three months left in her final cycle with Namaste, Mariana had not missed a payment. "The difference with the banks is that they want the loan paid back all at once. But you do not feel it as much if you pay little by little [like with Namaste]."

Mariana's levels and forms of participation in Namaste did not differ dramatically from that of her peers. She attended educational sessions and occasionally spoke up when asked a question. She rarely missed her one-on-one meetings, and her business adviser noted that Mariana implemented her adviser's recommendations in just over half of her monthly reports. In reality, Mariana's participation required little energy or effort, and compared to women participating in other NGOs, she had relatively little to say about the organization. She claimed she would not attend the educational and mentorship sessions without the loan, and when asked about the effects that her participation had on her life, she emphasized that Namaste had "helped [her] with the loan only, with other things, no."

Significantly, Mariana increased her monthly business profits by $100 while she was participating in Namaste, in just eighteen months. During that time she was able to smooth out her consumption, which normally varied depending on the support that her sometimes-employed children could provide. One hundred dollars a month was a significant increase for Mariana; it meant that her monthly business income at the end of her loan cycle was triple that of her monthly income at the start.

LARA

Mariana's neighbor, Lara, also benefited economically from her participation in Namaste. A sixty-six-year-old woman with a kind face and strong voice, Lara was one of the few women who genuinely seemed to value the educational side of Namaste's work during my observations. "When I was a child," she explained, "I wanted to study, but my parents said no, only boys go to school. Boys go to school because right after, they will get a job and they will put it to use." She continued to pressure her parents to let her go, so when one of her brothers dropped out, they allowed her to use his school supplies and attend classes. "Back then you used a little chalkboard and a piece of chalk and you wrote like this," she explained with a smile as she held out her left hand to represent the chalkboard and mimed writing on it. "You wrote and then you erased it, [making letters out of] little balls and little sticks." But after just one year, Lara's parents pulled her out of school, leaving her with limited literacy skills. As an adult, she attended literacy classes with CONALFA (the National Committee for Literacy). "They taught me how to write better. . . . I studied for two years there and learned how to write my name well. Before, I could not."

Well before Lara entered Namaste, she managed small informal businesses to supplement her husband's income as an agricultural worker and to support her large family. They had eleven children, two of whom died from unknown sicknesses. "I brought them to the doctor but it was too late. They could not recover." Despite their scarce resources and their large family, Lara was determined to give her children more opportunities than she had and made sure that every one of her surviving children had the opportunity to attend school up through sixth grade. "I asked permission at the school for my daughters to sell fruit during recess. I had to get everything all ready—the watermelons, the oranges—and at recess time they would run home and get the fruit and go and sell it. In that way, I paid for their schools supplies, their clothing, their socks. Because it was expensive. We had to buy books and everything."

When the violence of the armed conflict began affecting her community, they thought of leaving. "During this time the army killed many people. They persecuted people. . . . During this time we lost a lot of animals, and the owners of the farm got mad." It was likely that the army suspected the community of giving animals or meat to guerrilla forces. "I was very scared," Lara continued. "I remember one time I was pregnant and I heard the army come into a neighbor's house. And I was in bed and I threw myself to the floor. The army marched right here by the house with the people tied up. They killed many people. Even children." As a result of the violence, Lara confided, "we did not sleep well. We wanted to leave, but what were we going to do with the children? Where were we going to go? My husband said let us go, but I said they could kill our children while we are traveling. So we left it in God's hands. And thank God, nothing happened to us." Despite her statement that "nothing happened," however, Lara later revealed that her husband was in fact detained for a month because he supported the local agricultural workers' demands for higher wages.

At the time of our conversation, three of Lara's children worked in the capital, one lived in another community, four lived close by, and one had recently died in a work accident in a factory in the capital. The factory, however, was not held accountable for her son's death. They "did not give us anything, not even anything for the coffin. And it costs 850 quetzal [$106] for the burial." One of her sons was working on the plantations that populated the export-processing zone down the road, where workers protested low wages in the 1970s and 1980s and were met with repression. At the time of our conversation, workers were not organized. Unions in the sugar sector were effectively dismantled in the 1970s when their leaders were persecuted and killed, as Lara herself witnessed (Lawrence 2011). Although freedom of association and the right to collective bargaining were legally guaranteed in Guatemala, in practice these rights were violated with impunity. As a result, only 3 percent of the Guatemalan workforce belonged to a union (U.S. State Department 2006).

"Now, they go to the farms looking for work. They leave at four o'clock in the morning, at five o'clock they begin to work. At two o'clock they leave. It is a long day. [For this] they get paid 800 quetzal [$100] every fifteen days," a salary well below the minimum wage and the $513 a month needed to feed an average family, by the Guatemalan government's own estimates (Lawrence 2011).

At the time I spoke with her, Lara had managed her store for two years. It was painted bright blue, advertising Tigo, a mobile phone service provider, and located in a small building next to her one-room house. Her two grandsons walked in and out of the store and alerted Lara when a customer arrived. Lara explained that they were there because her son, the one who worked as a day laborer on the plantation down the road, injured his hand and had been unable to work and feed his children, so they were staying with her. She used the loan that she received from Namaste, her first loan from an MFI, to stock the store. When she had enough gathered together, she used the store's profits to buy animals. Lara proudly showed me her pigs and chickens. Gesturing to the pigs, she explained, "I buy them when they cost 300 quetzal ($37.55) and three months later I sell them for 700 quetzal ($87.60). I have this one that is pregnant. I will sell the babies for 200 quetzal ($25) each when they are two months old. I also have some that I buy to fatten up; I have just two for breeding."

Lara explained that when her business adviser visited her, she always "[had] everything arranged" (all of her figures gathered together). She noted that in Namaste, they have learned "how to sell" and that "you cannot have a short temper with clients." She continued, "Maybe we do not remember everything but when we are in the classes we say, yes, that is right. It is true, because if you are short with a client, he is not going to come back. I also learned that when I make my purchases to set some money aside for the [loan] payment, and there is still a little profit left. . . . I learned about how much each thing costs and that you should not use the money for personal things, just things that will help the business grow." As an example, Lara explained, "this year, I gave vaccines to my chickens. Because before, four chickens died. So I bought the vaccine and the rest are still alive." Lara claimed that because she had attended classes with Namaste, she would feel comfortable soliciting a loan that did not come with education. "Because now I know how to sell, how to work with my animals and everything." When asked what she would change about Namaste, Lara replied that the organization should give more money. "But only to responsible people. They have to [find] honest people when making groups. You have to know each other well."

Lara received two loans from Namaste for her store—the first for 1,250 quetzal ($156) and the second for 1,500 quetzal ($188). She attended educational sessions and felt comfortable asking or answering questions. She attended the majority of her one-on-one meetings, and her business adviser noted in half of her monthly reports that Lara had implemented her advice.

Over the course of these two loan cycles, she increased her monthly business profits by 589 quetzal ($74), which represented a 66 percent increase in her monthly business income. What is more, she was able to invest that money in another small business that, in addition to earning a profit, represented a savings "account" in the form of animals she could easily sell or eat in times of need. Lara had always been interested in education, so her participation in Namaste did not transform her interests. But it did allow her to take part in educational activities that she had missed as a child. She appreciated the lessons that Namaste taught her and applied them to her businesses, with positive economic results.

MICHELE

In Los Morelos, Michele had similarly positive experiences with Namaste. Michele was an outgoing woman in her late forties who hosted Namaste's monthly educational sessions in the tiny clinic next to her house. Michele explained that she allowed the clinic to be built on her land and had been working in it for the previous five years. The clinic was a welcome addition to Los Morelos. Although the adjacent community had a clinic supported by foreigners, traveling to it required a walk down, and then back up, a very steep hill.

Michele was born in the town next door to Los Morelos, one of nine children. "I would have to say that I had a difficult childhood because there were nine of us children and our father liked to drink a lot. Because there were so many of us, there was very little food," Michele explained. Their limited resources also meant that Michele only completed three years of school. "[My parents] sent me to school, but without any school supplies. . . . I got good grades, but it was hard without supplies. How was I going to write down what I learned? One of the teachers took manila paper, folded it half, and gave it me to use as a notebook. So in my fourth year, I left school. And my parents did not ask me why; I just went to work." Instead of continuing her studies, she went to fields to work, picking green beans, weeding, tending to the plants, and milking the family's one cow. She also helped out around the house, making tortillas and cleaning. When she married at the age of seventeen, she moved to her husband's hometown, Los Morelos.

"It was hard at first getting used to married life. Because of my young age, I did not have any experience or knowledge. I had never heard any talks [about family planning]. So I had three children one right after the other." Michele and her husband ended up having five children, who ranged in age from nine to twenty-four at the time of our conversation. When they first married, Michele would go to the fields to help her husband, who today works in the capital as a gardener. In 1998, she became a community health promoter. "There was a clinic that worked to unite the community. They worked with the sick, and worked to make sure that pregnant women would have monthly visits. And they named people to support their work. They asked my husband to do it but he could not because of his work. So I did it." The clinic paid her 50 quetzal each month ($6.26) as a stipend. Five years ago, the clinic promoted her to facilitator and started paying her 500 quetzal a month (roughly $63). "But," Michele clarified, "this is a stipend, not a salary. Because really I could earn more if I worked [somewhere else]."

Through her involvement in the clinic, Michele eventually participated in the Community Development Council (COCODE) as a health representative. "There are a number of groups there, groups of teachers, of health workers, a sports group. . . . We would get together and sign the project requests." Men dominated many COCODEs, as they did this one, so Michele's participation was relatively unique. "Usually there are only three female members there, one from the school and two in [the area of] health."

Michele had been working with Namaste for a year and a half when we spoke. She initially heard about the program from a flyer left by a FAPE representative, with whom Namaste was partnered at the time. Of the first group she joined with Namaste, only two of the original members ended up continuing on to a second cycle. "I think it is because they did not know how to administer [their money] well. They buy things that do not bring benefits to the business."

"Namaste is good because before I was selling bananas and Jell-O but I did not know if I was making a profit or not," Michele recounted. "Namaste taught me to separate my money, [to separate] the profit I make from my business [from] my personal money. They taught me about time [being] one of the costs of business." Once Michele realized her original business was not profitable, she switched to selling cosmetics out of a catalogue. "In the past, there would be sales and special offers, but I could not take advantage of them because I did not have a lot of money. And people would come and order things but I would be all out. Now I have the money to turn products around."

This was not Michele's first experience with loans or education, though. She had previously belonged to an agricultural cooperative called Four Pines (Cuarto Pinos) that had provided educational opportunities. "Once they taught us about raising rabbits. They had classes on cooking. . . . They gave us credit too, but we ended up in debt with this organization." In order to pay off this debt, Michele went with her eldest daughter to work in the fields, planting and fumigating.

What Michelle called fumigating was common work. One traveling through the Guatemalan countryside was likely to see Guatemalans, only sometimes with a face mask or a bandana tied around their mouths, spraying insecticides out of a tube that ran from their hands to the boxy containers strapped to their backs like poison backpacks. Guatemalans who lived near and labored on Guatemala's *fincas* were often exposed to toxic material—either when they were hired as "backpack sprayers" or as they worked or lived near lands that underwent frequent aerial sprays. As a result, Guatemalans in these areas had been found to have dramatically elevated levels of dichloro-diphenyl-trichloroethane (DDT) in their blood, and DDT had been found in cow's milk, fish, meat, greens, and drinking water. Guatemalan's exposure to toxins was intimately linked with their limited employment opportunities and a state that failed to enforce labor laws. In the United States, when less toxic pesticides were used, workers were banned from sprayed areas for seventy-two hours. In Guatemala, by contrast, workers often handled chemicals that had been banned in Europe, and those who left the fields during the spraying risked forfeiting their wages and losing their jobs (Cultural Survival 2010; Lawrence 2011).

In addition to the loans from Cuatro Pinos, Michele and her husband took out two loans with FONDESOL, an organization affiliated with the Catholic Church that specialized in rural microcredit. This was one of the larger MFIs in the country, lending at the time to more than seventy thousand borrowers, over 70 percent of whom were women. Compared to these other organizations, Michele viewed Namaste favorably. "They explain how to see if there is a profit, how to separate money, and the [emphasis on] savings is good. I set aside some money so if one day I need it, it is there." One of her favorite activities was traveling to Pana-jachel to attend the annual business conference.

Michele's experience in Namaste, then, was positive overall. Over the course of her time with Namaste, Michele's monthly cash flow increased by 1,203 quetzal ($150). She valued the business knowledge and skills that she learned in the educational sessions, both because she has found them useful in her everyday life and because, she said, "it is beautiful to learn." She attended the vast majority of her educational sessions and one-on-one meetings with her business adviser. Still, it was her prior experience, rather than her experience in Namaste, that made her more willing to participate actively outside of home. When I noted that she seemed to be the most talkative member of her loan group, Michelle explained, "That is because of my experience. For example, when my husband went to the capital, I would go with him. And I learned to come out of my shell, to relate with people. And in the clinic, people come here from other places." While her participation in Namaste did not transform her conceptions of self or her interests, or challenge the structural barriers that she had encountered in her life, it did yield pos-itive, tangible outcomes in a context in which such outcomes were rare.

The experiences of Mariana, Lara, and Michele highlight the multiple, over-lapping sources of structural violence that the poor, especially women, expe-rience in Guatemala, none of which Namaste is able to recognize, much less address, in the context of bootstrap development. The NGO does not address the unequal distribution of land and economic structures that privilege large, undertaxed landholders. It does not address the effects of trade policy on the daily lives, the health, and the economic livelihoods of the poor. It does not challenge a system that forces Guatemalans to endure insecure employment and unsafe working conditions, requires them to accept wages below the le-gal minimum, and prevents them from acting collectively. It does not invite women who have experienced tragedies in their lives—being denied educa-tion because of gender discrimination, losing children because of poverty, enduring and witnessing state-led violence—to reflect on these experiences and imagine different futures. But it does, for the most part, improve the daily lives of women like Mariana, Lara, and Michelle, at least in the short term, by teaching them concrete skills and raising their incomes.

Namaste's positive economic benefits, while significant in the short term, appear to come with very few of the spillover effects assumed to accompany microfinance. Although Namaste set the explicit goal of limiting the duration of women's participation in the NGO in order to promote their self-reliance, many women leave Namaste only to go on to solicit loans from one of the many other MFIs operating in their communities. Most of these MFIs claim a social mission but in practice provide little support beyond loans, focusing instead on repayment, expansion, and profits. Thus before, during, and after women's participation, the institutional environment in which Namaste operates undercuts its ability to meet its long-term goals for women and bootstrap development more broadly.

One of the well-publicized benefits of group-based microcredit is its ability to encourage women to create new social ties and build social capital (Sanyal 2009; Anderson and Locker 2002; Hashemi, Schuler, and Riley 1996). In the case of Namaste, just under half of former beneficiaries surveyed in 2013 reported that their relationships with their group members had improved as a result of their participation, saying that they "got to know each other" and they gained each other's trust because they "saw that they never failed to make payment." Yet these relationships appeared to be based largely on interaction surrounding loans and did not lead to collective action. Just as significantly, 39 percent of women reported that their participation did not change their relationships with other women at all, and a minority (12 percent) reported that their participation in Namaste had actually *worsened* their relationships with their peers—citing conflicts over repayment or jealousies among friends. Roughly a third of women surveyed reported giving advice or help to group members, with a slightly smaller percentage reporting receiving advice or help from group members during and after their participation in Namaste. The vast majority of examples related to encouraging peers to repay loans (which may reflect pressure rather than encouragement) or carry on with their businesses.

While encouragement from one's peers and getting to know other women likely enrich women's lives, Namaste's non-economic effects in reality appear to be quite modest. Given that other studies on different MFIs have found more dramatic results for their non-economic effects, this finding should push us to move past generalizations about NGOs or MFIs to examine what is actually going on inside these spaces that is driving variations in outcomes. That is, we need to start looking at the "how" of microfinance rather than focusing solely on the particular mix of loans and services provided.

Because women participated in Namaste for a fixed period of time, with limited ability and desire to use Namaste's narrow spaces for their own purposes, they were less likely to expand the basis of their relationships with other women beyond loans and business. They were also unlikely to undertake the critical assessments of their own identities and realities necessary to imagine alternative ways of living and expand their capacity to aspire (Appadurai 2004). Thus, Namaste's developers and beneficiaries together created sites of development that resembled hallways, channeling women into relatively uniform forms of participation that were efficient and effective for imparting concrete skills, raising some women's business incomes in the short term, and potentially expanding business networks and knowledge for some beneficiaries. But doing so also limited women's likelihood to act creatively, identify shared struggles in the face of social exclusion, or question and transform their identities or realities.

CONCLUSIONS

This chapter demonstrated that women do not form expectations of particular development projects and NGOs in isolation. Instead, they draw on their previous experiences and informal knowledge of other projects and judge them in relation to each other. The institutional environment in which Namaste is embedded, alongside its foreign identity and recruitment strategies, reinforces women's view of Namaste as just another MFI and therefore shapes their expectations that participation will be minimal. Once they enter the NGO, beneficiaries encounter and react to Namaste's employees, who are themselves enacting bootstrap development based on their own biases and goals.

For their own reasons, Namaste's policymakers, leaders, workers, and beneficiaries alike often value women's participation for instrumental reasons. For Namaste's policymakers and leaders, women's participation is seen as valuable as a means to the end of increasing their business incomes. For workers, women's participation helps them achieve status and keep their jobs. In order to pursue their respective goals, these developers contribute to hierarchical relationships with women, compartmentalize women's identities, and manage and monitor their behavior. Based on their own goals and environments, most beneficiaries similarly value their participation in Namaste's activities instrumentally—as a cost they pay in order to gain access to a loan. They react in a variety of ways to Namaste's attempts to manage and monitor their behavior. At times they expand the room for maneuver, but generally beneficiaries limit the time and effort that they dedicate to participation. As such, developers and beneficiaries jointly construct narrow development hallways in which concrete skills are taught, but in which there are fewer small encounters and little room for discussions of identities and the social exclusion that poor Guatemalan women so often endure.

CHAPTER FIVE

THE FRATERNITY'S
HOLISTIC MODEL

We aim for holistic development. Because it is not enough [for Mayan women] to have food [to] eat. . . . [They have to] work, [have] good health, knowledge, spirituality, connection with the four cardinal points, connection with nature[,] . . . psychological health, [know] what their obligations are, what their rights are—as women and as citizens. —ALICIA, DIRECTOR OF FRATERNIDAD DE PRESBITERIALES MAYAS

So explains the director of Fraternidad de Presbiteriales Mayas (the Fraternity), when describing the organization's goals. Like Namaste, the Fraternity offers its beneficiaries small loans and education, but the Fraternity arrived at this project design through very different networks and webs of meaning, resulting in vastly different development models, organizational values, and structures. The Fraternity is a grassroots, foreign-funded NGO that grew out of indigenous women's collective action in Protestant churches in 1980s. This prehistory, rooted in indigenous women's fight for greater inclusion in religious contexts, has shaped its organizational characteristics alongside its holistic model of development. This model embraces multiple nonquantifiable development goals at once. Founders and early policymakers drew on their habitus as Protestants and Mayan women activists while institutionalizing an organization based on their alternative vision of development. Thus, although the Fraternity uses similar technologies to Namaste (loans and classes), its developers imbue them with distinct meanings and apply them to different ends, based on their multifaceted view of poverty and development. Whereas Namaste uses small loans to enhance women's business incomes and involve them in business education, the Fraternity uses loans to draw women into the organization, where they encourage women to recapture their Mayan identity, revalue themselves as women, change their communities, and live more fully in their faiths—all in hopes of achieving its holistic vision of development.

As with Namaste, Fraternity's interactional origins were intimately connected to the NGO's subsequent trajectory. Early policymakers' histories and syncretic identities led them to view individual economic well-being as intimately connected with spiritual, physical, emotional, and community well-being, to see indigenous women as members of excluded groups rather than as individuals, and to recognize structural sources of inequality that the policymakers themselves had experienced firsthand. As a result, the Fraternity's policymakers eschewed specialization, viewed women's participation as inherently valuable, and embraced multiple, long-term goals at once. In turn, the expressions of the Fraternity's model of holistic development and its other organizational characteristics (its values, structure, and networks connections) have had long-lasting consequences for the practices and experiences of development on the ground, even though they continue to allow for room to maneuver on the part of workers and beneficiaries.

THE FRATERNITY'S PREHISTORY: PROMOTING MAYAN
WOMEN'S PARTICIPATION IN RELIGIOUS SPACES

The Fraternity's origins are intimately linked with historical developments within the National Evangelical Presbyterian Church of Guatemala (hereafter the Presbyterian Church or IENPG), which has maintained its presence in many communities in the Guatemalan highlands since the late nineteenth and early twentieth centuries. The founders and early members of the Fraternity initially mobilized to push for space for indigenous women's participation in the Presbyterian Church but later broke away to form an independent NGO. Because of this prehistory and its subsequent vision of and approach to holistic development, the Fraternity today resembles both a service-oriented and a culture-producing organization. Rather than simply serving women's interests, it explicitly seeks to change them, pushing the women to alter their values and priorities.

Historically, the Presbyterian Church in Guatemala limited women's participation to predefined channels, including women's societies (groups of women organized at the level of individual churches), women's presbyterials (groups that brought together members of women's societies within a geographic area), and the National Women's Society (the umbrella organization of all presbyterials, charged with evangelizing and social work). But women were barred from becoming pastors, deacons, or *ancianas* (elders), and they were therefore denied access to the most important leadership positions in the church.[1] In addition to experiencing gender discrimination within the most important institution in their lives (for many), the indigenous women of the Fraternity recounted feeling uniquely marginalized by the Presbyterian Church based on their ethnicity. Despite the country's ethnolinguistic diversity and the comparative strength of the Presbyterian Church among indigenous populations (discussed in chapter 2), indigenous women were not well represented in the limited spaces in which women were invited to participate. Instead, professional ladina women predominated in these spheres. Mayan women reported that they felt isolated from the National Women's Society and experienced discrimination even in their own presbyterials.

Resentments grew as state-led violence was increasingly directed at indigenous communities in the context of Guatemala's armed conflict, especially during the counterinsurgency of Lucas García (1978–82) and the scorched-earth campaigns of Ríos Montt (1982–3) (see chapter 2). These events, and reactions to them within the church, served to politicize divisions within the Presbyterian Church along ethnic lines. Internal debates within the IENPG in the 1970s and 1980s centered on, among other things, what to do in the face of the troubling political and social situation in the country (Schäfer 1991). Mayan populations were disproportionately affected by the ongoing violence, but they "often received little support from their Ladino brethren in the denomination" (Samson 2008, 80). Mayan Presbyterians argued for a shift toward social services (rather than evangelizing), while conservative ladino elements of the church linked such a shift with liberation theology, by then associated with the guerrillas. Many members of the Mayan presbyteries in the IENPG secretly set themselves against the military government, creating informal networks among themselves, while some ladino members of the church hierarchy actively collaborated with the government (Schäfer 1991).

The growing "ethnic self-confidence of the Mayans" (Schäfer 1991, 40), expressed in the founding of new Mayan presbyteries in the 1970s and 1980s, also created tensions within the IENPG. The ladino-led synod (central church council) initially assumed that Mayan leaders would play the role of "transmission belt" through which it could carry out its intentions with Mayan populations. But Mayan presbyteries rejected this role and instead crafted their own unique theological and practical positions that many ladino members of the IENPG saw as controversial. Mayan presbyteries oriented themselves toward contemporary social and political problems, targeted social work at entire communities rather than only at church members, and incorporated indigenous elements into worship services (Schäfer 1991; Samson 2007).

By the mid-1980s, the worst of the violence was over and the first competitive elections in over three decades signaled a democratic opening. Although they had previously been organizing for some years, it was not until this time that indigenous members of the IENPG felt comfortable organizing openly to "promote activities that would be perceived as social action in a political sense" (Samson 2007, 68). A number of Presbyterian pastors subsequently met at the Maya K'iche' Biblical Institute in San Cristobal to form the Hermandad de Presbiterios Mayas (hereafter, the Hermandad), an organization that consolidated the work of Mayan presbyteries in the areas of theological education and self-help projects. They also supported the creation of a lesser-known parallel organization focusing solely on indigenous women, which would become the Fraternity.

The Fraternity's four founders were women from different ethnolinguistic groups: two Mam, one K'iche', and one Kaqchikel. At their first meeting, these women drew on support and ideas from progressive male Mayan pastors and discussed the value of Mayan women's contributions to the church and obstacles to their active participation. They noted that indigenous women experienced discrimination because of both their gender and their ethnicity and suffered higher levels of poverty and illiteracy. They also noted that indigenous women were much more likely than ladina women to have been widowed in the recent wave of violence. They subsequently drew on their religious networks to mobilize indigenous women in their respective churches and presbyterials, pushing them to create their own groups for consciousness-raising, Bible study, and small productive projects.

The women traveled to Protestant churches across various Mayan ethnolinguistic groups to provide women with material, spiritual, and emotional support, often alongside progressive male members of Mayan presbyteries. It was in the midst of these travels that they named their emerging federation the Fraternity of Mayan Presbyterials, a name they chose because they felt that the word "fraternity" signified fellowship and unity between different indigenous groups. Leaders of the Fraternity distinguished their emerging organization from the IENPG's National Women's Society because for them, gender intersected with indigeneity in ways that could not be adequately represented in a ladina-dominated institution. They emphasized their shared indigenous identity and called for recognition of indigenous forms of worship that diverged from those of ladino presbyteries. The Fraternity's leaders made a conscious effort to include all ethnolinguistic groups, echoing strategies of the budding pan-Mayan movement. Luisa, one of the Fraternity's founders and early board members explained,

> We said we are Mayas and we are going to involve all the ethnicities . . . because of machismo, because of marginalization. . . . We will organize ourselves separately, we will preserve our culture, look after our work, our necessities. . . . We traveled to Q'anjob'al, Chimaltenango, Petén . . . motivating women. And organize they did.

The initial stages of organization were slow and frustrating. The Fraternity's leaders began by gathering indigenous women into groups in their churches, leading them in Bible study, and providing workshops to enhance women's sense of their own value. They drew on their local religious networks to recruit new members and on the international connections forged through the IENPG to fund group-based productive projects for indigenous women. Sister churches in the United States and Canada sent donations for activities such as farming or animal husbandry, which the Fraternity in turn distributed donations to groups of indigenous Protestant women.

During this early period, the founding members of the Fraternity did not have offices and often struggled to find funds for their activities. They gathered in each other's homes and traveled by public bus, often walking for hours down dirt roads to remote communities. According to Luisa, "We did not earn anything. What we earned was people's support." Thereafter, whenever these early Fraternity members gathered together, they laughed about this period, telling tales of broken-down buses and sore bodies. The difficulty of the task seemed to inspire founding members to act, lending support to the argument that in many cases "undertakings that have no precedent and whose successful outcome is not assured are felt as peculiarly noble." As such, the effort expended became "striving," and "*as though in compensation for the uncertainty* it is this striving that is endowed with the feeling of already of having a pleasurable experience" (Hirschman 2002, 89). That is, the costs of collective action were precisely the benefits in women's eyes.

In this period, Alicia, a woman who would become influential in the Fraternity, became associated with the organization. Raised and educated as a Catholic, Alicia joined the Presbyterian Church when she married her Presbyterian husband at the age of twenty-one. Having put herself through school and having been exposed to foreign Catholic missionaries who promoted women's active participation and rights, Alicia was highly attuned to issues of women's participation. She quickly became active in her women's society and traveled as a representative of her church to an Evangelical [Protestant] Women's Encounter. Here, Alicia was asked to give the message—and because she was able to do so confidently in both K'iche' and Spanish, the women of the Fraternity who were present saw that she was well educated and capable and invited her to work with them. Soon thereafter, Alicia became the coordinator of women's programs in the deacon's office, ensuring the Fraternity had a measure of support within the church hierarchy for the nine years that Alicia held the position.

By the early 1990s, the pan-Mayan movement was growing nationally, providing Mayan presbyteries the language and space to question more openly the long-standing racism within the IENPG (Garrard-Burnett 2004). The leaders of the Fraternity took on a more controversial role, mobilizing on the basis of their indigenous identity and partnering with the Hermandad to push for space for indigenous leadership in the church hierarchy and for officially sanctioned indigenous forms of worship. But the Fraternity's leaders also made gender-specific demands; they mobilized explicitly and controversially *as women*. The Fraternity's leadership focused on self-help groups and initially went through institutionalized channels to air their grievances—bringing them to the National Assembly rather than undertaking more public forms of protest.

They crafted frames that highlighted familiar Protestant themes of family and spirituality as an expression of their own beliefs and values that had been molded in religious spheres, rather than a clearly devised strategy. Women often drew on biblical passages to make their claims; indeed, many identified their religious beliefs as their impetus for mobilization itself. For example, Georgina, an early member in the Fraternity during this time, explained her decision to participate by highlighting that excluding women was a sin.

> Even . . . men that are Christians, pastors, they do not recognize women.
> . . . I have been with men who found biblical passages that say women cannot do things. But Jesus gave importance to the work of women. Jesus gave opportunity to women first. . . . Women were his prophetic voice.
>
> How? Why? Because the women were the last ones at his tomb when he died. Maria was there, Elena was there . . . and they were the last ones to retire, and retire to do what? Not to their houses, but to prepare a perfume for the next day. And when they came the next day, Jesus was

not there; it was a surprise. And who was there? The angels—and they said why are you looking for him here, go and tell the others [that he is risen]. And they went to tell their neighbors.

What did the men do? They did not believe the women. "It is not true" [they said]. And they were men that had been with Christ for a long time, walked with Christ. They did not believe that he had risen. But among the women, they confirmed it: "Yes it is true."

This is good to teach men—that Jesus gave women the opportunity, that he took them into account. Why do they not value women? They are sinners.

The Fraternity adopted goals that emphasized women's traditional gender roles and actively incorporated families. For example, in a 1989/90 internal evaluation, leaders of the Fraternity concluded that, among other goals, the organization should "highlight the importance of unity among families and communities." Founders spoke of women's value as wives and mothers. When they were accused of being feminists, they rejected the label with which they did not identify, claiming they were simply aiming for, in the words of Alicia, "mutual respect between women and men" and promoting projects that would help entire families, not just women. This framing resonated with the Fraternity's context but also reflected many members' strongly held beliefs that it was irresponsible to teach women about their rights "without teaching them about their responsibilities to their husbands and families," as Alicia explained, because doing so would be inappropriate in the Guatemalan context.

In the early 1990s, at the Presbyterian Church's National Assembly, the women of the Fraternity partnered with the ladina women of the National Women's Presbytery to petition the National Assembly. They demanded that women be allowed to hold leadership positions and that the synod explicitly recognize women's rights within the church. United, the Fraternity's leaders and ladina women also successfully pushed for a study of women's status within the church. Although the results confirmed that there was insufficient space for women's participation in the church, these findings failed to prompt any immediate reforms. It was not until five years later that women's ordination was officially sanctioned. Subsequently, women's pastoral ordination was very rare: by 2013, there had been only five women ordained as pastors in the IENPG in the entire country. Two of these five exceptional women were founding and early members of the Fraternity.

Synod members reacted strongly to women's demands at the National Assembly, associating these indigenous women with the guerrilla war in the

Guatemalan countryside. As was the case with many other Latin American women's movements, although members of the Fraternity did not "always attack the existing sex-gender system in as systematic and consistent a way as our present-day feminist theories may dictate," their criticisms and demands were stinging enough that conservative forces saw them as a threat (Wieringa 1992, 111). Alicia explained to me that members of the National Assembly claimed that the women of the Fraternity "were the right hand of the guerrilla." According to Alicia, detractors claimed that "everyone who [worked] in [social] projects" was a guerrilla. "[They said,] 'The women who work in health, the women who want to know how to read and write, they are guerrillas because they are promoting an ideology that is against the government [and] against the Church.'"[2]

This "persecution within the Church, from church members themselves," as Alicia described it, weakened the relationship between the IENPG and the Fraternity. According to members of the Fraternity, after the confrontation at the National Assembly, members of the synod worked to isolate them. Women who were in leadership positions during that time received threats from male members of the church. Conflicts between the Fraternity and church officials continued throughout the 1990s, and hostility was often focused toward Alicia and the Fraternity's founding members, who were exceptionally independent, articulate, educated, and well connected, and thus more threatening to conservative members. Critics argued that these women were creating divisions within churches between women and men and between ladino and indigenous members. Alicia conflicted with both ladino and indigenous men, received threats from anonymous sources, and was called a feminist (a strong insult in those spheres) and a *machista* (a chauvinist against men). She was eventually removed from her position in the deacon's office but continued to receive threats even after the Fraternity separated from the church.

In 1996, when Guatemala was celebrating the newly signed peace accords and Quetzaltenango was celebrating the election of its first indigenous mayor, the Fraternity was legally separating from the IENPG to become an independent NGO. The Fraternity's leaders felt that the IENPG was not only unresponsive to their demands but was also punishing the Fraternity's leaders, as two early leaders (Alicia and Georgina) separately recounted to me in interviews. The increasing number and popularity of NGOs during this time likely had an effect as well, as they gave members of the Fraternity a model to follow, the hope of capturing some of the new international funds, and a vision for an alternative future.

The Fraternity established an office just a few blocks from Quetzaltenango's bustling market and bus terminal. The NGO's official founding date (1998) makes it appear to be just one more drop in the tidal wave of NGOs formed in Guatemala following the peace accords (described in chapter 2). But in reality it had already undergone a significant period of contested organization and growth. This prehistory shaped the Fraternity's policymakers' vision of development, embedded the NGO in both local and international religious networks that provided them with access to new members, ideas, and resources, and affected the Fraternity's organizational structure as an independent NGO.

BUILDING AN NGO FROM THE GROUND UP:
AD HOC ATTEMPTS TO IMPLEMENT HOLISTIC DEVELOPMENT

Upon separating from the Presbyterian Church, the Fraternity secured support from the United Church of Canada, the Evangelical Center for Pastoral Studies in Central America (CEDEPCA, an evangelical consortium), and Presbyterian World Service and Development (PWS&D), the service arm of the Presbyterian Church of Canada. The PWS&D had previously been funding projects and services through the Presbyterian Church in Guatemala. At the time of the split, PSW&D's leadership decided to divert these funds toward the Fraternity because it viewed the NGO's work more favorably than that of the IENPG. Alicia was named the Fraternity's director, and many of the organization's founders and early members were placed on a board of directors. Together, they outlined their vision for the organization. Thereafter NGO leaders (the Guatemalan director and board of directors) simultaneously served as the NGO's key policymakers for years to come. Rather than simply providing material support, they decided that they wanted to help women recapture cultural values and raise their self-esteem. According to Alicia, they hoped that the material support they provided to women did not "hurt them" but instead encouraged them to "value themselves and develop their capabilities." This vision was intimately connected with the Fraternity's origins and subsequent struggles; they argued that "the marginalized . . . should not feel marginalized anymore" and that they "should not fight with those who marginalize [them], but rather develop [them]selves, [and their] capabilities," as a form of resistance.

The Fraternity subsequently progressed on a largely ad hoc basis. While Namaste's trajectory was driven by clear goals that were methodically adjusted along the way through pilot projects and systematic processes, in practice the Fraternity made changes that were primarily driven by the availability of external funds or by the whims of the organization's first director, Alicia. For example, initially the Fraternity incorporated programs related to literacy and adult education, only to eliminate them when they decided to give small loans, although no one could ever explain how this decision was made.

While it was operating under the Presbyterian Church, the Fraternity had provided group donations for small self-help projects. But after the Fraternity separated from the church, it replaced group donations with individual loans, although women would continue to be organized into groups. According to Georgina, the policymakers/leaders had previously noticed that when women were given group donations, "they used it up because they did not value it" and often invested in unproductive projects. As a result, they decided to provide women with loans instead of donations so that women would have an incentive to use the money wisely, because they would have to repay it.

Women received loans between $125 and $625 for small businesses, which they repaid after one year, that came with very low effective interest rates (under 5 percent).[3] Whereas Namaste looked to the market to determine their loan cycles and interest rates, the Fraternity's policymakers/leaders made these decisions without considering what other loan-granting institutions were doing, as they did not see the Fraternity as comparable to banks or MFIs. This distinction can also be seen in their decision to use the terms "revolving fund" and "recognition fee" rather than "loan" and "interest."

In 2010, the Fraternity funded over four hundred women across twenty-six groups, the vast majority of whom lived in mostly rural, indigenous areas of Quetzaltenango. Women's communities were characterized by low rates of female education and employment. Most beneficiaries were Maya Mam (75 percent), and a minority were K'iche' (19 percent) and Q'eqchi' (6 percent). Unlike in Namaste, the Fraternity's policymakers/leaders made no attempt to clearly define a target population beyond focusing on indigenous women; it did not expend any energy or resources on recruitment, waiting instead for women to learn of the program through word of mouth and approach them.

Although the Fraternity distributed revolving funds individually, it required women to organize themselves into groups of at least five, elect a board of directors consisting of a president, a vice president, a treasurer, a secretary, and one or more council members. In order to access the revolving fund, women were required to attend group classes twice a month, though in practice the frequency of classes and attendance varied. These classes rotated among programs that reflected the Fraternity's holistic approach, including the Women's Pastoral Program, which focused on self-esteem and mutual respect through a biblical perspective, and the Socio-Productive Program, which taught animal husbandry, agriculture, and handicrafts. Originally the organization addressed women's health through classes on medicinal plants and traditional medicine within the Women's Pastoral Program, but when a foreign missionary with expertise in nutrition arrived, they added a separate program that focused exclusively on health and nutrition. In time, and on an ad hoc basis, the Fraternity added larger conferences on diverse topics such as the environment and marital relationships.

Programs and topics were added according to the current interests of the director or the expertise of visiting missionaries. Alicia eventually became interested in environmental degradation through talks she attended outside of the organization. Thereafter she began scheduling conferences and classes through a newly created Education and Environment Program that she herself managed, focusing on issues such as global warming and littering. She often connected these topics with Christian values, health, and Mayan culture and spirituality, reflecting the belief that holistic development implied peace and justice, "for the earth, not just for human beings."

The Fraternity's workers also encouraged some women to enroll in more intensive courses in theological study, with course material provided by the Latin American Bible University (UBL), and later in health and nutrition, with course material gathered by a foreign missionary. Once women had completed the required coursework, which often spanned two to three years, they could lead classes in the Fraternity on a voluntary basis. By 2010, Fraternity's policy-makers/leaders had rethought the promoter program. They highlighted that training women in only one area of their work (theological study or nutrition) limited their impact and contradicted their vision in which the various facets of development overlapped. They transformed the promoter course into the School of Comprehensive Education, in which women were trained in the material from the Women's Pastoral, Socio-Productive, Health and Nutrition, and Education and Environment Programs. This transformation reflected and reinforced the Fraternity's holistic vision—allowing them to more explicitly draw connections between the different topics they discussed. The promoter program and later the School of Comprehensive Education provided some beneficiaries with the opportunity to take on new roles within the organization, including that of teacher, leader, and role model. Doing so often challenged them to develop new skills, relationships, and self-conceptions, as will be demonstrated in chapter 6.

Alicia's death in 2012 deeply affected the organization and its members. Initially Alicia's daughter was proposed as her replacement. After consulting with the Fraternity's funders, the board of directors decided instead to conduct a formal external search for a new director. They selected Antonieta, a K'iche' woman who had previous experience with other indigenous NGOs. Under her direction, the Fraternity continued to expand, serving more women even as their international funding decreased. By 2013, the Fraternity worked with over six hundred women across forty-two groups. The organization even began working with women from a new ethnolinguistic group, accepting four Kaqchikel groups. This implied substantial costs, as no one at the organization spoke Kaqchikel and some groups were located more than three hours away from the Fraternity's headquarters by car. The Fraternity's workers were unable to adequately serve the new groups of women, and their shrinking budget did not allow the organization to hire additional staff. The result was that some groups "felt abandoned" when they were not visited by the Fraternity's workers, according to a Fraternity employee.

Rather than retiring groups or limiting women's participation, though, the Fraternity called on women themselves to assist them in their work. Two representatives from each group were selected to attend trainings at the Fraternity's offices that they could then replicate in their groups. In this way, the Fraternity was able to supplement workers' visits with lessons taught by beneficiaries themselves. Antonieta envisioned involving these beneficiaries in other aspects of the Fraternity's work. By the end of 2013, she was formulating a plan for selected beneficiaries to visit their peers to monitor the degree to which they were implementing the Fraternity's advice. As we will see, the transfer of the directorship from Alicia to Antonieta, along with pressure from foreign donors and limited funding, served to make the organization flatter and more inclusive, affecting the organizational structure but not altering its holistic model of development, which was only reinforced over time.

THE FRATERNITY'S MODEL OF DEVELOPMENT
AND ORGANIZATIONAL CHARACTERISTICS

The Fraternity's Holistic Model of Development and Faith in God and Culture

Because the Fraternity's policymakers/leaders, as Mayans, Christians, and women, experienced social exclusion firsthand, they came to define development in a broad way that incorporated social, economic, and political changes and included women on the basis of their multiple, intersecting identities. Today, the Fraternity continues to address women's identities as mothers, wives, Christians, and community members, rather than solely as individual businesswomen, as does Namaste. It seeks transformations in women's economic situations but also in their identities, families, churches, and communities. The fact that the Fraternity was created to expand the spaces in which indigenous women could participate imbued the organization with lasting values. The organization's policymakers continue to encourage participation for participation's sake—seeing it as both instrumentally and intrinsically valuable.

Alicia explained this holistic model, which includes economic and noneconomic aspects of well-being and which targets women to inspire transformations in individuals, churches, and communities, when discussing her vision for the future. "My dream is that a woman does not just have a cow, but has a pretty stable, and that she is valuing the animals. . . . I want them to multiply. I want women to understand what holistic development [means] because for me, [it] is key to a spiritual life." For her, this means, "not only mental well-being, but spiritual, physical well-being." She clarified further that she wants women to "learn to develop and value their vocations, their gifts within the church so that one day the church will not separate the material and the spiritual," and that she wants women work to create "communities that are green, with crystal waters, with pure air."

The Fraternity's policymakers/leaders draw on their interpretations and reworkings of "traditional Mayan culture," Christian values, and their national and organizational histories in their educational material and everyday practices. The director, board members, and some workers emphasize that they cannot simply address one aspect of development but need to simultaneously address women's spiritual and physical well-being, mental health, self-esteem, and their economic livelihoods through both a Christian and a Mayan perspective. Women participating in the Fraternity attend classes with the Women's Pastoral Program "so they know why [they] should value the land and value [themselves]," Alicia told me. Drawing on material produced by CEDEPCA, foreign missionaries, UBL, and the Mesoamerican Committee for Peace, these classes rely on biblical lessons about the value of women in the hopes of improving women's self-esteem and draw on religious and Mayan values to reinforce women's commitment to their communities and to the environment. The Fraternity's policymakers/leaders see these topics as connected: in their view, the mistreatment of the environment results from low self-esteem, which in turn reflects one's lack of spiritual well-being.

Through the Socio-Productive Program, the Fraternity trains women in handicrafts, organic agriculture, and animal husbandry, all activities that fit with its emphasis on traditional values and environmental sustainability. An agronomist teaches women how to grow new types of vegetables and to make organic fertilizer, homemade chicken feed, and natural solutions to rid animals of parasites. Throughout, he emphasizes that women should avoid chemicals that damage the earth, in accordance with their Mayan and Christian values, in line with the strategies of the pan-Mayan movement, and against the long-term emphasis on Green Revolution technology in the country (described in chapter 2). The Fraternity's policymakers/leaders see these lessons as intimately linked to those on health and nutrition because they inform women "what is healthy to grow and eat," as Alicia described.

When discussing their loans, beneficiaries are taught that they "should not just sell things to sell things" in pursuit of their own economic well-being. Rather, they should sell food that is healthy as an expression of care for their neighbors and their communities, as the director explained in a 2009 interview. This guidance is based on an explicit rejection of individualism and consumerism of modern society. Because of this distinction, the Fraternity refers to women's businesses as their *proyectos* (projects), because they see them as part of lifelong endeavors to recuperate traditional values and care for themselves, their families, and communities in ways that align with their faith and culture.

Through the Health and Nutrition Program, the Fraternity teaches women about food groups and healthy eating habits and gives them hands-on opportunities to practice cooking nutritious meals for their families from foods that grow in their communities. According to the Fraternity's policymakers/leaders, the principles of the Pastoral Program are also connected with the nutritional program because if beneficiaries love themselves, they will care for themselves by consuming healthy foods. Because they see the topics they discuss as intimately linked and equally important, course material between the programs often overlaps.

Through its more intensive promoter classes and the School of Comprehensive Education, the Fraternity seeks to cultivate future leaders. Women are taught that God does not want them to suffer on this earth—echoing the teachings of liberation theology. Women are asked to discuss the ways they would like to transform their lives, their churches, and their communities. By pushing women to imagine other realities and think about steps to realize those realities, the Fraternity potentially encourages women to develop and exercise their capacity to aspire (Appadurai 2004). Graduates of these classes are subsequently dispatched to lead classes for new groups of beneficiaries. Some beneficiaries are therefore put in positions to further develop and teach new skills, following the multiplier model characteristic of many popular education programs in Latin America (Murdock 2008).

Women are encouraged to attend the Fraternity's yearly assemblies, where,

FIGURE 5.1. Women participating in the Fraternity make an organic solution to treat parasites in farm animals. Photograph by the author.

among other activities, beneficiaries choose between candidates for the Fraternity's board of directors. Candidates are themselves beneficiaries of the organization, oftentimes those who have participated in the organization for many years. Under Alicia, this board largely played a symbolic role. But under Antonieta, board members started to carry out important advisory and decision-making functions in the NGO's daily operations and programming. Thus, while Namaste primarily puts women in the role of recipients of knowledge, the Fraternity provides *some* beneficiaries with the opportunity to take on leadership roles in the organization and beyond. As we will see in the following chapter, these opportunities for leadership—when meted out by NGO leaders and workers with their own biases and in the context of the Fraternity's charismatic structure—are actually quite unevenly distributed. The minority of women who are assigned leadership roles, however, often transform their

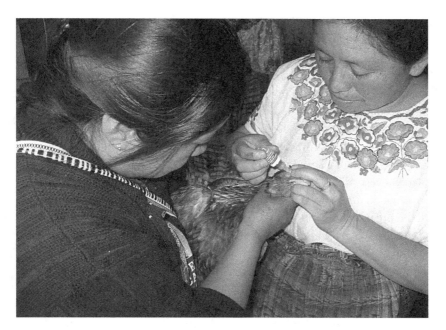

FIGURE 5.2. Women in the Fraternity learn how to vaccinate chickens.
Photograph by the author.

identities as a result of their participation, coming to see themselves as teachers and leaders in the organization, rather than customers or beneficiaries.

In practice, the Fraternity's policymakers/leaders neglect the one aspect of women's lives that Namaste's policymakers emphasize. Women are not trained in financial literacy or business management. Indeed, the Fraternity's policymakers/leaders do not give much importance to the loans they distribute, even though in many women's eyes it is central to the NGO's work. In its first decade of existence, the NGO's promotional material actually contained no mention of the revolving funds, and there has never been an employee dedicated to management of the loans, despite the fact that the loans represent at least 40 percent of the NGO's yearly expenses. Instead, the revolving fund is subsumed in the Socio-Productive Program and is in practice managed by the NGO's director, who is charged with numerous other tasks, including program management, fundraising, and communication with donors. Both of the Fraternity's directors, Alicia and Antonieta, have discussed the loan as simply the lure that attracts women to the organization. In any holistic organization, balancing short-term, practical interests with long-term, strategic interests and simultaneously seeking material benefits as well as internal transformations represent constant struggles. In the case of the Fraternity, policymakers/leaders prioritize women's internal transformations over their incomes. Doing so comes with very real tradeoffs, explored further in the next chapter.

The Fraternity's holistic model entails a view of development as a gradual, multifaceted process involving transformations in women, institutions, and communities. In its quest for long-term change, the Fraternity's policymakers/leaders hope to inspire women's sustained participation; thus, unlike Namaste, it does not limit the number of loans that women can receive and encourages them to participate in many activities outside of regularly scheduled classes. Alicia, for example, explained that she "laments that there are some women who form a group and then leave" because when women stay in the organization for a long time, "they are going to learn things and value themselves." Although some beneficiaries have participated in the NGO for just one or two years, a surprising number have participated for much longer, sometimes more than ten years. Developers' desire for sustained participation is intimately linked to their model of development. As an employee explained to me in a 2009 email, "we cannot approve that women work with us for just a year, because this is about holistic development," which requires deep transformations that are slow and ongoing.

The Fraternity also seeks sustained membership because the founders (who served as early policymakers/leaders) experienced historical marginalization within the church, which led them to imbue the NGO with norms that valued women's participation intrinsically. Josefina, an early board member explained:

> The National Church did not take [the founders] into account, did not value their work. They thought that because we were women, we were Mayan, that we were not worth anything . . . [and that] we could not do things. But they were wrong, because yes we can. . . . As we suffered, as we have lived, other women have lived . . . and we do not want it to continue. Because of this we have battled, we have established [trainings and classes] so that women can participate.

This view of participation as intrinsically valuable also affects the Fraternity's strategy—or lack thereof—for accepting women into the organization. Rather than outlining a clear target population (as Namaste does), the Fraternity accepts beneficiaries as they approach the organization, provided that funding is available and women agree to meet the Fraternity's requirements. The criteria for accepting new beneficiaries remains unclear even to the Fraternity's workers. One employee notes with confusion in a 2010 report that "there is a considerable gap in socio-economic levels in the same group" such that there are "cases in which one group member works [cleaning] in the house of the other group member."

Barriers to entry are low because the Fraternity's model of development leads the organization to value inclusion over efficiency, a strategy that comes with benefits and costs. Because the NGO accepts groups on an ad hoc basis and without any discussion of how many women it can actually serve effectively, the organization is often stretched very thin. Its workers are so busy that they rarely have time for planning or evaluation, affecting not only the NGO's daily functioning but also its beneficiaries' experiences in the organization. Beneficiaries often complain privately that activities are poorly planned and repetitive, workers arrive late or fail to remind them of upcoming meetings, and activities are inefficiently managed and last for too long.

Organizations like the Fraternity—those that are built from the bottom up and locate their roots in collective action—are often more likely to recognize the intersectionality of identities and social exclusion than are top-down organizations that are created to address specific problems, like Namaste. But even policymakers in grassroots organizations create simplified views of their beneficiaries. The Fraternity's policymakers/leaders, looking at their own experiences, goals, and dispositions as guides, assume that indigenous women are waiting for opportunities to participate in groups or will come to value participation if they are properly enlightened. As in Namaste, this simplified view of beneficiaries overlooks the diversity of women's experiences and goals. It generates blockages to achieving the NGO's goals while simultaneously generating opportunities for beneficiaries and workers to leverage this simplified view to their own ends.

Because holistic models are filtered through on-the-ground realities of NGO competition, scarce resources, structural inequalities, and people's diverse goals, they generate incoherencies that affect their daily practices, beneficiaries' experiences, and subsequent outcomes. On a day-to-day basis, the Fraternity's policymakers/leaders, workers, and beneficiaries struggle with the sometimes contradicting demands of short-term and long-term goals, as well as practical and strategic interests. Policymakers/leaders and workers confront the reality that NGOs and women do not have exclusive relationships and that beneficiaries have many responsibilities outside of participation in the Fraternity. Tensions between the Fraternity's expectations, its views of women, and its own interventions on the one hand and women's diverse realities on the other lead to mixed outcomes. In some cases, it limits women's willingness to undertake engaged, sustained participation in the organization, which is necessary for the types of internal transformations that the Fraternity's policymakers/leaders hope to inspire. In other cases, women fulfill a long-held desire to participate in groups or shift their interests to value engaged participation over time.

Because internal transformations are by nature slow and labor-intensive, and often require focused relationships, this diversity suggests that it is unlikely that *all* beneficiaries will benefit equally and in the same ways. Women have diverse experiences in organizations like the Fraternity because they vary in their expectations and desires, and in understaffed and underfunded organizations (especially those striving to expand) workers cannot take a special interest in every single beneficiary. In sum, the Fraternity's holistic model of development requires the organization's developers to make difficult choices on a daily basis about which goals and beneficiaries to prioritize. In the case of the Fraternity, these decisions are often based on personal idiosyncrasies (developers' biases, goals, and perceptions and beneficiaries' personal characteristics), affecting the nature and distribution of organizational benefits.

The Fraternity's Charismatic Structure

Despite romantic assumptions that grassroots organizations are more egalitarian than foreign transplants like Namaste, the Fraternity is in fact hierarchical and has been dominated for much of its history by the director. Whereas Namaste's internal hierarchy is organized according to task differentiation, formal rules, and technical expertise—hallmarks of bureaucracy—the Fraternity's hierarchy has long been shaped by personal characteristics, loyalties, and informal rules. I label the latter structure charismatic, drawing on Weber's discussion of charismatic authority, which is defined by the devotion to the exceptional character of an individual person and the "normative patterns or order revealed by him" (Weber 1978, 215; Beck 2014). This type of structure is quite common among NGOs, which are often affected by "leaderitis" (Lewis 2014).

Guatemalan organization, social movements, and governmental institutions are often influenced by personalism. But the Fraternity's roots in collective action additionally contributed to this charismatic structure, because "the requisites of mobilization tend to concentrate leadership quickly, especially in less developed democratizing countries, where skills and availability are scarce" (Brysk 2000, 157). Its roots in Protestant churches, where authority is concentrated around especially charismatic individuals, reinforced this tendency. In the case of the Fraternity, a handful of especially well-connected, educated, and experienced women led the process of mobilization, enjoyed disproportionate influence in the organization once it became an NGO, and institutionalized this influence by leveraging relationships with funders, workers, beneficiaries, and materials such as contracts, office space, and surveys. This reality affects the Fraternity's formal organizational structure as well as the informal rules that underlie its day-to-day operations.

The Fraternity's first director, Alicia, not only oversaw organizational matters and donor relations but also headed two of the Fraternity's four educational programs. In her role as coordinator of the Socio-Productive Program, she managed the revolving fund, giving her significant influence over decisions about loan recipients and quantities. In practice, this allowed for favoritism in the distribution and management of loans. Beneficiaries noted that the director would pressure some women who were late on their payments and refrain from doing so with others, or she would approve larger loans for some without a clear logic.

Alicia also assumed responsibility for all personnel decisions, which were often made without clear guidelines. Between 2007 and 2013, the Fraternity employed two different office managers, three different agronomists, and three different nutritionists, although other employees could only speculate as to why previous employees had been replaced. Workers were often left in the dark about other organizational matters as well. For much of the fourteen years that Alicia directed the organization, there were no regularly scheduled staff meetings, despite the fact that the staff was quite small (consisting of five to six workers) and could easily be gathered. Instead, Alicia called individual employees into her office when it suited her, leaving workers relatively ignorant of their peers' activities.

Eventually, Alicia began scheduling staff meetings. She explained that previously she had done "everything . . . [and] never shared [or] delegated" but that she had begun to think "it [was] necessary to consult, to get the support of the team." In reality, this decision also resulted from pressure that funders had been placing on Alicia to redistribute some of her responsibilities, according to a Fraternity funder. Even after incorporating regular staff meetings, though, Alicia continued to have the final say in decisions and often treated meetings as time to evaluate, rather than consult, staff. In one particularly telling meeting, Alicia scolded a worker for over twenty minutes for changing the name of a particular class without consulting with her, even though the content of the class had remained unchanged. Similarly, while the Fraternity's board of directors was meant to serve an advisory role and assist with policymaking, the director often used her meetings with the board as an opportunity to inform them of her decisions rather than solicit advice, limiting the board's policymaking role under her leadership.

Alicia was therefore positioned to have inordinate influence on the organization based on both her formal roles and informal authority. She made a number of decisions based on personal relationships—firing an employee with whom she had a personal conflict, bringing in her daughter as a member of the NGO's board, and even promising her children the Fraternity's office (partially registered in her name) as their inheritance. In one case, she contracted a relative's construction company to expand their offices rather than another company that submitted a lower bid. As the Fraternity's main funder refused to cover the difference between the two bids, the director asked the Fraternity's beneficiaries to sell their handicrafts in order to cover the extra costs of the expansion incurred by hiring her relative. Alicia's influence can be seen in the board's attempt to hire her daughter as the organization's director when Alicia died in 2012. It was not until funders suggested otherwise that the board decided to undertake a formal search to find different candidates.

Most seriously, under Alicia, personalism within the Fraternity allowed for favoritism and discrimination. While some beneficiaries were singled out for leadership positions and subsequently had transformative experiences within the organization, others were not offered similar opportunities. This uneven distribution of leadership opportunities for beneficiaries closely aligned with ethnolinguistic divisions within the organization. Outside volunteers and beneficiaries themselves noted that the NGO, headed by the K'iche' director and employing K'iche' and ladino staff, tended to favor K'iche' women over women of other ethnolinguistic groups, even though K'iche' women represented a minority of beneficiaries. On average, K'iche' women were given larger loans and were more likely to be encouraged to join the board, promoter classes, or the School of Comprehensive Education.[4]

The influence of the director's formal and informal authority was only mitigated by the fact that, unlike Namaste, the Fraternity did not value monitoring. The result was that the director rarely observed activities that she was not leading and was often only partially aware of what was taking place "in the field." This allowed some room for creativity on the part of the Fraternity's workers and beneficiaries, despite the hierarchical structure.

More recently, however, the Fraternity's hierarchical structure has shown possible signs of transformation. By the end of 2013, the board of directors played a more significant role in the Fraternity's day-to-day operations. After Alicia's death, board members took on more formal responsibilities, and the new director, Antonieta, regularly phoned or met with them in between official meetings to ask for their advice. One longtime board member reported that she felt respected by the new director, in stark contrast to her experience under the previous director, who met with some members of the board without informing her and minimized the role of the board by failing to "inform [the board] about anything until the board meetings."

Antonieta came from outside of the Fraternity; she therefore relied on the board to inform her of past successes and failures, communicate with groups with whom she did not yet have a relationship, and make key decisions about the future. She explained that she saw the relationship between her and the board as one of "mutual respect and assistance." Ironically, bringing in a director from outside the organization served to expand the role of longtime members of the organization.[5]

It is often found that external funders' demands contribute to NGOS' professionalization and hierarchy (Alvarez 1999; Markowitz and Tice 2002). But in the case of the Fraternity, funders' demands and reduced funding in fact had opposite effects. Canadian funders repeatedly suggested that Alicia devolve some of her responsibilities to other staff members, pressure that led Alicia to make a number of symbolic changes, such as holding regular staff meetings and assigning more responsibilities (at least on paper) to the board of directors. Under Antonieta, however, these symbolic trappings gained real influence in the organization, thus reducing the gap between the front-stage and backstage functions of staff and board meetings (Lund 2001). Alicia's and later Antonieta's decision to accept new groups even as funding was reduced introduced a crisis in the organization that was resolved by redistributing workers' responsibilities in instruction to beneficiaries themselves. Thus, rather than falling victim to the "iron law of oligarchy" (Michels 1911), as the organization expanded, the Fraternity actually showed signs of becoming flatter, relying more on relatively undereducated beneficiaries than professional staff.

Whereas Namaste was designed meticulously from the top down and incorporated monitoring and evaluation, the Fraternity was designed over time through the layering of formal and informal institutions and failed to systematically monitor or evaluate its efforts, creating significant gaps between formal rules and actual practice. The Fraternity only recently made any attempt at collecting the most basic information about its beneficiaries. As late as 2010, it lacked an up-to-date list of the active groups or beneficiaries or their basic contact information. In order to perform their duties, workers share information that they have collected on their own and rely on beneficiaries to pass announcements on to group members, even though this is an unreliable method of dissemination. Beneficiaries often learn of meetings when the Fraternity's workers arrive in their communities and the first group members they encounters run from house to house to gather the remaining members.

As a result, classes often start and end late, sometimes cutting into the time women require to prepare lunch or dinner for their families, to beneficiaries' distress.

In response to funders' pressure for evaluation, the Fraternity has begun administering surveys, documenting activities with photographs, and producing formal reports, although they often do so in ways that funders do not intend. Policymakers instruct workers to collect information on incoming women without thinking about its purpose—for example, asking about the sex of women's children but failing to gather more relevant information about literacy levels or primary languages. In the Fraternity's hands, surveys have been used to test beneficiaries rather than evaluate the organization's effects. At one point, workers administered surveys in Spanish to number of women who only spoke Q'anjob'al, many of whom were illiterate and did not even know their own ages. Yet workers administered surveys that included questions in Spanish such as "what does holistic development mean?" and "how do you know you are making a profit?" Similarly, for much of its history, returning beneficiaries were required to complete a three-page form created by the director before receiving their next loan. The form included questions that confused even the NGO's workers assisting illiterate women. The director later admitted this form was a "test" to see if the women had been participating in the workshops, in part to shame those who could not answer the questions so that they would be encouraged to participate more in the future. Upon their completion, the director placed the forms in a filing cabinet, never to look at them again.

The results of these attempts at collecting information and evaluating performance have not been easily accessible to the NGO's own workers and funders. At the time of my research, filing cabinets containing this material, along with reports and suggestions from visiting missionaries or volunteers, were locked in a filing cabinet located in the director's office. I only gained access to some of those files after three years of on-and-off observation with the organization, and funders often complained that they were not given access to these files or basic information about the NGO's programming, funding, and budget.

Beneficiaries' attendance at the Fraternity's activities is formally required but only sometimes enforced. There is no clear basis for accepting new groups or retiring existing groups. Groups are "retired" for various reasons: because its members are not regularly participating in activities, are receiving loans from other organizations, or are failing to invest their revolving fund responsibly. But there have been many groups that fit these descriptions that have stayed active, such that the decision to terminate a group has appeared somewhat arbitrary to both beneficiaries and NGO workers. On a number of occasions, workers have started working with a group only to find out in the middle of a course that the group was being "retired," without warning or explanation.

The Fraternity's organizational structure contributes to its inefficiency, which often frustrates its beneficiaries, for whom time is scarce. The Fraternity's events often start late and last for hours. On many occasions, women are forced to wait for long periods of time in the Fraternity's offices, conference venues, or women's homes before activities begin. This means that women spend more time together and experience more small encounters than do women participating in Namaste's comparatively more efficient and targeted activities. The Fraternity's looser organizational structure also provides room for creativity on the part of NGO workers and beneficiaries. Because they are given very little support and are rarely observed in the field, workers have de facto room for maneuver. The agronomist, for example, often begins each course asking women what they want to learn and then sets about designing educational programs to meet their needs, a strategy that would not be possible if education was closely monitored, as it is in Namaste.

In contrast to Namaste, then, the Fraternity relies less on formal rules and more on personal characteristics and relationships, which in turn opens a large gap between formal institutions and actual practices. These characteristics inform both blockages and opportunities. They reduce efficiency and allow for favoritism within the organization, such that women have varied experiences depending on their personal characteristics and connections with the Fraternity's workers and policymakers. But these organizational traits also give the Fraternity's workers and women themselves more opportunities to interact and act creatively. The following chapter will demonstrate that together the Fraternity's developers and beneficiaries create open, ambiguous spaces in which many things are possible, including *both* empowerment and disempowerment. In contrast to Namaste's development hallways, the Fraternity's sites of development resemble multipurpose rooms—spaces that can be put to multiple ends and in which diverse experiences and outcomes are possible.

Organizational Networks:
Leveraging International and Local Networks

The Fraternity's origins, trajectory, and founders' networks not only affected its development model, values, and organizational structure; they also embedded it in both local and international religious networks. The Fraternity's origins in the Presbyterian Church and its early mobilization strategies that emphasized face-to-face contact and small group projects embedded the

NGO in local networks. In 2000, one of the Fraternity's founders helped to found the Mam Association, an umbrella organization uniting Mam women involved in the Fraternity, and thereafter a parallel K'iche' Association and Kaqchikel Association were formed. Most women hear about the Fraternity through their pastors or through members of these associations, which each have their own boards of directors. Associations assist women in drafting requests for revolving funds and submit requests to the Fraternity's director. Thus, the Fraternity expends little effort on recruitment, in stark contrast to Namaste, because its beneficiaries take on this role themselves, performing unpaid labor in the process. What is more, because of its local, religious character, potential beneficiaries often see the Fraternity as distinct from and more attractive than other MFIs. Women's spouses often see women's participation in the Fraternity as an extension of their religious participation and therefore relatively unthreatening.

While members of the Fraternity's board of directors were initially former founders, board members are now longtime beneficiaries of the Fraternity, many of whom continue to receive the revolving fund and participate in classes with their respective groups. Thus, unlike Namaste, the Fraternity provides its beneficiaries with some voice in the organization, even if at times it has been only symbolic. Under Alicia, the board served a largely advisory role and had minimal influence on the organization's operations, although in key moments members pressured her to be more transparent. Upon Alicia's death in 2012, the board was central to the process of locating and hiring a new technical director and its influence was thereafter maintained. In contrast to Namaste, the Fraternity's director, its board members, and many of its workers live in the very communities in which beneficiaries live, and beneficiaries and other community members often travel to the Fraternity's offices, further strengthening the connections between the NGO and its beneficiaries and the perception that the Fraternity is not "just another MFI."

In addition to embedding the Fraternity in local communities, the Fraternity's origins in the Presbyterian Church also connected it to international religious networks through which it subsequently accessed funding, visits from missionaries and volunteers, logistical support, and ideas. Beyond funding, visits from foreign missionaries, members of sister churches, and representatives from other associations expose the Fraternity to new ideas about gender roles and development. For example, the Mesoamerican Committee for Peace and CEDEPCA send representatives to lead classes at the Fraternity, provide the organization with educational material, and even sponsor international travel for selected workers and beneficiaries. Issues of globalization, justice, and politics are central in this education. Early on, the United Church of Canada (UCC) sent a missionary to work with the Fraternity for three years to provide theological training and develop a course of study appropriate for cultures that learn by oral tradition. The course that the missionary developed with the Fraternity had a progressive bent that mirrored some of the central tenets of liberation theology: it focused on rectifying suffering and inequalities on earth, rather than waiting for their rectification in heaven. The Fraternity's policymakers/leaders, workers, and beneficiaries do not passively accept these ideas but actively reinterpret, adjust, and at times resist them.

The Fraternity's identity as a grassroots, Mayan, women's organization is attractive to many of its funders and supporting the Fraternity serves their own interests. In the face of the growing "economy of humanitarianism" in which "culture is a precious commodity" (Nuñez 2009, 113-17) and in which women are associated with development, supporting an organization of indigenous women who wear colorful *trajes* (indigenous clothing) and speak Mayan languages is attractive to international donors and their contributors. The Fraternity's religious nature also provides it with a measure of autonomy and allows policymakers/leaders to emphasize difficult-to-quantify goals that make sense to religious donors (such as internal transformation), even though it is dependent on international funding (Dicklitch and Rice 2004; Bakewell and Warren 2005). A representative of PWS&D explains further that the Fraternity satisfies its donors. Although PWS&D is the charity arm of the Presbyterian Church of Canada, it mostly funds secular grassroots organizations, to the confusion and, in some cases, protests of the parishioners whose contributions are central to its operations. Thus, including the Fraternity in its portfolio of partner organizations satisfies PWS&D's contributors because its gender, ethnic, and religious identity make the relationship between the Fraternity and PWS&D mutually beneficial. Even though donors have in the past complained that emails went weeks unanswered, requested documents never arrived or arrived incomplete, and information was not openly shared, they continued to value their relationship with the NGO.

The Fraternity's history of grassroots mobilization, its policymakers/leaders' and workers' identities, and its continued connection with local churches and religious organizations allow the Fraternity to maintain its identity as a local organization, despite its reliance on international funding. As a result, the Fraternity's developers and current and potential beneficiaries see the NGO as a different kind of organization, one that is not just another MFI.

As demonstrated in the next chapter, this local identity and association with religious spheres shapes women's expectations of the organization. Beneficiaries actively assign meaning and expectations to the Fraternity, and they often base these on comparisons with religious groups or indigenous groups rather than other MFIs. They are therefore more tolerant of time-consuming participation. A minority, in fact, view (or come to view) the time spent participating in the Fraternity as a benefit rather than a cost, although this view is far from universal among beneficiaries.

CONCLUSIONS

The Fraternity's roots in indigenous women's social mobilization and the experiences and dispositions of founding members informed the NGO's subsequent trajectory and characteristics. Drawing on creative combinations of Mayan and Protestant values and beliefs and their own personal histories, early policymakers/leaders operated according to a holistic model of development, which included nonquantifiable goals such as community well-being, culturally different citizens, indigenous women's voices, and inclusion, as well as a revalorization of nonhuman life. Its policymakers/leaders materialized this vision by developing programming and materials that reflected this model of development, although it did so in an ad hoc, bottom-up way. The Fraternity's origins and subsequent trajectory additionally contributed to a charismatic structure in which decisions were often made based on personal loyalties and characteristics and there existed significant gaps between formal policies and actual practices. They also embedded the Fraternity in local religious and cultural networks, while simultaneously allowing it to leverage international connections developed in the organization's prehistory and over time thereafter. Although the Fraternity reflected broader international trends that valued microfinance, incorporating women and indigenous peoples in development, and bottom-up development, seeing its characteristics as caused by those trends would overlook the contingent, interactional processes of translation and composition that produced them.

The following chapter focuses on how these organizational characteristics affect, but do not determine, the nature of interactions between developers and beneficiaries in the Fraternity. The organizational characteristics described in this chapter influence how women view the Fraternity, the expectations they place on their participation, and the demands they are willing to make, but they leave significant room for creativity on the part of workers and beneficiaries such that interactions at the Fraternity's interfaces yield diverse and mixed outcomes. Some but not all women transform their identities and interests, increasing their "power within." But the NGO has limited effects for women's economic livelihoods, unevenly distributes transformational opportunities, and attempts to manage women's behaviors in ways are at times disempowering.

CHAPTER SIX

THE UNEVEN PRACTICES
AND EXPERIENCES OF
HOLISTIC DEVELOPMENT

Alicia, the Fraternity's director, stood facing roughly thirty K'iche' women seated in teal plastic chairs. Projected on the white concrete wall behind her were the words "family economy." Once the chatter quieted down, she began: "Today we are going to talk about income, costs, and resources." She explained, "It used to be women married for love, but now they say the woman who marries wants a house (*la mujer que casa, casa quiere*). This is the effect of free trade. What we want is equilibrium for everything—this is something Mayan cosmovision values." Alicia pointed to the words on the wall and asked, "What do we understand about the importance of family economy?" Without waiting for an answer, she continued. "It is important to recapture what was described by God, that which was established from the beginning of creation—good administration." Alicia then clicked forward to a slide that outlined what she meant by this, reading aloud the listed aspects of good administration, which included (1) respecting life and that God is the owner of everything; (2) learning to share; (3) making a budget, establishing objectives and matrimonial and individual goals; and (4) teaching children the value of work (money) and a more dignified life.

Alicia explained, "We need to ask how much we earn as a couple and talk about what our objectives are. Sometimes men say, 'you are home all day,' 'you do nothing.' But fine, if we did nothing all day, we would see how the house is." To illustrate, Alicia later broke women up into small groups and distributed worksheets labeled with "analysis of incomes and costs." She instructed women to record, using words or pictures, what they did every day, how much money and time they spent in different activities, and what they earned as a family. After roughly twenty minutes, Alicia called on various women to share their answers. Women recounted their daily household and business activities—rising early to prepare breakfast, going to the market to buy food or sell their products, cleaning the home and tending to the children, feeding the animals, and preparing lunches and dinners. Some stated their monthly incomes based on on-the-spot mental estimates rather than the worksheets; others did not even bother to estimate incomes.

The contrasts between business education in the Fraternity, described here, and business education provided in Namaste (in the opening of chapter 4) reflect the diverging meanings, functions, and practices attached to the two NGOs' similar development technologies. Namaste's business classes are concise activities that focus on teaching women concrete concepts and skills that they can apply directly to their businesses. The Fraternity's classes are less efficient. The activity just described began over an hour late and, rather than having a clear ending point, continued on even as women quietly left to rush home to prepare lunches for their families. The conversation meandered from women's businesses, to their relationships with their husbands, to the damaging effects of consumerism. Namaste rarely references women's roles as wives and mothers, focusing instead on their identities as individual businesswomen. The Fraternity's developers, by contrast, often focus on women's roles in other spheres, most commonly the family. In other activities, they additionally highlight women's roles in their churches and communities alongside, through, and sometimes instead of their identities as businesswomen.

The Fraternity's activities, unlike Namaste's, tend to prioritize emotions, identities, and self-esteem over business matters—even activities that, according to official reports, focus on businesses. Much of the family economy class described here emphasized the importance of recapturing traditional values, conceived of as Christian and Mayan values. It also addressed women's self-esteem. By detailing all of the reproductive and productive activities that women undertook in a given day, women recognized that they contributed a good deal to the household in terms of their time and energy, even if they did not contribute monetarily. This activity did not, however, actually teach women how to calculate their profits or losses or create a family budget.

In these and other ways, the Fraternity's model of holistic development and other organizational characteristics affect the day-to-day practices and experiences of development, although both developers and beneficiaries actively react to and transform interventions on the ground. As with Namaste, beneficiaries assign meaning and expectations to the Fraternity based on their initial interactions with the NGO, previous experiences, comparisons with other institutions, and diverse personal goals. Although the majority of women join the NGO to access low-interest loans, women develop a different view of the Fraternity than they do of Namaste: based on the Fraternity's grassroots origins, local networks, and everyday strategies, most women conclude that the Fraternity is *not* just another MFI.

Driven by multiple goals—seeking short-term and long-term, internal and external, material and nonmaterial transformations—the Fraternity's many activities unintentionally end up being inefficient and time-consuming. They focus on emotions, identities, and syncretic understandings of beneficiaries' worth as Christians, Mayans, and women. These activities move beyond women's individual identities to allow for discussions of their roles in their families, churches, and communities. In its quest for holistic development, the Fraternity's developers additionally attempt to manage women's behavior to produce "good, Christian, Mayan women" subjects by using loan conditions, contracts, "tests," biblical verses, educational sessions, and scolding.

Beneficiaries, however, are not passive recipients of policymakers' programming and "lessons." Rather, they react in diverse and creative ways. Although the Fraternity's policymakers/leaders view women's participation as both instrumentally and intrinsically valuable, only some of its beneficiaries share this view. Others, like Namaste's beneficiaries, see their participation as a cost necessary to access low-interest loans and subsequently participate at minimal levels. The variation in how beneficiaries view their participation in the Fraternity springs from two sources. First, the fact that women often enter the Fraternity through religious networks and see the organization as something other than an MFI means that women join the Fraternity with a greater variety of goals and expectations than do women joining Namaste. Second, *some* women who are initially attracted to the Fraternity by the loan alone and see their participation as a cost subsequently undergo transformations within the organization through their interactions with people and course materials. Their identities change as they come to see themselves as role models, teachers, or leaders, and therefore their interests change such that they view their participation as intrinsically valuable. Others, marginalized by the personal biases of the Fraternity's developers, are blocked from these opportunities for transformation. Thus, developers and diverse beneficiaries interact in the

Fraternity to co-constitute sites of development that resemble multipurpose rooms—spaces in which many things can and do happen, including empowerment *and* disempowerment.

The varied practices, experiences, and interactions that unfold in the Fraternity are connected to its diverse, mixed outcomes. Beneficiaries do not seem to benefit economically from their participation, but some transform their self-esteem and identities. Yet such benefits are unevenly distributed, and the NGO at times reinforces inequalities among its beneficiaries.

HOW WOMEN COME TO VIEW THE FRATERNITY AS "NOT LIKE A BANK"

Because the Fraternity is embedded in local religious networks and communities, women often hear about the NGO through their pastors, members of their women's societies, or members of the Mam, K'iche', or Kaqchikel Associations who themselves participate in the NGO. Once interested women undertake the unpaid labor of gathering together at least five group members, the appropriate ethnic association's board (also uncompensated) helps the group draft a letter of interest that they submit to the Fraternity's director and board. This process diverges from that of the vast majority of MFIs in the area, who undertake recruitment strategies that are similar to those of Namaste—sending representatives (who are often seen as outsiders) to communities to knock on doors and distribute flyers.

Because the Fraternity views *all* indigenous women's participation as intrinsically valuable, the organization does not regularly turn women away. When facing resource limitations, its policymakers/leaders prioritize previously funded groups. This is in contrast with other MFIs, which often screen women based on their resources and credit history, and Namaste, which screens women according to levels of need and potential for business growth. Even when the Fraternity arguably has insufficient funding and staff, it continues to accept new groups. The lack of selection criteria, which contrasts with Namaste's increasingly narrow vision of its ideal beneficiaries, reflects Fraternity policymakers/leaders' holistic model of development, which is associated with a view of participation as intrinsically valuable and a tendency to value inclusion over efficiency.

The Fraternity's recruitment strategy is possible because of its local connections and religious identity, themselves born of its grassroots origins. Women actively develop simplified views of and expectations of organizations based on their initial impressions and experiences with other organizations they deem comparable. Because they access the Fraternity through their social networks, and develop expectations based on peers' experiences, the Fraternity's incoming beneficiaries are less likely to view the NGO as just another MFI, even in the face of other MFIs offering similar-sized loans. The Fraternity reinforces this tendency by labeling its loans "revolving funds" and interest rates "recognition fees." In activities, the Fraternity's workers emphasize this difference, highlighting that the Fraternity is "not like a bank that just gives a loan and then charges high interest rates" but rather encourages women "to be different, to change."

Although the majority of the Fraternity's beneficiaries join the organization in order to access a loan, few see the Fraternity as just another MFI and many associate the NGO with religious or cultural networks. Their expectations for participation are thus less colored by their experiences with, or the reputations of, other MFIs, and they are more likely to see Fraternity as trustworthy. Most beneficiaries learn of the Fraternity through members of ethnic associations or through their churches, women's societies, or pastors, networks in which women's participation is encouraged, albeit to a limited degree. In addition to attending services multiple times a week, participating in youth groups, church societies, and project-specific committees, and serving as elders, members of Protestant churches are also often encouraged to do readings, lead prayers, and take part in services in a direct way. Women's participation in religious spheres is often undervalued compared to that of their male counterparts and in many cases conforms to traditional gendered divisions of labor. Still, Protestant churches provide women with opportunities to undertake and observe various forms of participation similar to those that are common in the Fraternity, helping women form expectations and shaping their perceptions of their participation in the NGO.

Some women see their participation in the Fraternity as an extension of their church participation. For example, Sandra, a K'iche' woman, explains that she attended classes with the Fraternity in part because her pastor encouraged her, but also because she felt that she "needed the fund [loan], and to learn more, and to have knowledge in different spheres of life and to share it in the church." At the time we spoke, she had been participating in the Fraternity for five years. In an exceptional case, one woman's church participation pushed her to join the Fraternity solely to access education; she decided to forgo the loan altogether. Gabriela had only reached the third grade as a child and saw the Fraternity's promoter classes as a chance to gain the skills she needed to fulfill new roles she was being assigned in her church:

[When I first started coming to church services] they asked me to [direct services] but I was not motivated to do so because before I had not participated in anything. And I knew women participated in a course [at the Fraternity]. "But I cannot do anything," I said. I went [to meetings of the women's society at the church], and was observing. Twice I led [the services]—and I was sweating and sweating, and they could see I did not want to do it. Later, I started to participate more. And later they elected me president . . . and I was worrying because if no one arrives to give the sermon, I have to do it. And I could not do it. I said, "if I had only studied."

Gabriela was so worried about leading church activities that she sent her nephew to the Fraternity to inquire about the classes that women in her church were attending. When she discovered that the Fraternity's classes were free, she eagerly enrolled. Gabriela continued to attend promoter classes at the Fraternity and to take part in conferences and activities, all without ever receiving a loan.

Even women who explicitly join the Fraternity to access a loan associate the Fraternity with religious networks. Paula, for example, first heard about the Fraternity through a pastor in her church. "He said, 'listen sister, there is a fund. And if you are in agreement, you have to get together with each other [to form a group] and take out a loan. Not a loan, a fund.'" She subsequently recruited women from her church to join her loan group. Once Paula had gathered enough women together, they submitted their request to members of the Mam Association in a meeting of her presbytery. Thus, the entire process of joining the Fraternity—from initially hearing about the organization, to forming a group, to finally submitting a request to join—took place in religious contexts.

Because of the Fraternity's local connections and identity, women's first interactions with the organization are colored not by its association with other MFIs but rather by its association with Protestant churches. This reality shapes women's expectations for their participation in the Fraternity: they are subsequently more tolerant of long group activities and classes that mirror church services in that they often last for a long time, begin and end with prayers, reference biblical verses, are led by a charismatic leader, and call on women to give testimony. Women are also less likely to view other MFIs as equivalent substitutes for the Fraternity, making exit less desirable, even in the face of dissatisfaction (Hirschman 1970; M. E. Warren 2001). Because the Fraternity's policymakers/leaders' goals require engaged, sustained participation on the part of its beneficiaries, these perceptions and expectations serve the NGO well.

WORKERS' INTERPRETATIONS OF HOLISTIC DEVELOPMENT AND WOMEN'S CREATIVE REACTIONS

Developers Contributing to the Fraternity's Disorganized "Classrooms"

Although, like Namaste, the Fraternity creates development classrooms, the lessons imparted and teaching styles diverge from those of Namaste. The activities that unfold there are inefficient and unfocused, frustrating women but also allowing them more time and space to interact and act creatively. The Fraternity's classrooms are put to multiple uses. Rather than focusing solely on concrete business skills, the Fraternity seeks internal changes, opening up spaces for the exploration of emotions and identities. Unlike Namaste, the Fraternity provides women with the opportunity to move up in the organization, encouraging some to take on new roles and transform their identities and interests in the process, although these opportunities are unevenly distributed.

IXIM ULEW

In the rural, K'iche' community of Ixim Ulew, women wandered in and out of a large open room in Blanca's house. It was cleared of all furniture except for a herd of more than thirty mismatched plastic chairs facing a white sheet pinned to the wall. Women were waiting for the day's activity, which was supposed to start forty minutes ago, to begin. They leaned over in their chairs or wandered out to the enclosed dirt courtyard to chat. Beneficiaries had been notified of today's activity just last week and were urged to arrive on time. Still, the Fraternity's representatives, Alicia and Natalia, arrived over half an hour late and were still struggling to set up the projector and the laptop for a presentation of the Fraternity's homemade video, "Hidden Landfills."

Finally, Alicia stood in front of the room and waited for the women to sit down. She greeted them in K'iche' before switching to Spanish. "Today we are going to learn about how our communities are, how the environment is in our country. There are many religions, many churches, that have pretty names but what do they [actually] do? One has to think about doing things. We want you to change your lives. How have you changed your lives?" When no one answered, Alicia offered herself as an example: "For example, I only watch television to watch the news. I do not watch soap operas because they encourage violence and prostitution. One can become addicted." She continued, "We have to think about what is best for us, what is best for our children. . . . This is the value of being a woman. This is why we talk about self-esteem. Imagine a young girl who says, 'I am stupid. I am not good for anything. I do not know how to read or write. I am ignorant.' She gets to heaven and they say, 'what have you done with your life?' and she says 'nothing.' They are going to say 'go back and do it again.' [That is why] our participation as women is important. That is why we want to see you make changes."

Alicia then introduced the video for the day, which demonstrated how Guatemalans had damaged the environment by throwing their garbage on roadsides and in rivers and valleys. But when Alicia tried to play it, nothing happened. The women sat uncomfortably and eventually began milling about while Alicia and Natalia fiddled with the laptop once again. I overheard a group of women congregated outside of the doorway, whispering worriedly about what to do if the event did not begin soon, agreeing that their husbands would be angry if they were not home to prepare lunch. Finally, Alicia and Natalia decided to show a different movie, one that depicted the earth as a melting ice cream cone, explained the process of global warming, and concluded with a number of recommendations for combating it that seem out of context. Women were instructed to take fewer hot showers, even though few had hot water in their homes and some lacked running water altogether, and to use energy-efficient light bulbs, which were unavailable in their communities even if the women had electricity and could afford them.

During the video, a man arrived with a DVD player. Blanca and her family distributed snacks—pieces of bread and hot drinks made of chocolate, water, and rice—while women talked among themselves. Alicia and Natalia finally figured out how to play the originally scheduled video on the DVD player, and the women settled back into their seats. The video was only half completed, though, when a few women ducked out to return home to prepare lunch. Alicia, sensing the restlessness in the room, stopped the video halfway to conclude, "Now you see what it is like in your communities. What we want is each group to write a letter within the next two weeks to the K'iche' Association to ask for their accompaniment to secure a meeting with your mayors to express your concern. Then we are going to put up a billboard in a prominent place expressing concern and inviting the population and the mayor to reduce the amount of garbage [in our communities]." Natalia stood up with a crumpled piece of paper and began to take attendance as women gathered around her.

This activity demonstrates that the Fraternity's activities are often less focused and efficient than those of Namaste. Activities often start late and last for anywhere between an hour and a half and four hours. A few times each year, women attend daylong conferences on topics of the director's choosing. Others have written about the disempowering effects of forcing the marginalized to wait (Auyero 2012). In the context of the Fraternity, beneficiaries often feel frustrated by the amount of time they spend in the Fraternity's activities and waiting around. In the previous activity, women discuss with each other how to leave the activity in time to prepare lunch but feel uncomfortable telling the Fraternity's workers that they are worried about repercussions at home. In this sense, the women's waiting shows the subtle ways that the Fraternity restricts their mobility at the same time that it provides them with legitimate spaces for participation. It is both an expression and a reinforcement of asymmetrical power dynamics at work within the NGO.

In stark contrast to women's experiences in Namaste, women are asked to come together for numerous, long activities and are encouraged to keep participating for many years. The NGO's policymakers/leaders see these activities as central to women's lives, even though the women often do not feel the same, and they therefore ask the women to give more time and energy to their activities than many of the women are willing and able to give. Beneficiaries, however, have their own goals and strategies and react in diverse ways to the Fraternity's expectations. Some accommodate the Fraternity's demands in order to avoid risking access to a loan; others fail to attend required events like the one just described. Some arrive late, walk in and out of activities, answer their phones or carry on side conversations, or leave early. Others complain privately to members of their respective ethnic associations, who advise the women and relay complaints to the Fraternity's policymakers/leaders.

In practice, numerous long activities and extended waiting times produce many more small encounters among and between beneficiaries and workers

FIGURE 6.1.
The chaotic
process
of taking
attendance in
the Fraternity.
Photograph by
the author.

(figure 6.1). This provides for richer (if more frustrating) participatory experiences and allows beneficiaries to use their time in the organization creatively—for example, using waiting periods to discuss familial or church matters or complain about the Fraternity itself. Indeed, my interviews with the Fraternity's beneficiaries often lasted much longer than interviews with their counterparts in Namaste because the women had more to say about their participation in the organization (both positive and negative), had more experiences to share, and were more likely to draw connections between their participation in the Fraternity and other areas of their lives. The Fraternity's policymakers/leaders' demands often come with significant costs: some women resent the time and effort that participating in the organization requires. Yet, because changes in identities and relationships often happen incrementally through repeated small encounters, the Fraternity is more likely than Namaste to inspire intended and unintended changes in women's relationships and identities as it offers women more chances to interact in both planned and unplanned ways.

The fact that women receiving small business loans are asked to attend classes on environmental degradation and to approach government representatives, as they were in the previous vignette, demonstrates the Fraternity's desire to inspire transformations beyond the economic realm and beyond the individual. Policymakers/leaders explicitly seek to change women's values, identities, and activities and, in so doing, transform churches and communities. Based on these varied goals, policymakers/leaders and workers encourage women to discuss and reflect on their opinions, feelings, and experiences in their families, churches, and communities. These multifaceted goals are similarly demonstrated in the following vignette in which a worker enrolls stories, pictures, biblical verses, and women's own experiences in order to promote women's self-esteem.

TINULCO

Women sat in a semicircle in a concrete house in the Mam town of Tinulco. Natalia—a K'iche' woman with a kind, plump face, round glasses, and graying hair pulled back into a low ponytail—introduced the new theme "Me and You." "Today we are going to focus on the first part of this, who am I? . . . We are going to have a dialogue with ourselves, discover ourselves. . . . Every single person needs [time to] reflect. This is how we start making a change." She gestured to the circle of women: "What does it mean to make a change?" One woman responded, "To set forth to do new things, instead of continuing to do the same things as before." "Yes," Natalia replied, "we want a transformation, but it needs to start with ourselves. Take the cloth bags [you made earlier this year] for example. Before you said you could not make them because you did not have a machine. But then you realized that yes, you can." She looked around at the women as they nodded and murmured their agreement. "There are women who say 'I cannot do anything [because] I cannot read or write.' But you can weave [and do handicrafts]. Do you need to know how to read or write to weave?" The women—many of whom, like almost 70 percent of women in this community, were illiterate—shook their heads. Natalia smiled: "No, you do not."

Natalia then removed a manila folder from her cloth bag, opening it up to begin reading a story aloud entitled, "I Want to Be a Person." The story described a woman who felt trapped and alone in her own home and was thinking about her dreams. When she finished, Natalia walked around the room showing the women a piece of paper divided in two. On one side, a woman looked sadly at a window that was blocked; on the other, a woman surrounded by flowers looked out an open window. "What do you see?" One woman replied, "The woman on the left is sad." Another added, "She is enclosed. She wants to see out the window but cannot see."

Natalia then taped a piece of butcher paper to the wall and pointed to the questions written on it. "We are going to break up into small groups and answer these questions: Have you felt this way before? What did you do to change your situation, or did it stay the same?" Women spent fifteen minutes in their groups, talking about the questions, gossiping about other topics, switching between Mam and Spanish. They recorded their responses on a piece of butcher paper, using some words but mostly pictures, laughing at their stick-figure drawings. When they had quieted down, Natalia invited each group to stand in front of the group to present.

The representative of the first group explained, "One of us said that her husband used to enclose her in the house but that now she goes to meetings. Another had a similar situation but now she works and is able to get out of the house." The second group's representative said that when one of the women had problems "she goes for walks with her mother to forget," and that another woman's husband used to drink too much, "but that was before they joined the church. Now he does not drink and now they are not in this problem." The third group's representative summarized: "Some of the women had problems not because of drinking but because [their husbands had] other women. But now things are getting better. Others said they have problems but they go to church to get out of the house, because this is when the problems come, when one is alone in the house." The representative of the fourth group explained, "Before when we were not [Protestant], my husband used to drink and sometimes he came home and hit me. Now we are [Protestant] so we do not have these problems." The final group's representative explained, "One of us had these problems when her husband was alive. He would not allow her to go out to do the shopping; he was jealous. Now that he has died, she has the opportunity to go to the market, to attend meetings. Two of us have husbands that are understanding. For me, my husband is understanding [when I want to go out] because he knows that I am alone with the children during the day."

Natalia came to the front of the room: "So we have seen problems with jealousy, with feeling enclosed and isolated, with infidelity. This is how women feel sometimes. Marriage is hard. But when we change our lives, it is a blessing. Look at this woman, a widow who now has the opportunity to be here and to be in the Mam Association."

Later Natalia announced, "Now we are [going to] talk about self-esteem" while she opened up her Bible. She drew on biblical verses: "See, the Bible says that a bird does not fall without God knowing and that God has counted all the hairs on your head. So you should not worry because God loves you more than many birds. If God loves us so much, what should we do?" A beneficiary responded, "Care for ourselves." "That is right"—Natalia smiled—"care for ourselves and accept ourselves as we are." The women spent the rest of the class discussing the "symptoms" of low self-esteem and the various ways that women could care for themselves.

This activity would not qualify as an appropriate development activity according to a narrow, resource-based model of development like the one adopted in Namaste. But the Fraternity's leaders see poverty as both a lack of resources *and* a lack of self-esteem and cultural identity, and they define development in a way that includes (rather than overlooks or instrumentalizes) changes in the private sphere. Thus an activity that focuses on personal experiences, emotions, and self-esteem fits with their holistic model of development. The Fraternity's policymakers/leaders see women as potential agents of change but assume that before they can change their families and communities, they have to undergo personal transformations, leading the organization to focus on women's power within and alongside (and sometimes rather than) their material well-being.

In the hierarchy of knowledge in the Fraternity's interfaces, developers' expertise is afforded more weight than that of beneficiaries. Yet the Fraternity's developers also encourage women to share their personal testimonies as a part of lesson plans in ways that are similar to traditions established Protestant church services. Women quickly become accustomed to sharing and resharing their life stories. Doing so produces more flexible spaces than those created by Namaste; in these spaces, women's stories, emotions, and experiences shape the nature of the activities undertaken in them. The activity just described has been repeated many times, but because it incorporates women's experiences as

FIGURE 6.2. Women in the Fraternity pose with their handmade cloth bags.
Photograph by the author.

part of the lesson, it varies across different groups. In this case, the discussion allows each woman to discuss her marital relationship. In a different group of beneficiaries, the activity took on a different focus when one woman, upon listening to the story "I Want to Be a Person," began to cry. She explained that she understood the way the woman in the story felt because she has felt alone since her daughter's father had abandoned them. She wept: "Sometimes I think . . . I do not know what I am good for. I do not know why God made me," and the "lesson plan" was broken down and reconstituted by both Natalia and beneficiaries themselves. They focused on consoling the young woman rather than breaking into small groups to discuss their relationships with their husbands.

Even when lessons focus on concrete skills, such as animal husbandry, textiles, or farming, they incorporate discussions of self-esteem, identities, or women's relationships with and responsibilities toward their churches, communities, and environments as Christians and Mayans. In the activity in Tinulco described previously, Natalia drew a connection between women's experiences learning how to make cloth bags and their ability to overcome obstacles (see figure 6.2). Readers may remember from chapter 4 that in Namaste, when women complained that they could not make a particular type of purse without sewing machines, women were told that a good businesswoman was "someone who overcomes obstacles." The Fraternity's workers consistently communicate a similar message—that women are able to overcome obstacles—but they connect this skill with their identities as women, as Christians, and as Mayans. Furthermore, because developers in the Fraternity are less concerned with providing women with concise, targeted, preplanned lessons, they can take the next step by actually teaching women how to make cloth bags by hand. Workers are then able to point to this accomplishment to demonstrate that beneficiaries are capable of more than they thought.

DEVELOPERS ENCOURAGING SOME WOMEN'S
PARTICIPATION WHILE DISCRIMINATING AGAINST OTHERS

The Fraternity's policymakers/leaders, through their personal experiences, recognize that all too often indigenous women are denied equal access to participatory opportunities and leadership positions. The NGO's history has informed an organizational habitus which includes a view of indigenous women's participation as intrinsically valuable, rather than just instrumentally so, which in turn has influenced the decision to create spaces for beneficiaries to take on new responsibilities and roles in the organization. Yet the NGO's charismatic structure and developers' personal biases ensure that these opportunities are not equally available to all beneficiaries, despite the Fraternity's formal objectives and public transcripts.

The first avenue for beneficiaries' leadership is the board of directors. Current beneficiaries nominate and vote on board candidates at the Fraternity's annual assembly. Board members, who are supposed to serve two- to three-year terms, are drawn from beneficiaries' own ranks. Women are therefore more likely to see the Fraternity's board members as one of them because they are from the same communities, receive loans from the Fraternity, and often have similarly low levels of formal education. Serving on the board is potentially a transformational experience for those who are elected. Women are given opportunities to develop and practice civic skills—they lead meetings, write letters and acts, review the organization's official reports, share their opinions, and relay messages among the Fraternity's director, beneficiaries, and workers.

Victoria, for example, was an early member of the Fraternity. She was selected to serve on the board as a council member because of her experience in the organization, even though she had only reached the fourth grade and initially felt uncomfortable speaking Spanish rather than her native language, Mam. She served in this position for six years before being promoted to secretary, a role with which she struggled because it entailed writing acts, and she lacked confidence in her writing skills. While she claimed that the director at times made her feel like she was a "bad secretary," by the end of her eight years in this position she explained that she gained confidence because other board members "told [her] that yes, [she] could do it because if [she had] the will and the desire, the Fraternity [was] there" to help. By 2013, Victoria was elected president of the board of directors. In this position she led board sessions, received reports from the director and program coordinators, and visited loan groups. Victoria explained with pride that her job was to "see how they are working, if there are problems, or if all is going well, and to make sure the groups are doing well."

Beyond learning new skills, enjoying the prestige of leadership, and having the opportunity for one's voice to be heard, board membership provides beneficiaries with an opportunity to meet women outside their loan groups and establish more intimate relationships with fellow board members, alongside whom they serve for many years. Sofia, who at different times has served as the board's secretary, treasurer, and president, explained that women often leverage board meetings for other purposes, such as to discuss problems at home or past experiences. She recounted, "When we come together as members we [find that] we have had different pains, different joys. [We talk about] how our families act. And sometimes women are suffering, so we share, and give words of encouragement and console each other. In this way we move forward." Thus board meetings provide elected beneficiaries with more small encounters and new opportunities that they put to creative uses—to discuss their personal problems and emotions, develop relationships, and help other women like themselves.

Yet these opportunities are not evenly distributed. In theory, members of the board are supposed to rotate every two to three years to provide more women with opportunities to take on more active roles. In reality, this is not the case. Beneficiaries often assume that significant experience is required to fulfill the board's responsibilities, and less experienced women are therefore less likely to run or receive votes for board positions. Although beneficiaries themselves technically nominate candidates, in reality the Fraternity's director and workers often informally encourage certain women to run. Serving on the board requires a good deal of time, energy, and responsibility but does not come with a salary or material benefits, so many beneficiaries are hesitant to stand as candidates unless they are singled out by the Fraternity's director or employees. Some who are elected retire before their term is complete, at which point the Fraternity's director and remaining board members choose their replacements, often drawing from previous board members. As a result, board positions in practice often rotate among the same group of women, leading one funder to suggest that the organization's board has become "stagnant." The tendency of Fraternity's policymakers/leaders and workers to single out women they favor (based on their own perceptions and biases) combines with the women's own understandings of the positions' requirements such that leadership opportunities are unevenly distributed among women, with some receiving/taking advantage of numerous leadership opportunities and others receiving/taking advantage of none.

This pattern is also repeated in promoter classes and the School of Comprehensive Education, in which the Fraternity's beneficiaries enroll to receive further training to become voluntary educators. These trainings are time- and labor-intensive. For example, initially the promoter classes in theological study required women to complete thirty-six classes designed by UBL, spread out over the course of three years. Upon completion, women received credit and a certificate from UBL and became qualified to lead group classes for the Women's Pastoral Program on a voluntary basis. These types of programs thus challenge beneficiaries to move from seeing themselves as students to seeing themselves as teachers, and provide them with opportunities to experiment with new roles. Indeed, the Women's Pastoral Program's coordinator herself was a member of the first generation of promoter students. Once a beneficiary, she became a student and now serves as a permanent, paid educator who has instructed hundreds of women and trained subsequent generations of promoters.

In order to recruit students to promoter classes (and later to the School of Comprehensive Education), the Fraternity's director and workers identify beneficiaries they see as especially promising—by undefined criteria. Women are singled out because they are especially articulate, demonstrate interest in a particular subject, have fewer family responsibilities, or have close relationships with staff. Some are selected because they are longtime beneficiaries and familiar with the program; others are selected because they are new to the program and are young and energetic. Even women who are reluctant to enroll feel uncomfortable refusing a direct invitation, and thus being singled out is incredibly important for beneficiaries' subsequent participation in more extensive classes. Favoritism within the charismatic organization therefore contributes to the diversity of women's experiences of holistic development. As we will see, these diverse experiences are linked to the NGO's varied outcomes for women, with those who are signaled out and who undertake engaged participation benefiting comparatively more than those who are not selected and maintain minimal levels of participation.

Promoter courses and courses in the School of Comprehensive Education are not required to receive a loan, and women's participation in them comes with no extra material benefits. This, coupled with the fact that these courses are time-intensive, means that progress is slow and limited. Out of a given class of ten or twelve women, usually only two or three complete the whole program. Still, even for those who do not graduate, these classes are often transformative. Beneficiaries feel important because they are singled out. One woman explained that what she had been missing before was "love, esteem, and attention," but that the Fraternity's worker who signaled her out valued her participation, which motivated her to continue. In the context of these classes, as in board meetings, women are often encouraged to practice civic skills and develop new relationships. They are also exposed to new ideas and encouraged to develop new capabilities. For example, Sandra explained that the promoter classes in the Women's Pastoral Program were initially "hard for [her] to understand" because they had pushed her to question the reality of her family, community, and country. She continued,

> [The teacher] said often we pick out a text of the Bible to share with the church, and we only think of that which is spiritual. We pray, we come together, and continue without seeing the need that surrounds us. . . . So that is when I started to understand that we need to pay attention not only to what is going on inside the church, but also outside of the church.
>
> . . . I was a little scared because one of the sisters [from the Fraternity] . . . she spoke with us about politics—whether it was good for the church to be involved in politics or not. "What do you think?" she said. We said, "It is not good." This is what they taught us in the church, that politics are not good, it is [an area of] sin. Those who get involved in politics do it because they want money, they want fortune, and what is more, women should never involve themselves in politics. This is what they taught us in the church.
>
> So through the questions that the sister asked, and the lessons, we learned politics is good, it is good to participate. . . . So, for me, personally, it helped me a lot to understand things that the church had not taught us, that we did not understand.

It is in the context of these classes that many women apply lessons and question the teachings and practices of their churches, often doing so in ways that draw on biblical teachings. Sandra explained, "A Bible passage says give to God what is God's and give to Caesar what is Caesar's. So us, as leaders, have to carry out the obligations and responsibilities we have in our communities and our country."

When Fernanda entered the Fraternity's promoter class she was illiterate and unable to speak Spanish. But after three years of participating in these more intensive classes she was able to converse in Spanish and was able to read simple passages. Developing these skills not only increased Fernanda's ability to develop relationships with non-Mam speakers and participate in the Fraternity in a more active way, it also raised her confidence. She explained, "Now I am happy because I can read a little, although I cannot write. I am happy [in the classes because] before, I was only with the cows. Now I know things I did not know before." This new knowledge included how to care for the environment and which foods to eat and which to avoid. Fernanda first learned about colonization from the Fraternity; before she assumed that the Spanish-speaking population had always controlled Guatemala. Through her participation in the Fraternity and her newly acquired Spanish skills, Fernanda had begun listening to the news and hoped that the Fraternity could address her questions, explaining, "I have heard that they are going to take out the gasoline, gold, and carbon [from the land], but I do not understand it," in reference to the controversies over the new mining laws in the country (described in chapter 2). In a country in which 85 percent of women reported that they *never* discuss politics, Fernanda's desire to do just that stands out (Azpuru, Pira, and Seligson 2006).

Through promoter classes, beneficiaries develop closer relationships with the Fraternity's workers, to whom they often turn for advice or help. Alma contacted the Health and Nutrition Program coordinator when her children refused to eat the vegetables that she had learned were so important for their development. When Daniela had problems in her loan group and her church, she shared them with her teacher and classmates in her promoter class. When Lorena's health deteriorated, a worker convinced the director to help with her medical expenses and locate a specialist in natural remedies to meet with her.

Promoter classes and classes in the School of Comprehensive Education encourage women not only to develop new capacities related to communication and literacy but also to cultivate the capacity to aspire. For example, one activity (itself co-created by the Fraternity's workers and a foreign missionary) calls on women to share their own experiences of gender discrimination and discuss what life is like for women in their communities. Women are asked to what extent their communities reflect God's vision and to think about what their roles should be in shaping their community to align with this vision. Activities like this one push women to imagine other realities and think about steps to realize them. As a result, some beneficiaries come to see themselves as leaders. Patricia explained that she wanted to continue studying because "through my experience I can help a lot of women. They feel alone. And maybe they will not share all of their problems but at least I can tell them that God lives and that He will listen to them and that He has helped me, and He can help them." She then confessed to me that she dreamed of becoming the Fraternity's director after Alicia retired, a role that she would have never previously imagined herself capable of performing.

Beneficiaries who are singled out and who are selected to join the board of directors or attend more intensive classes represent a minority of the Fraternity's beneficiaries, usually less than 10 percent at any given time. Beyond the personal relationships that affect the likelihood of belonging to this group, ethnicity plays a role in a way that favors K'iche' beneficiaries. Despite the fact that the vast majority of beneficiaries are Mam, the Fraternity has never employed anyone who could speak Mam; all of the employees either have been ladino or have belonged to the same ethnic group as the K'iche' director. Given that Mam women are much less likely to speak Spanish than K'iche' women, this fact greatly affects the Fraternity's work and the experiences of Mam women themselves, who often sit through classes in Spanish with limited ability to actively participate. Because promoter classes and board meetings are conducted in Spanish, Mam women are less likely to be invited to participate in these positions or see themselves as qualified to do so.

A number of volunteers and beneficiaries have noted that Mam women are marginalized in the organization for reasons other than language barriers. Some of the Fraternity's policymakers and employees, real people with their own biases, see Mam women as more difficult to work with because they are less educated, less "hygienic," and more backward. Alicia, for example, explained to me that it was more difficult working with Mam women because of historical differences. "Historically [Spanish colonizers] used the Mam to pick coffee, plantains. So they were mainly in the fields and they ate mainly tortillas and beans, or chiles and tortillas, just that. On the other hand, the K'iche's were servants in the feudal houses—they said, 'fix yourselves up, brush your hair, and put on this uniform. You have to be able to speak Spanish because you are going to care for our children and cook our food.' So you can see us K'iche' we look a little bit more put together because of this history." This perception of Mam women as backward contributes to limited leadership opportunities within the organization for Mam women and to patronizing behavior on the part of some of the Fraternity's developers.

Mam women participating in the Fraternity live in more isolated areas, are poorer than their K'iche' counterparts, and are less likely to speak Spanish. Yet the Fraternity does not consider different strategies for working with them; instead the policymakers/leaders and workers apply, with few adjustments, their work with K'iche' women to their work with Mam women. Despite the real and perceived differences between Mam and K'iche' communities, the organization has failed to hire anyone who is able to communicate in Mam or is from a Mam community. In the midst of the Fraternity's search for a new program coordinator, for example, two Mam women (a former and current board member) canvassed their communities for qualified Mam candidates and informed the director of a number of options. Yet, for unknown reasons, the director did not interview these applicants, deciding instead to hire another K'iche' woman. Understandably, Mam beneficiaries are less likely to identify with Fraternity workers and have less motivation to attend the Fraternity's classes and workshops, which are conducted in a language that some have difficulty understanding and speaking, even though occasionally bilingual beneficiaries are asked to translate. K'iche' participants, on the other hand, benefit from the fact that the Fraternity employs a number of K'iche' staff and attend classes that are taught in a language they can understand.

In board meetings and promoter classes, Mam women are underrepresented. Victoria was the only Mam woman on the Fraternity's board in 2009, yet I commonly observed meetings and activities held in which all board members except Victoria were in attendance. Although she had an overall positive experience on the board, she noted that at times she felt humiliated because she could not speak Spanish as well as the others. Spending time in the office allowed her to overhear conversations with which she felt uncomfortable: "Sometimes the director says the Mam women this, the Mam women that. I do not like it. 'The Mam women do not know anything' [she says] . . . [but] not having studied is not one's fault."

Those who are singled out for more intensive participation and leadership opportunities have very different experiences of holistic development than do most beneficiaries. The Fraternity's policymakers/leaders and employees single women out based on their personal perceptions, biases, and, at times, ethnic stereotypes. Those who are singled out are encouraged to take on new roles, and their participatory experiences are richer and made up of more small encounters. Those who are singled out are therefore more likely to change their identities and question their realities. Thus, women's diverse goals and perceptions of the requirements of leadership positions, the Fraternity's charismatic structure, and developers' biases combine to generate diverse experiences of holistic development.

Addressing Women's Multiple Identities in the Fraternity

The activities described in this chapter thus far demonstrate that in its daily activities the Fraternity's policymakers/leaders and workers often view beneficiaries as members of marginalized groups; emphasize women's roles in their families, churches, and communities; and attempt to reconstitute beneficiaries' identities as women, Christians, and Mayans. This is in stark contrast to Namaste's focus on women as individuals and its tendency to compartmentalize beneficiaries' identities as businesswomen. In the Fraternity's interfaces, women are encouraged to discuss their familial relationships, interact with local-level politicians to enact change in their communities, revalue cultural practices, and discuss their feelings about themselves as women.

Over time, the Fraternity has increasingly incorporated families and communities into its work, in part because the NGO's policymakers/leaders see the revolving fund as serving families rather than women alone, as Antonieta explained to me in a 2013 interview. In 2007, the NGO began explicitly involving men, initially inviting a male representative for each woman (a husband, son, or father) to the Fraternity's offices to attend an annual afternoon activity. In the first such activity, nineteen boys and men (ranging in age from eight to mid-sixties) gathered in the Fraternity's offices, facing Alicia standing at a whiteboard. After describing the loan that the Fraternity gives to women, the director broke the men into groups to answer the questions written on the whiteboard, which included (1) What do we think of our wives' or mothers' work? (2) What changes has my wife or mother made? (3) How has the fund helped our family? (4) What successes has [the fund] given our family?

After deliberation in their groups, men nervously presented their answers, which focused on how the loan had helped them earn a little extra money to buy various products—food, clothing, their children's notebooks, animals, or fruit. Later in the activity Alicia asked the men to break into their groups once more to answer one final question: What are you going to do as a husband or son to support your wife's or mother's project? Group representatives came forward one by one offering both general responses, such as "encourage her to move forward with her project," and more specific examples of ways they could contribute to women's businesses by running errands or helping their wives/mothers feed their animals or transport their goods.

By 2008, the Fraternity expanded on this activity, establishing an annual conference focusing on couples' self-esteem. Husbands now accompany their wives for these daylong conferences in which they discuss marital relationships and women's and men's self-esteem from a Mayan perspective (with a Mayan spiritual guide), a Christian perspective (with a church representative), and a social perspective (with a social worker or psychologist). Eventually, the Fraternity began incorporating discussions of alcoholism and drug addiction in these conferences because they learned from women's own stories how deeply they were affected when their husbands struggled with substance abuse. By 2013, the Fraternity's director was considering adding Father's Day celebrations as a way to draw men into the organization, both to support their wives' participation and to learn lessons they could apply in their homes. Policymakers/leaders and many workers see men's attendance in these types of events as progress in and of itself because it demonstrates that men are willing to support their wives', mothers', and daughters' participation. Thus the Fraternity's multifaceted view of women's roles and identities leads developers not only to encourage women to discuss their experiences in the private sphere but also to incorporate family members themselves in its programming.

In addition to seeing women as wives, the Fraternity's developers reinforce women's identities as Christians and at times (intentionally or unintentionally) open up spaces for women to critically reflect on their experiences in their churches. This has led some women to challenge the teachings of one of the most important institutions in their lives. Some of the Fraternity's classes challenge the notion that politics are "dirty" and Christians should avoid them. In other cases, women creatively draw on the Fraternity's educational material to identify oppression in their own churches, even when this is not the intended purpose of a given activity. For example, during one promoter class in the Women's Pastoral Program, beneficiaries discussed the concept of discrimination in their country. It prompted one woman, Daniela, to draw a connection to happenings in her church:

> In my church, there are around four hundred people, and they were asking for money to go to the construction of the church. Only around fifty people contributed. . . . The first time, they asked for 1,000 quetzal [about $125] from the women and 2,000 from the men [about $250]. They said words without deeds mean nothing. . . . So I gave my 1,000. . . . And the second time around they asked for 2,000 quetzal from the women and 4,000 [about $500] from the men . . . and they gave a slip of paper to those who contributed the first time and at the end of service one day they asked those with the paper to stay to discuss something . . .

and those without papers could go or stay. . . . That was not fair, because some people could not afford to contribute but they should still be consulted.

Another beneficiary responded, "That is not right. . . . My parents always said there are so many who need rice, a bag of sugar. . . . Think of how many people you could have helped with that 1,000 quetzal!"

Daniela said, "I know!" She put her hand over her face in frustration. "I kept thinking I should go talk to the pastor but kept getting disheartened. . . . There is a women's society [at my church]—and they ask each woman to give 500 quetzal [about $65]. It is not fair to use Bible verses to try to get the poor to give money."

Later, when I interviewed Daniela privately, she highlighted the Fraternity's promoter classes as crucial to recognizing such injustices, saying that when she started attending these classes "[her] mind woke up." Thereafter, when the women's society in her church asked for donations from its members, she started questioning their intentions. "One time [the woman's society] asked for 25 quetzal ($3.13) from each person, and I was left thinking, there were twenty-nine of us—twenty-five times twenty-nine—how much money is that? And I talked about it with my sister, and I went in and asked, and all of this money, where is it going?" By the time of my departure, Daniela had been stripped of privileges in her church, in part as a result of challenging the women's society, but she continued to attend promoter classes at the Fraternity. Daniela's experience demonstrates how women creatively assign meaning to the Fraternity's activities, transforming written lessons through their interactions with the material, beneficiaries, and workers, interweaving their experiences inside and outside of the Fraternity.

In other cases, the Fraternity's policymakers/leaders and workers actively encourage women to reinterpret Christian values. The Fraternity's developers repeatedly emphasize two lessons that challenge what some women have previously learned in their churches. First, they argue that humans, not God, are responsible for many of life's negative aspects. During an activity on environmental degradation, for example, Alicia began, "Some say that God is the cause of everything. But is it God who planned the bad things that happen? Or us? . . . God made us all beautiful . . . but if we are ugly, it is because we do not care for ourselves. Contamination has produced illnesses [that] come from us, not from God." In another class, Natalia stated, "I have heard some people say that [with] global warming, the lack of rain, God is punishing us. What do you think? Is God punishing us? No, God is not punishing us with the effects of global warming. . . . We ourselves are hurting the environment." Natalia then drew on a biblical verse to highlight that they were administrators, not the owners, of the land.

This lesson connects with the second: that God does not want people to suffer and wait for salvation to find happiness and well-being; instead, God's will is for them to change themselves and their realities in this lifetime. Echoing insights from liberation theology and new ideas from foreign missionaries, the Fraternity connects the acts of changing one's behaviors and beliefs and fighting for change in one's family, church, or community to women's deeply held faith.

Putting these lessons into practice, the Fraternity's developers encourage women to interact with municipal authorities, undertake projects in their communities, and participate in other spheres. Beyond encouraging women to approach local government officials to express their concern about littering, Fraternity's developers and beneficiaries have approached the local forestry program to explain their concerns about deforestation and to coordinate a reforestation project across various municipalities. These projects are proposed by the Fraternity's policymakers/leaders, not beneficiaries. They therefore do not represent a political awakening among beneficiaries. But they do call upon beneficiaries to interact with local government officials in ways many have not previously done, potentially affecting their willingness to do so in the future.

While the policymakers/leaders initially shied away from electoral politics, wanting to depict the organization as apolitical, they eventually began incorporating discussions of political participation and citizenship in the Pastoral Program following suggestions from international missionaries and volunteers. In the period leading up to the 2011 presidential elections, the Fraternity invited representatives from Supreme Electoral Tribunal (Tribunal Supremo Electoral, TSE) to give workshops on the importance and process of voting. An employee described the activity to me in 2013: "The point was for [women] to recognize their rights to vote and to analyze well who to vote for" rather than to instruct them to vote for particular candidates. Thus, over time, the Fraternity's holistic model of development led its policymakers/leaders to expand its scope and include more types of participants (family members) and more topics, even as levels of funding decreased following the 2008 financial crisis.

The Fraternity in many ways acts as a culture-producing organization, one in which developers and beneficiaries together craft syncretic identities of themselves as Christians, Mayans, and women. Developers undertake identity work in their daily interactions with beneficiaries in hopes of promoting women's sense of self-worth, efficacy, and action, based in part on the assumption that indigenous women suffer from low self-esteem, lack of efficacy, and inactivity in community affairs. They encourage women to value their Mayan identities by associating it with their Christian faith. Rather than seeing Mayan spiritual beliefs as incompatible with their Christian beliefs, Fraternity developers emphasize points of commonality as well as difference. When asked what drove her to be exceptionally active in social organizations and in the church, for example, Alicia invoked both her Christian and her Mayan identities in ways that were characteristic of her conversations with beneficiaries:

> Ancestral spirituality is very important. Because there are those in the church that choose some to have certain privileges [special responsibilities/roles]. But the Bible says we need to find the gifts that God has given us. And this is what I tell women. They do not know what their gifts are that God gave them; they do not know their *nahuales*. I have my *nahual* and it indicates that I have work on earth—and this work is good for my fellow man and is good for myself.

Here, Alicia sees her unique nature as both a gift from a Christian God and the reflection of her *nahual*—in Mayan cosmovision, a spirit being or animistic entity associated with a person, determined by the day she is born and affecting her personality and talents. Similarly, Luisa, one of the Fraternity's founders and early board members explained, "If I compare the Mayan religion with the Bible—sometimes they agree a lot."

Some of the NGO's beneficiaries echo beliefs about the complementarity between Mayan and Christian beliefs. Georgina stated,

> It would be a pity for us, if I as a [Protestant] did not give importance to . . . Mayan values and beliefs. For example, to give thanks to God, the creator and maker of life, owner of the land, owner of the water, the plants, the trees, bread, everything. . . . This is what the Mayan culture says, value nature. . . . We sleep in the night, and open our eyes and see the light, see his greatness, see his mountains—this is the Mayan culture—thank the creator and maker of life that gives us all of this. Corn, beans, these are things that the Mayan spirituality places highly, right? Give value to what is. Thank you Lord for this corn, thank you for these beans, thank you our Mother Earth. . . . In the Mayan spirituality, you light a candle—and they are going to say she is a witch, and it is not like that. She is giving thanks to God for the four cardinal points . . . the four corners that God has given us.

Still, even women who find overlap between Mayan and Christian beliefs, identities, and values often distance themselves from Mayan "witchcraft" that they see as un-Christian, arguing that they are not "very radical" and eschew practices that they have heard about, including "[going] to a special place [to] burn a bunch of things," asking for "curses," or "[killing] chickens over the fire so that [someone] has headaches, dies, or loses her money."

Instead, developers and many beneficiaries within the Fraternity draw on their Mayan identities when they speak of caring for the earth, using natural medicines, and recapturing ancestral values and practices, while simultaneously seeing these expressions of their Christian faith. Classes within the Women's Pastoral Program especially emphasize these values. For example, in one such class, the pastoral coordinator drew connections between biblical verses and traditional practices and values.

> NATALIA (NGO worker): If we are the image of God, what should we do?
>
> BENEFICIARY: Care for our bodies.
>
> NATALIA: And how do we do this?
>
> BENEFICIARY: From what I understood, first we have to care for our health. Then we have to remember our traditional customs—wear the traditional clothing, drink *atol* [a drink made of corn, sugar, and water or milk] and eat potatoes instead of Coca-Cola.
>
> NATALIA: Yes, sometimes we sell our beans [that we grow] and then buy canned beans. We eat Maseca [a brand of prepackaged corn flour] instead of *nixtamal* [corn women soak in water and lime and make into corn dough or *masa*]. We sell our traje and buy T-shirts. But if we are the image of God, we will care for ourselves.

For the Fraternity's developers, caring for oneself is tied intimately with the recapturing of "traditional" values and customs, and it is deemed a fundamentally Christian act.

On another occasion, the pastoral coordinator used the story of the Good Samaritan and the commandment to love one's neighbor within a discussion of traditional practices in Mayan communities. The coordinator broke women into small groups, asking them to discuss how one valued and loved her neighbors in the Mayan culture. One beneficiary discussed the traditions practiced in the past that had become less common.

BENEFICIARY: [Before], for example, when a mother gave birth for the first time, usually a more experienced mother would come to help her—to teach her how to take care of the child, because new mothers often do not know how. . . . In the past, when the first ear of corn was picked, they would have a big party. And they did not drink coffee—it was atol in the morning, atol at lunch, and atol at night.

NATALIA: Yes, and they were stronger then. Now, we use a stove or microwave for cooking but in the past, they cooked over fire. . . . I still do this sometimes. . . . It is not just for cooking, it also unites the family because everyone gathers around, telling stories, talking. . . . It is time to remember, to recuperate, revalue these traditions.

Natalia then read the story of the Good Samaritan, using it as a way to draw a further contrast.

NATALIA [writing "mutual help" on the poster]: What does this mean?

BENEFICIARY: You help me, and I help you.

NATALIA [writing "individualism" on the poster]: Today we have this in our minds. What does it mean?

BENEFICIARY: We are divided.

These lessons were developed in part by drawing on material and instruction from the Mesoamerican Committee for Peace—a secular organization that criticizes the Western, capitalist focus on individualism and celebrates community-based projects. In the Fraternity, however, the material is reinterpreted using the language of faith and tradition, which are closely tied to the Fraternity's roots and its developers' interpretations of Christianity and Mayan culture.

Similarly, the Fraternity's activities connect women's gender identity to their faith in order to encourage them to revalue their identities as women. The Fraternity's policymakers/leaders, workers, and particularly active beneficiaries alike speak of the tendency to celebrate the birth of a son more than a daughter or to provide schooling for boys but not girls, understanding these practices as rooted in misplaced beliefs that women are less valuable than men. To challenge these beliefs, the Fraternity's workers draw on biblical stories in which women play prominent roles and address biblical verses that seem to devalue women by placing the Bible in a historical context, explaining

that it was written by men during a time when women were considered property, unclean, and unimportant.

The ways in which the Fraternity attempts to combat *machista* beliefs, however, do not fit neatly into Western feminist frameworks. Like many women's
movements and organizations in Latin America, the Fraternity's developers
often emphasize women's value by drawing on their traditional roles as wives
and mothers, discourses that are echoed by beneficiaries. For example, Georgina, a longtime beneficiary of the Fraternity who had taken on numerous
leadership roles in the NGO explained that she had learned that through their
reproductive labor, women are in fact present in both the private and public
spheres:

> If you say to [men] that women are important, they say all their lives
> they are in the house, they do not do anything. But you have to ana-
> lyze this, to think. Women, we are in the house, with the family, in the
> church, in society, in the fields. How? In the fields because the woman
> gets up at four o'clock, five o'clock in the morning, to make tortillas.
> For what? For the husband to eat, and [to make] more tortillas for the
> husband to bring to work. At eleven or twelve o'clock during the day,
> the husband sits to eat tortillas and beans. Who made it? So the woman
> is present here. . . . She is in society because there she is, she is with the
> family. Making tortillas, washing clothing, caring for the children. Ev-
> erywhere. So this is what you have to clarify, so [women] wake up. Men
> are not the only ones to work in the fields. The women are there too, in
> their atol, their drinks, their tortillas, their beans, the woman is present.

The Fraternity's workers often echo Georgina's point of view, emphasizing
the value of women's reproductive labor for families and societies, although
this does not mean that they blindly accept patriarchal norms. Instead, they
place activities that women are already pursuing (planting and harvesting,
animal husbandry, weaving or sewing, doing housework, discussing the Bible, caring for their families) in a new framework. By doing so, they encourage women to view their often-devalued activities and roles as sources of
pride and prestige, with varying levels of success. Encouraging beneficiaries
to recognize their value as wives and mothers can be profoundly political
work—both because it challenges communities' assumptions about women's
worth and because it challenges women's assumptions about their own value.
By celebrating women's reproductive roles, the Fraternity's developers attempt
to teach women that they fulfill crucial roles, deserve to be treated with respect, and should be given a say in household and community decisions.

This expansive view of development activities, which not only focuses on women as individuals but also incorporates their multiple roles and identities, does not come without costs. The Fraternity's policymakers/leaders, like those in Namaste, looked to their own experiences, meanings, and goals when developing views of women. Although this leads them to recognize women's intersecting identities and multiple roles, it also encourages them to presume that other indigenous women wish to participate in the NGO's activities and delight in doing so—or at the very least will come to value their participation once they are properly enlightened. They thus overlook that some women are already active in other spheres or see the Fraternity's activities as overly burdensome or relatively unimportant. Policymakers/leaders' simplified views of beneficiaries obstruct their ability to read women's subtle expressions of discontent regarding the number and length of activities and to recognize the full diversity of goals and meanings that women assign to their participation in the NGO.

WOMEN'S DIVERSE MEANINGS AND ACTIONS CHALLENGING DEVELOPERS' PREDICTIONS

While the Fraternity's policymakers/leaders view indigenous women's participation as intrinsically valuable, its beneficiaries hold varied views of their participation in the organization. Many join to gain access to a loan, explaining simply, "We went there for the money, to get the fund." Thus, upon entering the organization, many women in the Fraternity, like those in Namaste, see their participation as a cost incurred to gain access to a loan. Because they view the Fraternity as a source of loans, it is difficult for these women "to understand all of the implicit obligations apart from those related to the loan," according to a Fraternity employee. Addressing multiple goals requires significant investments of time and energy on the part of both the Fraternity's workers and its beneficiaries, as well as beneficiaries' sustained, engaged participation. Many women who join simply to access low-interest loans feel that too much is being asked of them and that they are not developing skills that will help them in their businesses. These women use the NGO strategically to pursue their own goals; when they are confronted by what they see as unrealistic demands, they only sometimes comply, as we will see. When loan groups do retire, they often explain that participating in the Fraternity entails too many activities.

Some beneficiaries see their participation as an extension of their church participation; others view it as an opportunity to pursue the education they have previously been denied and therefore view their participation as a benefit in and of itself. These beneficiaries are more tolerant of the Fraternity's many, often long activities and are more likely to enjoy the chance to get out of the house and socialize with others. Still others enter the NGO looking for a loan and valuing participation instrumentally but, through the course of their participation, come to see their participation as intrinsically valuable as they transform their identities and therefore their interests. Often they undertake these transformations after being singled out by the NGO's workers or policymakers/leaders, being assigned leadership roles, or being convinced to enroll in more intense courses. As demonstrated, however, the opportunities for this type of transformation are not universally and equally distributed. The majority of the Fraternity's beneficiaries join in order to gain access to a low-interest loan and continue to view their participation as a cost thereafter.

Thus, the Fraternity's holistic model of development, its loose and charismatic structure, employees' biases, and women's diverse goals all interact to produce sites of development in which many different things are happening at once and in which many meanings and goals are pursued in relation to the Fraternity's activities. These sites resemble multipurpose rooms rather than hallways—they are not efficient, nor do they channel women in uniform directions. Instead they are flexible spaces in which diverse experiences of participation, and therefore diverse outcomes, are possible.

Beneficiaries are able to act creatively in these contexts, although not all choose to do so. Developers' and beneficiaries' at times contrasting views of participation inspire unscripted action. Women learn that they cannot avoid all mandatory activities without risking loss of loans or prestige, so some develop hidden transcripts in which they complain among themselves about the time spent in activities. Limited attendance at supposedly required activities is a perpetual problem that the Fraternity's workers and policymakers/leaders confront. At times, Mam women leverage stereotypes about them and the reality of linguistic barriers to avoid attending activities they do not find useful. A leader of the Mam Association told me privately that she instructs Mam women participating in the Fraternity to attend activities only if they can understand Spanish, even though attendance is technically mandatory for all.

Some have also come to realize that they can miss a few activities, as long as other members of their loan group attend, because the Fraternity is unlikely to discontinue a group if the majority of its members usually show up. Members of the some groups therefore alternate attending activities, drawing on implicit agreements among themselves. In the activities themselves, some beneficiaries arrive on time and actively participate, whereas others, realizing attendance is usually taken at the end of activities, arrive late, step outside to use their phones in the middle of activities, or talk to other attendees, indicating that women agree to attend "required" activities but do not give them the level of import that policymakers expect (a subtle compromise). Thus the tension produced by developers' and beneficiaries' conflicting views about the value and centrality of development activities in women's lives generate multiple responses from beneficiaries including hidden transcripts, guile, and compromise.

Women's agency is expressed not just by women pursuing their diverse goals, actively transforming their goals, and undertaking the types of un-scripted activities described here, but also by applying the Fraternity's lessons in creative and unintended ways. Many of the beneficiaries I spoke with no-ticed favoritism within the Fraternity and used the language that they learned from the Fraternity's developers to discuss it with each other and with me. Barbara, for example, complained that the Fraternity's developers treated women who were late with their payments differently depending on their re-lationship with each woman. She explained that while the workers and direc-tor did not punish another woman who was late with her payments, she was treated harshly, and she drew explicit comparisons between the Fraternity's rhetoric and actions in doing so.

> What I regret is to see [is] that there exists, between us, discrimination. Discrimination and pride. . . . Because sometimes they give us classes about discrimination—that we should not discriminate against each other, but I am sorry the truth is that I have even seen it in the Frater-nity. . . . Last year, we [paid back the fund] in June . . . and my husband had just died so I was left a little in debt because of his death. It is was *very* hard gathering the money together for the fund . . . and I fell a week behind and [a Fraternity worker] talked to me very harshly . . . up to the point that she said she was not going to take me into account anymore . . . so on one hand they say help people but on the other, they discriminate.

Unlike women in Namaste, women in the Fraternity display diverse levels and forms of participation. This diversity comes from a number of sources. First, because beneficiaries see the Fraternity as something "other" than an MFI, they join for a greater variety of reasons and attach diverse meanings to the organization. Second, once they enter, women encounter a variety of par-ticipatory experiences based on their incoming goals, but also based on their relationship with developers and their personal characteristics, including their ethnicity. Some women become dissatisfied with the many activities and participate at minimal levels, many accommodate the Fraternity's demands in order to ensure continued access to loans and avoid shaming, some delight in the experience of participation from the beginning, and still others develop an interest in participation along the way. Throughout, beneficiaries exercise agency by acting in unscripted ways to meet their own goals and enact their own meanings. These diverse experiences of holistic development are made possible by the Fraternity's loose, charismatic structure, developers' biases, and women's varied personalities, goals, and strategies.

THE FRATERNITY'S ATTEMPTS AT CULTIVATING GOOD CHRISTIAN, MAYAN WOMEN SUBJECTS AND WOMEN'S CREATIVE REACTIONS

In its quest to achieve its vision of development, the Fraternity's developers attempt to manage women's behavior to produce good Christian, Mayan women subjects by leveraging interactions with beneficiaries and materials. Using loan conditions, contracts, "tests," biblical verses, educational sessions, and scolding, the Fraternity strives for its particular vision of women's empowerment but does so in ways that are, at times, disempowering.

The first steps the Fraternity takes to create good Christian, Mayan women subjects involve establishing ideal values and discouraging certain types of businesses and behaviors through loan contracts. Policymakers/leaders ban women from using their loans to stock *tiendas* (small stores), which many poor women operate out of their houses to earn extra income. Tiendas in which women sell sodas, waters, chips, and sweets are so popular that just under one-third of Namaste's loans have supported these types of businesses. But the Fraternity does not support any because, even though they can be quite profitable, they violate the organization's values. Managing a tienda means selling products that are unhealthy, packaged in plastic (and therefore bad for the environment), and made by foreign companies, like Coca-Cola, that promote a materialistic "consumer" culture.

Because policymakers/leaders do not want women to "just sell things to sell things," as Alicia explained, they incorporate business classes that align with its multifaceted model of development. Women are taught how to compost and use organic fertilizer even if their businesses involve buying and selling scarves; to make cloth bags to use instead of plastic bags even if their businesses involve raising pigs; and to care for vegetable gardens even if their businesses involve embroidery. Through these socio-productive classes, the Fraternity communicates and promotes its ideal of a good Christian, Mayan woman subject: one who raises animals and makes her own organic chicken feed; has

FIGURE 6.3. Women in the Fraternity learn to grow cabbage using organic fertilizer. Photograph by the author.

her own vegetable garden fertilized by organic compost (see figure 6.3); makes traditional handicrafts and wears a *traje* rather than a T-shirt and jeans; cares for the environment and prepares healthy foods for her family; and carries out and teaches traditional Mayan values that focus on community, rather than individual, well-being.

Loan contracts reinforce these values. While they include provisions that might be expected (requiring women to attend classes and apply loans to their businesses), they also include behavioral and value-based provisions. For example, in order to receive a loan, women have to formally agree that they will not use plastic bags, feed their children unhealthy foods, or contaminate the environment.

These values are reinforced in the organization's day-to-day practices. On one occasion, the director presented a video (in Spanish) on environmental degradation to a group of Mam women. She concluded the activity by going around the group, pointing at each woman, and asking questions—"Is it good to use plastic bags?" "Is it good to have garbage on the roadside?"—waiting for each woman to shake her head no before moving on to the next. On another occasion, when a worker arrived to an activity, she found the women waiting outside while their children stood at their feet, snacking on chips and sweets in the small, glossy bags sold in any tienda. When the activity began, she scolded the women, saying, "Are you caring for the earth? Because look at your children with their junk food [in plastic bags]. Did you forget? Do these nourish our children?" The women looked down and mumbled no, and the worker continued: "What should we give our children instead of junk food?" A few women responded, "Fruit" or "nuts." The employee nodded. "There are children who are sick, who are malnourished. And whose fault is it? Is it the children's fault? No, it is the mother's fault. Because she knows better."

The Fraternity's developers also attempt to regulate the ways that women manage their own bodies, encouraging them to consume foods deemed traditional—such as atol, handmade corn flour, fruits, and vegetables—rather than soda, store-bought flour, and chips or packaged sweets. Policymakers/leaders and workers also encourage women to wear the traditional traje rather than Western clothing, even though the traje is much more expensive. Classes on self-esteem often focus on the ways that women can care for themselves by maintaining a clean house, bathing oneself, and "putting oneself together." For example, when a worker asked a group to review what it had learned about self-esteem, one beneficiary stood up to respond,

> I am going to talk about how to make ourselves up. See? [She takes her hair down.] My hair is not brushed and my son is a little dirty. We have to put into practice what we learn. To put ourselves together . . . not just for special occasions but also for day-to-day life. When I go even just to the mill, I try to put myself together. . . . Doing this, fixing ourselves up, fixing our houses up, making our children look nice, this increases one's self-esteem. Because remember the Bible says that we are formed in the image of God. What does it mean then if we don't take care of ourselves, if we walk around with our hair unbrushed?

The woman's response reflects the Fraternity's lessons that encourage women to regulate their bodies by consuming foods that are deemed healthy and consistent with their cultural heritage, to wear traditional clothing, and to challenge the stereotypes of indigenous women as backward and unwashed by bathing frequently, wearing clean clothing, and brushing one's hair. As wives and mothers, they are also tasked with teaching their families to do the same.

Through its everyday interactions with women, the Fraternity communicates its vision of the ideal Christian, Mayan woman subject and in both obvious and subtle ways rewards good behavior and punishes bad. Women are tested on what they have learned in surveys that are required to receive a new loan. Rather than asking for women's feedback, survey questions often have clear right and wrong answers, as do many of the verbal questions women are asked in the context of group classes. The Fraternity's developers reinforce good behavior by inviting well-behaved women to take on leadership positions or increasing their loans, and punishes bad behavior by scolding women, testing them in these surveys, and threatening to discontinue their loans.

This type of moralizing work is often overlooked in grassroots organizations pursuing alternative visions of development, but it is an inevitable part of the daily operations of development organizations, which exercise power externally and internally in order to promote their particular models of development. This reality demonstrates the elusive nature of power in NGOs: even NGOs founded with the explicit goal of empowering the marginalized may end up exercising their power over and through beneficiaries in ways that are in fact disempowering. A qualitative account of power, like the one provided here, elucidates how empowerment and disempowerment can in fact occur at the same time and in the same context. The Fraternity's policymakers/leaders simultaneously encourage women to challenge the status quo and enact *their own* vision of the good life, which may or may not accord with that of beneficiaries.

Women accommodate the Fraternity's demands by repeating answers that have been emphasized as correct, although some do so simply to get through activities more quickly. Others transform the Fraternity's attempts to manage their desires and behaviors in various ways. Some verbally agree with the Fraternity's lessons but in practice implement only some, or none, of them— continuing to use plastic bags or enjoying a bag of chips. In other cases, women do not consistently attend the Fraternity's formally required classes. When confronted with a disjuncture between the Fraternity's teachings and their own practices, women feign misunderstanding. Others use jokes to resist. For example, during one of the breaks at the Fraternity's yearly assembly, the director tried to convince a group of beneficiaries to go for a walk with her to use the time in a more healthy way and to connect with the environment. One of the women, implicitly highlighting the differences between the director, who sat behind a desk all day, and the women, who worked in the fields and often traveled on foot to run their various errands, laughed and responded, "Listen, sister, I walk *every* day."

Even though the Fraternity uses loans as a disciplining force and deploys multiple strategies to institutionalize its position and manage beneficiaries' behaviors, beneficiaries are not powerless in these spheres. Although they rarely exercise as much power as does the NGO they face, beneficiaries can react in a variety of ways—by accommodating the Fraternity's demands, maintaining distinct public and hidden transcripts, leveraging stereotypes, or using jokes to push back in acceptable ways.

THE MIXED OUTCOMES OF THE FRATERNITY'S HOLISTIC DEVELOPMENT: PERSONAL TRANSFORMATION FOR SOME BUT LIMITED BENEFITS FOR MANY

The diversity of beneficiaries' goals, meanings, and strategies alongside the Fraternity's holistic model of development and other organizational characteristics interact to generate sites of development that are akin to multipurpose rooms—relatively open spaces that can be put to many different uses and in which many things are possible. In some cases, women learn skills that will be useful for political activism; even when they are not intended to do so, group activities and promoter classes give some women a chance to develop and practice communication and literacy skills. Women are asked to push for changes in their communities, contact local government officials, challenge the church's teachings, or develop dreams for the future. In other cases, women draw on the language they learn in the Fraternity to express their discontent with their churches, communities, or even the Fraternity itself, thus encouraging them to practice the art of voice.

Some women are encouraged to take on leadership roles in the organization, giving them the opportunity to practice civic skills, expand their social networks, and see themselves as leaders. Sofia, for example, had suffered through an abusive relationship before eventually leaving her husband, joining the Presbyterian Church, and entering the Fraternity. There, she was repeatedly asked to reflect on and share her own life story. Although she had previously been ashamed of her past, through the telling and retelling of her story in the Fraternity, she began to see her hard life as a source of strength and as allowing her to help others. She explained that she continued to participate in the Fraternity because "it is a source of support" for the other women in the Fraternity. She explained further: "Sometimes they say to me, sister Sofia, what do you think? Sister Sofia, your experience has been very hard, nevertheless you are here with us. We want you to help us." She reiterated that there were women who suffered as she had suffered and that she could be a role model for them. Another woman, Blanca, became a promoter in the Fraternity because "as a woman, [she] should think of other women," and felt that her continued participation in the Fraternity was important because women "need to prioritize [their] own participation . . . [and] have to make people aware of the utmost importance of participation, for women's well-being." Thus Blanca explained her participation in the Fraternity as a form of service, rather than a way to access a loan.

But the Fraternity's results are not uniformly positive. The NGO achieves mixed results that are unevenly spread across women. Classes that focus on budgeting, like the one described in this chapter's opening, do not in reality teach concrete skills. Rather, the Fraternity's workers transform these classes into discussions of women's worth and identities. Many of the women who have been participating in the Fraternity for years are not able to determine if the businesses in which they invest their loans are operating at a profit or a loss. Policymakers/leaders themselves are unable to assess the impact of its revolving funds on women's incomes, and they do not make any attempt to do so. Women appear to generally maintain the same standard of living even after participating in the Fraternity for many years, even as much as a decade. Thus, when faced with multiple goals and limited time, expertise, and funding, the Fraternity's policymakers/leaders prioritize transforming women's self-esteem and identities over raising their incomes.

While some women develop new skills, increase their self-esteem, or transform their identities, many others go through the motions of participation relatively unchanged. The experiences of a few women will help illustrate both the mixed effects that the Fraternity has for any given woman and the uneven effects it has across beneficiaries.

LORENA

Lorena, whom we met in the book's introduction, had an overall positive experience with the Fraternity, but even this success story demonstrates the Fraternity's mixed results. Lorena grew up in Izpan, one of eleven children. Her siblings were allowed to study up through sixth grade, but after that point, her six sisters were not allowed to continue because her parents saw further education as a waste for girls. Lorena herself only made it through third grade before her parents let her drop out. "I liked studying," she explained, "but the other children insulted me. . . . I washed my traje, but I only had one to wear [so] they did not think I dressed well."

Thereafter, Lorena learned how to operate a sewing machine, working first in a nearby textile plant and then traveling with her sister daily to a much larger nearby city to work in various boutiques. When Lorena married, she moved in with her in-laws and became pregnant with her first daughter and, soon thereafter, her second. Although she wanted to see a doctor for prenatal care, her husband and her in-laws argued that it was too expensive and prevented her from doing so. Lorena explains, "[My husband] did not give me any importance. He did not treat me like a wife." A few years later, her husband was arrested and sent to prison. Because the land on which Lorena and her family lived was registered in her in-laws' name, her in-laws were able to take the little piece of land she had, leaving Lorena "with nothing."

Lorena was forced to move into her mother's house, where she and her daughters continued to live. The cinderblock house was perched by itself on top of an embankment by the main road of the village of Charaja, on the outskirts of Izpan. Nearby was the first textile plant in Guatemala, which had employed Izpan's residents for over a hundred years, although it had recently struggled in the face of international competition, leading to waves of layoffs. Many of the roughly 3,500 residents of Charaja either worked in the textile plant, as Lorena did as a teenager, or harvested beans, corn, or vegetables. But while in the past the clothing Lorena made sold like "hot cakes," by the time I met her, Lorena's hands no longer served her. After a decade of illness without adequate health care, she could not do agricultural or factory work or make the clothing she once sold. At one point, Lorena explained, she was bedridden for six months. These battles with an unknown illness aged Lorena; she looked much older than her forty-five years. But her health started to improve after the Fraternity paid for her to visit a new doctor and a specialist in natural medicines.

Lorena had been receiving loans and attending classes in the Fraternity for six years at the time of our interview. During group classes, she took notes in shaky handwriting, asked and answered questions regularly, and stood up when she had something especially important to say. She attended conferences that the Fraternity periodically held for women on topics such as environmental degradation or self-esteem. She even attended a conference for married couples by herself. For the previous two and a half years, she had been participating in more intensive promoter classes in the Pastoral Program. This meant that upon completing the course she would be considered qualified to teach classes to other groups of women in the Fraternity, although up until recently she had thought the classes were simply for extra education. Lorena was invested; she was committed to the Fraternity despite the fact that she could have received the same loan if she participated as did many of the other women in her loan group, who attended "mandatory" classes sporadically, remained relatively silent throughout, and did not participate in promoter classes.

Lorena initially joined the Fraternity to gain access to a loan so that she could earn more to support her daughters' education. She used the loan to buy scarves in bulk that she sold in the market and to purchase fabric that she turned into aprons with her daughter's help. But Lorena was pulled into engaged participation when workers gave her special attention in classes and encouraged her to take on leadership roles. She explained, "They paid attention to me." She joined promoter classes when one employee, Natalia, "called upon [her] to study," even though these classes did not come with additional material benefits. Eventually Lorena began to see her participation as intrinsically valuable and as a way to help other women. She explained that her participation in the Fraternity led to internal changes: "I feel that God is using me now. . . . Now I love myself a lot. . . . I still cannot make tortillas or do the wash. But I know I am something important. I know households in pain—and I try to help. Because if you have two pieces of bread, you should give one away."

Lorena's experience, however, had not been purely positive. Fraternity activities often lasted multiple hours, as Lorena's loan group waited for tardy beneficiaries or workers to arrive or workers to cover redundant material in hopes of achieving ambiguous goals. This was time that women like Lorena could be spending participating in other organizations or selling products in the market. More troubling, despite six years of working with the Fraternity, Lorena had yet to learn how to calculate her business's profits or losses, and she had become dependent on the loan. She explained, "Sometimes it is difficult to gather the money to repay the loan. And although we are very punctual repaying the loan, sometimes the Fraternity delays a little [in distributing the next loan]. Sometimes as much as a month, and it is like we are living without water." The Fraternity had given Lorena space to transform her identity and sense of self-worth, but it had not helped her improve her material well-being in the short or long term. Instead, Lorena became dependent on the Fraternity's loans for survival.

NATALIA

Natalia, a soft-spoken K'iche' woman, started with the Fraternity as a beneficiary, became a promoter, and then was one of the organization's three program coordinators. Natalia was born in Sacatzal—a small, rural K'iche' village—one of five children. Her father worked at a factory. When Natalia finished primary school, she wanted to continue studying, but her father refused: "He said 'no you are too old [to keep studying]. You are a woman; you are going to marry. Your job is to be in the kitchen.'" Still, she "always had in [her] mind to learn something," so even after she married and had six children, Natalia found ways to pursue this desire, first in the church and then by enrolling in sewing and nursing classes and, later, theological classes with the Fraternity. She connected this continued desire for education with her experience as a child, explaining, "I did not have the opportunity to have an academic education. And when you have the desire to continue but you are not able to do it . . . you feel, I do not know, oppressed. You feel that your dreams are unrealized."

When Natalia married at eighteen, she joined the Presbyterian Church, to which her husband belonged. She found that while there was "not complete women's participation" in that sphere, the church "always gave women the opportunity to choose a Bible passage or give the message," opportunities she enjoyed. She began to participate more, serving on the board and as the president of the women's society before being named as one of two representatives to the women's presbytery. It was here "where the idea of continuing studying theology [in the Fraternity] was born."

Natalia joined the Fraternity as a member of a loan group but a year later decided to forgo the loan and instead concentrate on her theological studies at the Fraternity. A member of the first promoter class, Natalia studied with a visiting missionary to become an educator in the Women's Pastoral Program. Eventually, Natalia began traveling with the missionary to teach classes to women's groups. These experiences visiting other women solidified her dedication to the Fraternity's work and her participation as a leader. She explained, "It was when I went to the communities that I opened my eyes to the needs of women. So I said inside myself, so women *need*, like I needed help and experience, and I too lacked education. So with this training, I need to teach women.

And this is what I put as my goal. . . . The *little* I am learning, I am going to teach." As a result, Natalia organized a number of women in her surrounding communities, encouraging them to form groups to solicit funds and education from the Fraternity. At one point, Natalia began having serious marital problems because of rumors that she was using her work with the Fraternity as a pretense to be unfaithful. This was a common accusation leveled against socially active women in Guatemala that, in effect, served as a form of social control and a way to limit women's mobility. In the face of these problems, however, Natalia considered leaving her husband but never considered leaving the Fraternity.

Years later, when the missionary left the Fraternity, Natalia took over her role and eventually became a full-time employee. By the time of our interview Natalia had worked with hundreds of beneficiaries. She enjoyed seeing women undergo the changes that she herself had experienced:

> When I started in the women's society, I was embarrassed to even say my name. I was scared to introduce myself to a group. . . . And I see that women are like that when they start [in the Fraternity]. So I motivate them to start and little by little, one loses this sense of fear or embarrassment, timidity. One comes to have confidence in herself and confidence in God. . . . Some of the women I trained now preach in their women's societies, some are members of the board—secretary, treasurer; now they do not have problems with . . . let us say, leadership among women. . . . A sister that does not know how to read or write, [can] now direct [services], now she can do something with the sisters. Now she feels capable [to do] all of this work.

The Fraternity allowed Natalia to pursue the education she felt she lacked and gave her the opportunity to act as a leader among women. Her material well-being improved because she was offered full-time employment, not because she was given a loan. Thus her positive experience, which yielded both material and nonmaterial rewards, was not representative of that of most beneficiaries. Yet her story highlights one of the benefits of the Fraternity's approach—the potential cultivation of new leaders who can act as agents of change and whose individual-level effects can spill over into organizations and communities.

Regina lived in an adobe house with a crooked metal pipe from which smoke twisted and turned into the foggy air of Los Alarcones. Los Alarcones was a tiny community that did not even appear on maps, located on the outskirts of a larger community of just over one thousand residents, Acolillo. Without a truck with four-wheel drive and a brave driver, Los Alarcones was only accessible by foot—requiring a traveler to walk one of two narrow dirt paths from the center of Acolillo. As they had traditionally done, the overwhelming majority of residents of Acolillo—almost all Mam—worked in agriculture, planting and har-vesting corn or potatoes. Here, there were few sources of employment outside of agriculture, and most lived in poverty. Seventy percent of Acolillo's residents never attended school; only 22 percent of women and 36 percent of men were literate (Instituto Nacional de Guatemala 2009).

Growing up in a different but equally remote part of Acolillo, Regina led a life deeply affected by both poverty and isolation. Regina's father came down with a fever and diarrhea when she was young, and without a clinic nearby, he died because they "did not know a remedy." Without a father to help support the family, Regina's mother and her eight sib-lings worked in the fields, planting wheat and corn. They often did not have enough food to eat. There was no school nearby, so Regina and her siblings did not attend a single day of classes. "I do not know even one letter," she explained. Regina moved to Los Alarcones after she married. When asked how she met her husband, Regina giggled: "Nothing more [happened] than he asked my mother. We were not talking before. We did not know each other." Together they had three children, though only two survived. She explained that she thought her husband was smarter than she was because "he knows Spanish and knows things like where to go to vote."

Regina first heard about the Fraternity from a cousin, who was al-ready participating in the NGO. Because the area was so remote, and because most women, like Regina, only spoke Mam, few MFIs operated there, so Regina saw the Fraternity as her only opportunity for a loan. She since received two loans from the Fraternity, which she invested in her business raising cows. Using the loan, she bought a calf for 1,500 quetzal (roughly $188) and a year later sold it for 2,000 quetzal (roughly $250). But she did not keep track of how much she spent raising the cow and so was not sure how much of a profit she was making. Her cow's corral was poorly maintained because Regina rarely felt capable of physical labor; she had suffered on and off from an unnamed sickness for eight years. Regina dreamed of building a house for her children next to hers but did not know where she would get the funds; animal husbandry had not proven profitable enough to save any money.

Overall, Regina's life had not changed significantly as a result of her participation in the Fraternity. She said that her relationships with the other women in her loan group had not changed, and while she liked listening to lessons about the environment, she sometimes missed classes because she was not feeling well. She could not recall the other topics they had discussed. She explained that she had a hard time participating actively because lessons were conducted in Spanish and she primarily communicated in Mam. When one of the other women translated for her and the others, she more or less understood the classes, but she felt reticent to speak up. Because the Fraternity did not keep records on women's profits, it was difficult to know the economic effect of her participation. She was able to start her animal husbandry business with the Fraternity's help, but it was clear to Regina that without another loan, her business would be in jeopardy.

The stories of Lorena, Natalia, and Regina demonstrate the Fraternity's mixed effects and the uneven nature of those effects. Even women who have been participating in the Fraternity for five or ten years do not note any significant changes in their material well-being, and many women's businesses are dependent on the Fraternity's very-low-interest loans for survival. But a minority of women do undergo transformation in how they view themselves and their realities: they increase their sense of self-efficacy, come to see themselves as leaders and role models among women, and question powerful institutions and long-standing marginalization. Others benefit from other forms of support. Lorena, for example, developed a close relationship with the Fraternity's developers and therefore could count on their emotional support when confronting her illness. The Fraternity further helped Lorena cover some of her medical expenses and made contact with a naturalist, providing her with care that accorded with the organization's values.

But material and nonmaterial support is not evenly distributed. In contrast to Lorena, Regina, who similarly suffered from an unknown illness, was not given any extra help—financial or otherwise. Like many of her Mam counterparts, her leadership was not cultivated, and the Fraternity failed to ensure she could participate actively in classes. The unevenness is also reflected in the material benefits, as K'iche' women like Lorena regularly receive larger loans than Mam women like Regina.

CONCLUSION

All loan-granting NGOs are not alike, nor are they all primarily interested in women's incomes. When we get inside development organizations, we see that the same technology can be put to multiple ends, and the effects of that technology depend critically on how it is deployed and the meanings that developers and beneficiaries attach to it. Based on the Fraternity's local identity and networks and women's initial interactions with the NGO, women come to see the organization as something other than an MFI, even though it distributes loans. Thus, the women who enter the Fraternity assign it a greater variety of meanings and leverage it to pursue a greater variety of goals when compared to women entering Namaste. Thereafter, the Fraternity's daily practices reinforce women's view of the Fraternity as different, in ways that women perceive positively and negatively, depending on their goals and interactions with developers.

In contrast to Namaste, the Fraternity emphasizes women's intersecting identities and multiple roles, and it uses loans as part of a broader strategy intended to promote syncretic understandings of women's worth and responsibilities as Mayans, Christians, and women. In its view, women's participation is both instrumentally and intrinsically valuable. The NGO's policymakers/ leaders therefore worry less about efficiency and include many activities that often last hours. This frustrates many women, but it also allows for a greater number of small encounters and more flexibility.

The organization encourages some women to move beyond required activities to undertake additional participation and leadership roles and attempts to cultivate its vision of good Christian, Mayan women subjects. In so doing, it challenges the ways that some women view themselves and their realities. In policymakers/leaders' eyes, transformations in women's identities, self-esteems, values, behaviors, and relationships are not just instrumental to development; they constitute it. Yet these opportunities for transformation are not evenly distributed and often end up reinforcing rather than combating long-standing inequalities.

Developers alone do not determine the daily experiences and outcomes for the Fraternity's beneficiaries. Women react to developers' attempts to manage them in various, often subtle ways. Some beneficiaries eschew active participation, some feign it, and still others embrace it. Women's varied interests, meanings, and decisions, alongside the Fraternity's organizational characteristics and daily practices, lead to heterogeneous patterns of participation, which are in turn linked to mixed outcomes and benefits that are unevenly spread across beneficiaries' lives.

CHAPTER SEVEN

THE IMPLICATIONS OF SOCIALLY CONSTRUCTED DEVELOPMENT

This book moves beyond debates about what "authentic" development is in order to explore the diverse interactions, practices, and experiences that take place under the label "NGO" and the guise of "development." It therefore views development as "neither an ideal nor a catastrophe" but rather an object of study (Olivier de Sardan 2005, 25). While internationally funded development projects have been criticized for their failures, they continue to be imbricated in and to reshape local-level interactions and meanings across the global south, with numerous intended and unintended effects. Understanding the interactions in and around development projects is therefore key to understanding social life in the global south. But this understanding is hindered by popular trends that depict development interventions either as operating with a hidden agenda or as self-contained, apolitical treatments for poverty alleviation, both of which obscure development's messy, power-laden processes on the ground. Developers may "abstract from practice" (Mosse 2005, 231) in their project descriptions and evaluations, but researchers should resist this urge. After all, it is in the quotidian practices and experiences that we see development projects actually impacting the global south, spinning off new processes of interaction and meaning-making. By focusing on what development is supposed to do, we are missing how it is made and what it actually does.

Prioritizing the socially constructed nature of development projects stands to transform how we study and pursue development, starting with the very way we conceptualize it. Rather than viewing development as a northern intervention into the passive global south, the findings presented here suggest that researchers and practitioners should instead see it as a set of relationships being worked out on uneven terrain characterized by inherent tensions and navigated by people using different conceptual and experiential maps. This conceptual shift implies a focus on the agency of and interactions among developers and beneficiaries alongside an accounting of the formal policies, development models, and types of goods/services being provided. It forces us to see policymakers and project leaders as socially embedded actors who often act with the very best of intentions but are affected by their own biases and goals in ways that obstruct their ability to see the world and development projects through beneficiaries' eyes. It also encourages us to see development workers as doing much more than implementing previously established policies. By assigning development projects a variety of meanings and goals (including future employment), adjusting plans according to their contexts and perceptions of beneficiaries, or ignoring formal policies altogether, workers actively transform projects in unexpected ways that are rarely captured by evaluation reports focusing on inputs and outputs. Most importantly, the findings presented here reveal that beneficiaries are not passive recipients of development projects. Rather, they are savvy individuals who leverage projects for their own ends and engage with, pick apart, and sidetrack projects, all while recognizing that such projects tend to be fleeting and rarely transform their lives and communities in any dramatic way.

Yet recent trends in international development research have moved further away from this line of thinking. Instead, the academic literature (especially in the United States) has been bifurcated between two schools, neither of which sufficiently addresses the socially constructed nature of development projects.[1] The first focuses on the global political and economic context in which development has emerged, highlighting the unequal political and economic terrain of development and the various ways that development interventions replicate inequalities that exist globally on a local scale. Studies in this vein rely on discourse analysis or broad assessments of development trends, such as philanthrocapitalism (Edwards 2010) or transnational business feminism (Roberts 2012, 2015), to demonstrate how development projects represent cogs in an antipolitics machine (Ferguson 1994).

In the field of microfinance, for example, critical scholars have argued that microfinance projects serve to "entrench and manage the contradictions of neoliberal development" (Weber 2014, 545) and mold beneficiaries into neoliberal subjects who "act in accordance with the 'market principles of discipline, efficiency and competitiveness'" (Karim 2011, xvii). These critical scholars tend to overlook the socially embedded agency of those involved in development at all levels, depicting development as more or less authorless (Brigg 2001; Lairap-Fonderson 2002; Keating, Rasmussen, and Rishi 2010; Moodie 2013). Effects and intentions are conflated in ways that obscure the multiple meanings, goals, and social relations that produce development policies and shape development practices on the ground.

In the cases presented here, policymakers and NGO leaders leveraged microfinance for very different ends, with limited success. Namaste's policymakers in many ways intended to cultivate entrepreneurial subjects that aligned with notions of neoliberal governmentality set forth by critical scholars. But workers focused more on figuring out ways to manipulate their interactions with paperwork and beneficiaries to ensure that they recruited enough borrowers, collected data efficiently, and performed well enough to keep their jobs. For their part, beneficiaries only sometimes took up Namaste's values and meanings. Often, they went through the motions to secure access to a loan, took what they could from Namaste's educational material, and discarded the rest after exiting the organization.

On the other hand, the Fraternity's policymakers/leaders sought to use microfinance to attract indigenous women into the NGO, where they taught beneficiaries to reject the trappings of neoliberalism—individualism, consumerism, and Western products—and recapture their interpretation of traditional values. Thus, the Fraternity infused the same technology that Namaste utilized (microfinance) with vastly different meanings, pursuing goals that ran counter to critical scholars' assumptions about microfinance. Similar to those women participating in Namaste, only some women participating in the Fraternity internalized the Fraternity's lessons and meanings. Others followed along with the Fraternity's scripts about valuing the environment, community, and rejecting Western products in order to access low-interest loans without significantly changing their beliefs or quotidian practices.

A second group of researchers and practitioners ignore the broader critiques of development just described to address issues of monitoring and evaluation. In the last two decades, there has been a noted shift "to a more control oriented upward accountability" that emphasizes results-based management and impact assessment (Chambers 2010, 10). This shift has been accompanied by billions of dollars being invested in increasingly sophisticated evaluation techniques best exemplified by randomized controlled trials (RCTs), which are increasingly seen as the "gold standard" (Chambers 2010, 14; Davidson

2006; Faulkner 2014). In essence, these researchers attempt to transform complex global networks of funders, policymakers, NGO leaders and workers, and beneficiaries into treatments akin to pills in medical studies. By depicting development projects as free-floating, self-contained treatments, scholars ignore development projects' porous borders and overlook how policies result from intersecting biases and interests rather than objective measures of efficiency and effectiveness alone. Their excessive focus on anticipated outcomes over emergent processes leads them to ignore the contingent ways that development actually unfolds on the ground and to overlook the various unanticipated effects it has on people all along the development chain (Beck 2016; Beck and Radhakrishnan, forthcoming).

In the field of microfinance, these types of scholars generally ask if microfinance works rather than exploring "the workings of microfinance" (Taylor 2012, 602). Of late, they tend to compare pipeline and existing borrowers or, even better in their eyes, use RCTs to evaluate the effectiveness of microfinance in increasing incomes and consumption, improving businesses, contributing to education and health, or expanding women's mobility, autonomy, and decision-making power (Karlan and Zinman 2014; Pitt and Khandker 1998; Mosley 2001; Park and Changqing 2001; McKernan 2002; Bernasek 2003; Banerjee et al. 2013; Angelucci, Karlan, and Zinman 2014; Khandker 1998; Copestake, Bhalotra, and Johnson 2001; Copestake 2002; Hiatt and Woodworth 2006; Brau, Hiatt, and Woodworth 2009). These researchers rely on quantitative measures and before-and-after comparisons with the hopes of uncovering best practices, replicating projects in other contexts, or scaling up (Beck 2016).

Viewing Namaste's and the Fraternity from the top down and then from the bottom up demonstrates the flaw in viewing development interventions as replicable, scalable, self-contained treatments. There is no linear path between policies and outcomes. In between the "before" and the "after" in Namaste and the Fraternity, we observed emergent interactions among socio-material contexts and diverse people acting creatively, and often unpredictably. Thus Namaste's workers—in attempts to keep and succeed in their jobs—surveyed their environments—populated by a wide variety of MFIs, NGOs, and businesses targeting increasingly savvy women—and emphasized loans in their interactions with potential borrowers. At times these workers minimized the amount of time that they and their beneficiaries dedicated to education by focusing on data collection rather than providing detailed advice in their one-on-one meetings. Although the Fraternity formally encouraged the participation and leadership of all indigenous women, in practice its developers singled out some beneficiaries but not others, based on their idiosyncratic preferences and personal biases, including discriminatory assumptions about certain ethnicities. Someone operating with a treatment view of Namaste or the Fraternity might attribute whatever outcomes she found to each NGOS' formal policies and programs, without realizing that practices on the ground did not actually match those policies.

MOVING BEYOND BINARY ASSESSMENTS
OF PROJECT SUCCESS

Critical scholars tend to judge development projects according to their hidden agendas, evaluating the degree to which they reproduce global inequalities. In contrast, treatment views of development interventions tend to prioritize stated goals, judging the treatment as successful or unsuccessful based on the average effects across individuals or groups. Yet recognition of development's social construction forces researchers and practitioners to focus on a wide variety of outcomes, intended and unintended, direct and indirect. It calls on researchers to deploy diverse and creative categories and modes of evaluation derived from multiple perspectives. It also encourages scholars and practitioners to move beyond a focus on average effects to pay close attention to varied experiences and outcomes across individuals and groups.

The analysis of Namaste and the Fraternity presented here clearly demonstrates that development projects have many more effects than those anticipated and that those involved in projects often operate according to varying definitions of success. Thus, rather than evaluating these types of projects in binary terms (success/failure), researchers would be better served by exploring the fulfillment or blockage of the multiple goals assigned to development projects. More generally, researchers may ask what kinds of agency certain development relationships constrain, what kinds of agency they enable, and for whom—remembering that beneficiaries are differently affected by their participation in development projects, as are workers, NGO leaders, and policymakers themselves.

For example, the ways that developers and beneficiaries in Namaste interacted over time to resolve the tensions they faced between their perceptions of themselves and others in the context of competitive environments enabled women's agency as consumers, allowing them to pick and choose between, in their view, similar MFIS and to exit when they were dissatisfied. But it also reduced their incentive to exercise their agency as members, giving them little reason to use voice to change NGO practices. Many women who borrowed from Namaste did not actually want to expand their businesses despite policymakers' assumptions and goals. Thus beneficiaries may have judged their participation a success because it allowed them pay back another loan or access cash in the short term, even if there were no long-term consequences for business growth or development, to policymakers' disappointment.

In contrast, interactions between developers and beneficiaries in the context of the Fraternity allowed some women's agency as members and leaders to be expanded, although this possibility was limited to an extremely small group of mostly K'iche' women. Some internalized the NGO's project, participated at higher levels, and took on new roles that encouraged them to see themselves differently—transforming women's self-esteem, self-efficacy, values, and civic skills. Others stayed in the NGO but exercised voice when they became dissatisfied. This group of women often drew on the very language of discrimination taught in the Fraternity to accuse the NGO of hypocritically favoring some women over others, thus developing and practicing the art of voice in unintended ways. Despite Fraternity policymakers/leaders' goals related to personal and community transformations, many women conformed to policymakers/ leaders' scripts simply to maintain access to a loan, remaining relatively unchanged in their views of themselves. Yet despite the absence of deeper transformations, these women often considered their participation in the Fraternity successful because it gave them access to an extremely low-interest loan.

The findings presented here also demonstrate that we can learn a great deal by moving beyond average effects to pay careful attention to the ways that effects vary across beneficiaries. This can most obviously be seen in the Fraternity, in which, on average, K'iche' women benefited much more than did Mam women from their participation in the NGO. By moving beyond average effects, we discovered that one of the unintended consequences of the Fraternity's work was to increase inequality and (in some cases) tensions between ethnic groups. In Namaste, while many women reported that their relationships with their loan group members improved as a result of their participation in Namaste, examining average effects would have blinded us to the fact that there were other cases in which social networks were damaged, with potential serious consequences for women who often relied on kin and non-kin survival networks to get by.

Examining Namaste's and the Fraternity's mixed outcomes and how they varied across women demonstrates the benefits of moving beyond simplistic generalizations about success or failure. It encourages researchers to think about whose agency is expanded/constrained, what kinds of agency are expanded/constrained, and the distributional consequences of development projects across a variety of actors. Although this book focused on the construction of NGO projects and their varied effects for beneficiaries, one could fruitfully apply a similar approach to determine how developers' agency is variously exercised and affected by development projects.

To be clear, the mixed outcomes described here were not merely products of Namaste's and the Fraternity's top-down development or NGO models. Rather, they were critically linked to the ways that beneficiaries participated in the NGOs, the meaning they assigned to that participation, and the ways they interacted with developers, other beneficiaries, and their environments. Of course, Namaste's and the Fraternity's models of development and other organizational characteristics influenced leaders' and workers' quotidian practices and meanings as well as their beneficiaries' perceptions, expectations, and strategies. But organizational characteristics alone cannot explain the NGOs' mixed outcomes, because things could have turned out differently if people were operating in different contexts, made different choices, assigned different meanings to these NGOs' projects, or interacted differently thereafter. Thus, different organizations operating according to bootstrap or holistic models of development—applied to different populations, involving different workers, and embedded in different environments—would be unlikely to yield the same particular mix and variety of outcomes observed in this book.

Because actors' meanings, goals, and actions are likely to diverge across time, context, and groups, so are any interventions' outcomes. This realization should serve as a note of caution for those seeking to replicate or scale up development projects that policymakers or researchers deem successful. Others have made arguments against "cookie-cutter" strategies—often highlighting the importance of context in mediating projects' effects. But this book's findings about the social construction of development projects add to this line of argument by demonstrating that "cookie-cutter" projects are not so "cookie-cutter" on the ground. Even "one-size-fits-all" policies are inevitably transformed in practice by the contingent interactions between diverse actors and their environments. To expect similarly designed projects to consistently yield equivalent outcomes is to overlook the critical role that human agency and context play in constituting development interventions on the ground.

SHIFTING THE TYPES OF GENERALIZATIONS WE SEEK

This book's findings suggest that researchers of development would be well served by abandoning the search for the "best" (or "better") development intervention or approach through case studies or other means. Case studies of development projects, like those presented here, are useful because they allow us to better understand the nature of development interactions, human agency, and the landscapes that funders, policymakers, NGO leaders, development workers, and beneficiaries co-produce and encounter. But they do not allow us to conclude that microfinance "works" or that participatory methods are "better" than top-down methods. This is because "microfinance" and "participation" are likely to be constituted differently depending on the interactions that occur under their names. Rather than fruitlessly chasing impossible generalizations about the "best" approach, researchers would be better served by focused on uncovering generalizations about the topography of development's interactional terrain.

For example, the comparison between Namaste and the Fraternity, NGOs that embody diverging development models, organizational types, and international trends, revealed generalizable tensions that I believe exist within *any* given NGO-led development intervention. These tensions emanate from two sources: (1) the intersection of diverse lifeworlds/habitus at development's interfaces and (2) the confluence of NGOs' organizational and developmental goals.

Because developers and beneficiaries' goals, expectations, and meanings arise from their different histories and networks, interactions at development's interfaces necessarily proceed through series of "mutual misunderstanding[s]" (Rossi 2004, 559). When developers' and beneficiaries' contrasting lifeworlds, including their simplified conceptions of each other, collide in the context of development projects, blockages as well as room for maneuver are generated.

For example, Namaste's policymakers developed an intervention based on their assumptions about poor Guatemalan women's need for credit, desire to expand their business and become independent entrepreneurs, and ignorance of good business practices. Policymakers therefore drew on their own experiences and needs as Western businesspeople to provide loans and business education, to develop conferences that allowed for networking and innovation, and to introduce metrics that calculated women's hourly wage (a measure that made intuitive sense to policymakers). Drawing on their habitus and seeing their project as central to the lives of workers and beneficiaries, they placed a high premium on measurement and data collection, asking employees to complete many detailed forms, enter data into computer systems regularly, and craft personalized advice for each "beneficiary," all in the hopes of tracking and improving women's businesses.

Many women, however, in fact had ample access to loans, saw Namaste as just one of many MFIs, viewed business education as a cost, and saw conferences as a time to have fun and socialize. Few separated their productive duties related to running their businesses from their reproductive duties of caring for the household and children. They would, for example, complete housework and look after children in between customers to their home-based stores, fruit stands, or other businesses. This made calculating an accurate hourly wage nearly impossible, and the resulting figures relatively meaningless to women themselves. For their part, workers often felt overwhelmed by their many tasks. Some performed them out of a sincere desire to help women, others complied in order to keep their jobs, and still others focused largely on those tasks that were easily monitored (completing forms and entering data) to the detriment of their other work.

The discrepancies between policymakers' assumptions and perceptions of Guatemalan women, on the one hand, and Guatemalan women's lived realities, meanings, and goals, on the other, introduced obstacles to Namaste's goal of encouraging women to expand their businesses and developing local economies. But these same discrepancies also opened up room for maneuver for workers and beneficiaries. Workers gained status and continued employment by positioning themselves as "teachers" helping "ignorant" women, got through paperwork more quickly by colluding with women to estimate figures for hourly wages, and pitched the program as a loan to women but emphasized the importance of education while in the presence of higher-ups. Similarly, women could feign interest in business education in order to be more attractive beneficiaries or conform to assumptions about their lack of knowledge by claiming ignorance of policies when they did not want to comply with them. If they did comply with the business advice offered by workers, beneficiaries usually only did so during the time they were participating in Namaste, abandoning these practices upon leaving the NGO.

Similarly, the Fraternity's policymakers/leaders drew on their own experiences of collective action when establishing the NGO. They were motivated to participate and enjoyed doing so, and thus they assumed that other indigenous women had similar untapped desires and capabilities and would view the Fraternity's project as central to their lives. Because they projected their views about the value of participation and education onto beneficiaries, policymakers/leaders labeled many of its activities mandatory and often organized a number of extra activities, such as daylong conferences, alongside regularly scheduled classes. The Fraternity's policymakers/leaders saw these additional activities as extra benefits, but beneficiaries did not necessarily share this view.

A close analysis of women's daily lives reveals some in fact were already socially active—serving as midwives, participating in their churches or in parents' associations. While a minority of women saw (or came to see) the Fraternity's many activities as additional benefits alongside the revolving funds, most saw these inefficiently run and time-consuming activities as cumbersome and felt frustrated at the amount of time and energy that the Fraternity required of them. In response, these women deployed a variety of subtle strategies, such as developing hidden transcripts, colluding with their peers to alternate skipping activities, or arriving late to or leaving early from activities. More broadly, many women appeared to simply go through the motions of participation. They often said one thing in the context of the Fraternity's classes but did another outside of the NGO.

In the Fraternity, policymakers/leaders' assumptions about women's desires and needs created opportunities for *some* previously inactive women to fulfill or develop desires for education, participation, and leadership. It also provided room for maneuver in which women could choose hidden transcripts, guile, and compromise and to deploy the language of participation and self-esteem instrumentally, to please developers and ensure continued access to loans. But these same assumptions also introduced blockages in the Fraternity's work, such that developers at times acted in paternalistic and controlling ways that alienated some of the very women they were trying to enroll in their projects. Developers' assumptions also made it more difficult for beneficiaries to complain about activities openly and directly, for developers to register women's subtle expressions of discontent, and for policymakers/leaders to reconsider programming.

In both cases, tensions arising from the various lifeworlds that came together in the context of development interventions prevented the complete realization of policymakers' previously established goals, while allowing room for maneuver in which workers and beneficiaries could pursue their own goals that diverged from those of policymakers.

Another source of tension in NGO-led development projects can be found in the fact that NGOs are simultaneously influenced by developmental and organizational goals, which often conflict. Both Namaste and the Fraternity were established based on sincere desires to help Guatemalan women and contribute to development, and with implicit visions of "developed" persons that were instrumental to and constitutive of their development goals. Yet they lacked technologies with well-established links between given inputs and their desired outputs, complicating the task at hand. Moreover, in addition to their development-related goals, as organizations, they were unavoidably influenced by drives for organizational survival and growth. In response, the

NGOs creatively managed the tension between their developmental and organizational goals by leveraging materials, information, and ignorance in ways that allowed them to protect their core practices and reinforce existing projects (for similar findings, see Ebrahim 2003).

Using paperwork, databases, educational material, and business advisers, Namaste attempted to govern women's behavior, craft a world in which there were linear processes and clear links between inputs and outputs, and justify its existence and growth. It also substituted its ambitious goals of poverty reduction, development, and democracy for more manageable, measurable goals that were assumed to have these as spillover effects. Policymakers developed a single indicator as a proxy for success: return on investment, measured by how much women's business incomes increased for every dollar spent. Yet, in so doing, the organization also leveraged ignorance by failing to collect data on increased incomes' supposed spillover effects for beneficiaries, families, and communities.

The tension between developmental and organizational goals also intervened in Namaste's learning processes. For example, when Namaste's policymakers realized that their projects were not adequately helping the poorest of the poor women (their original target population), they simply adjusted their target population rather than questioning their core programs. Thus Namaste's failure only served as an impetus for similar future projects, although targeted at different beneficiaries. Namaste's emphasis on quantitative measurement also made certain forms of feedback illegible to higher-ups. Its focus on relatively short-term timetables and quantifiable goals and its tendency to isolate women's identities essentially put blinders on the organization, making it less able to read nonstandardized or nonquantified forms of information. Policymakers were unable to perceive long-term processes, such as the way the NGO affected women's environments, identities, and relationships over time. Developers were also less sensitive to women's narratives and multiple, intersecting identities, which were not easily quantified and therefore not easily understood using a feedback system designed to deal with numbers.

The Fraternity dealt with the tensions between its developmental and organizational goals differently. The NGO relied on surveys, contracts, educational programming, and workers in order to manage its beneficiaries' behavior and encourage women to work on themselves. It also leveraged headcounts, photographs, and anecdotal stories to link inputs and outputs in evaluation and donor reports, while regularly decoupling these from practices and programming. Whereas Namaste substituted its more ambitious goals with a singular measure with assumed spillovers, the Fraternity maintained its focus on multiple long-term goals. The organization managed the uncertainty that this generated by emphasizing process over results. Highlighting the slow nature of internal changes and community transformations allowed developers to remain confident in the face of uncertainty as long as they could point to small changes in the right direction or anecdotal stories as evidence of their eventual success. Drawing on the language of process, developers could easily interpret a variety of behaviors as proof of women's internal transformations. For example, developers regularly pointed to women's attendance in NGO-sponsored activities as evidence of their transformation, even though this participation was mandatory. They cited women's bathing as evidence of their self-esteem, use of organic compost as evidence of recapturing indigenous values, and vague statements in the context of NGO activities as evidence of a newfound sense of self-efficacy.

The Fraternity's strategies in the face of the tensions between developmental and organizational goals had implications for the nature of learning in the organization. The Fraternity's emphasis on process over results and its recognition of women's multiple identities allowed it to perceive unanticipated constraints on women's participation and empowerment. For example, developers were able to process women's stories about marital problems and spousal abuse in a way that Namaste's metrology could not. They subsequently incorporated husbands and fathers into their activities and created programming around couples' self-esteem, alcoholism, and substance abuse.

Yet, unlike Namaste, the Fraternity did not experience the same type of regular, easily interpreted feedback, nor did it include clear end points that called for self-evaluation. This meant that the organization had no sense of when a given group had graduated from the program, nor was it able to read its limited effects on women's economic well-being or its role in increasing inequality between ethnic groups. This reality constrained the Fraternity's ability to detect deficiencies in its programming and ensured that various forms of feedback could be used to justify future programming. In both Namaste and the Fraternity, then, the tension between developmental and organizational goals was creatively managed in ways that allowed the NGOs to justify their survival and the reproduction of their core activities.

EXPLAINING DEVELOPMENT PROJECTS' PERSISTENCE

The finding that Namaste and the Fraternity manage their developmental and organizational goals in ways that lead to the reproduction of their projects has implications for the broader field of development, which often repackages previous mentalities and strategies. Despite discursive shifts, very little actually ever disappears in the field of development. This can be clearly seen not just in the discussion of Namaste and the Fraternity but also in broader trends in development in Guatemala, outlined in chapter 2. The repeated focus on Green Revolution technology, nontraditional crops, and discourses of entrepreneurial self-help in Guatemala demonstrates that old technologies and project mentalities do not disappear with the introduction of new development models or international trends. Instead, they are recast using new buzzwords and repositioned within new frameworks. The result is that Guatemalan development has reproduced past contradictions and inequalities, while still allowing room for maneuver on the ground.

Similar trends have been observed since the birth of modern international development. On a number of occasions, critical academics and practitioners alike have made useful suggestions about the need to abandon one-size-fits-all strategies, take context and people's diversity seriously, and examine a wide variety of projects from the bottom up—from women's empowerment and involvement in food production, to distribution of public services, to disaster relief, among others (Hirschman 1967; Jaquette 1985; Pirotte, Husson, and Grunewald 1999; Pritchett and Woolcock 2004; Cornwall and Brock 2005; Andrews 2013; Mowles 2013). Yet we have seen time and again that these suggestions either fail to be incorporated or are incorporated only half-heartedly such that on-the-ground practices are simply repackaged using new discourses or new technologies. And despite these words of caution, practitioners today continue to search for ways to scale up and replicate development projects.

This tendency can perhaps be best seen in the history of participatory development. In the 1970s and 1980s, scholars and practitioners, inspired by the work of Paulo Freire, Ivan Illich, and Robert Chambers, among others, promoted participatory development in which poor members of the global south would be seen as experts in their own circumstances and needs, owners of development projects, which were to be designed from the bottom up (Freire 1970; Chambers 1983; Illich 1997). Yet scholars who embedded themselves in participatory projects often found that, "no matter how firm the commitment to good intentions, the notion of 'powerful outsiders' assisting 'powerless insiders' [was] constantly smuggled in" (Long 2001, 89). Conflicting developmental drives to help and organizational drives to manage explain why behind even participatory rhetoric, one often finds projects as usual. As organizations, generally accountable to external donors, NGOs face high demands for effective management, requiring central control and meeting preestablished objectives. These demands often run counter to those of bottom-up participation, which entail relinquishing control and accepting potential inefficiencies and uncertainties (Craig and Porter 1997; Mosse 2003, 2005; Quarles van Uf-ford 1993; Nauta 2006). Although this tension can be managed in a number of ways, scholars with in-depth knowledge of particular interventions have often noted that even projects designed to cultivate local participation "tend to be more managed than participatory," with the "balance of control (and project resources and funds) [ending] up inside the organizations which are managing the projects" (Craig and Porter 1997, 229). Projects are thus able to creatively "integrate critics and critiques in their policy discourse [for ex-ample, regarding bottom-up participation] with limited effect on practices" (Bierschenk 2008, 10).

Similarly, nowadays, projects are no longer the favored tool of international development; they have been replaced by partnerships with governments in the design and implementation of comprehensive development frameworks. Yet, even though we are supposedly past the era of projects, project mentalities—which among other tendencies, focus on policies and results rather than pro-cesses—persist. Indeed, some trends, such as international actors moving away from direct implementation to supporting government-led programs, may separate practitioners and researchers even further from the on-the-ground practices and experiences of development (Mosse 2005). And, as in the past, development interventions continue to be characterized by a "'se-ductive mix' of development 'buzzwords'" on the one hand and "a striking lack of progress in relation to a wide range of development indicators" on the other (Lewis and Mosse 2006, 8). But if development projects fail to live up to expectations, why do they persist? Why do we seem to see a continual repackaging of past trends and projects even as important critical works have convincingly pushed against them?

A close examination of how interactions between diverse actors and mate-rials constitute development projects and how those projects actually unfold on the ground helps explain this puzzle. After all, even large international organizations that shape worldwide development policies are made up of real people and interactions like those studied here. Examining the multiple mean-ings and goals assigned to development projects demonstrates how, over time, developers and beneficiaries often interact to produce something not quite intended but something that can be recast by various agents as success, thus contributing to projects' persistence (Long and Long 1992; Mosse 2005).

As shown in this book, affected by the tension between development and organizational goals, NGOs often interpret ambiguous feedback as evidence of success or negative feedback as the impetus for launching new projects.

Policymakers, NGO leaders, and workers assign a variety of goals and meanings to the NGOs and their projects, including status, a sense of purpose, and employment, alongside their developmental goals. These goals and meanings are wrapped up in organizational survival and growth. Developers, as socially embedded actors, draw on their own habitus in order to assign meanings to development projects and construct expectations of beneficiaries and their environments. Thus, often acting with the very best intentions, developers unintentionally generate their own incapacities and blockages to double-loop learning, which involves questioning underlying goals and assumptions that, in this case, might call into question the very value of the project or NGO.[2]

To illustrate, in many ways, both Namaste and the Fraternity are able to position themselves as successful. Namaste not only meets its short-term goal of increasing women's incomes but also successfully leverages the language of results and quantified measures to garner new connections and funding, which in turn provide further evidence of Namaste's success. The Fraternity can point to transformations among a minority of beneficiaries as evidence of its success in raising women's self-esteems and revitalizing cultural practices and religious values. Like Namaste, it has maintained long-standing local and international connections that it can point to as signs of success. Yet the previous chapters demonstrate that these narratives of success are incomplete even as they reinforce existing strategies of action.

Beneficiaries themselves also play a role. Potential and current beneficiaries are likely to ask for what they think developers are willing to give, based on their past experiences with and perceptions of developers. Those targeted by development interventions additionally may present themselves in ways that fit developers' expectations, based on images cultivated through repeated interactions over time (Bending and Rosenda 2006). This allows them to access resources or build networks with resource-rich or otherwise powerful allies, but it also reinforces developers' expectations about beneficiaries and ideas about the best way to go about helping them. The result is that NGOs are further buffered from feedback that could potentially lead to double-loop learning. Because beneficiaries appropriate, selectively adapt, and sidetrack development projects with their own goals and meanings in mind, they may view their participation as successful even if the project does not meet its intended goals, as seen with beneficiaries of Namaste and the Fraternity. This further explains why even failure can contribute to project reproduction: projects that fail to accomplish their intended goals may continue to receive positive feedback and buy-in from beneficiaries and communities.

Thus, tendencies on the part of *both* developers and beneficiaries, as socially embedded actors attempting to, respectively, make a difference and get by, help explain the persistence of development interventions. Development projects thrive because of (not in spite of) their tensions and inconsistencies, because they allow people to assign multiple meanings and goals to development projects and to view them as successful even if they fail to develop communities or countries.

MOVING FORWARD, WITH A HEALTHY DOSE OF SKEPTICISM

If development projects are interactional, relational processes rather than executions of previously formulated plans, then researchers and practitioners should not be surprised by gaps between policy, practice, and outcomes. Instead, they should expect these gaps as the inevitable result of human agency and interaction, and embrace them as valuable sources of information about development's possibilities and blockages. Gaps between policy, practice, and outcomes should be seen as productive rather than problematic or manageable through better design or implementation. For example, researchers and practitioners could focus on studying and learning from how the diverse actors being targeted by development interventions are actually using these projects in order to acquire a better understanding of people's diverse environments, goals, and identities. But this type of approach would require greater costs and considerably more flexibility, humility, and creativity than many current methods of project design and evaluation allow.

That said, while this book's findings about the socially constructed nature of development and its central tensions should affect how practitioners conceive of, study, pursue, and evaluate development, I am skeptical that it will. My skepticism is rooted not in a view of developers as malicious or willfully ignorant but rather in my understanding of them as real people who are juggling multiple goals and are influenced by their own worldviews. Yet, despite my skepticism about the degree to which the insights presented here will fundamentally transform the way that development is done, perhaps naively, I would like to encourage development researchers and practitioners to grapple with some difficult questions that this project has inspired, acknowledging that I myself am unable to answer them satisfactorily at this time.

Studying development projects over time has raised the question of how can we move beyond the tendency of single-loop learning, which focuses on improving existing projects, to increase the likelihood of double-loop learning in the field of development. That is, when simplified perceptions of the other collide or when organizational and development goals conflict, how can we encourage scholars and practitioners to question the value of a project's fundamental goals, meanings, and even its existence, rather than merely ask how that project can be improved? How can we encourage funders, policymakers, workers, and even researchers to incorporate diverse categories and modes of evaluation, derived from the multiple perspectives inevitably involved in any given development projects, as messy as this process may be? And perhaps most difficult to answer, how can we all take to heart James Ferguson's point that "there is no guarantee that our knowledge and skills will be relevant" (Ferguson 1994, 287), as uncomfortable as that might make us?

APPENDIX: *Research Methods and Ethical Dilemmas*

When I first visited Guatemala in the summer of 2006, I was struck by the number of NGOs I encountered; I became interested in the role of foreign-funded organizations in local understandings and practices of development, especially in a country so dramatically influenced by foreign intervention throughout its history. Thereafter, I focused my trips on conducting key informant interviews with NGO leaders, journalists, and government officials about the role of development NGOs, participant observations with women's NGOs, and archival searches related to women, development, and NGOs. Based on this research, I selected Namaste and the Fraternity for my comparative analysis, because while they were similar in terms of scale, activities, and target populations, they embodied diverging international trends in the field of development and NGOs and provided windows into Guatemala's overlapping development histories.

Thereafter, I coupled ethnographies at Namaste and the Fraternity's interfaces with analyses of NGO archives and with informal and formal interviews with funders, policymakers, NGO leaders, workers, and beneficiaries. Interviews with developers that focused on personal and organizational trajectories, alongside data gleaned from NGO archives, were crucial to understanding the sources and nature of development models, values, structures, and networks. Participation in staff meetings, informal conversations, and observations of developers' and beneficiaries' interactions revealed how these organizational characteristics were interpreted, put into practice, and adjusted on a daily basis by diverse people. I was able to analyze the ways that policymakers, leaders, and workers talked about their work and about beneficiaries, as well as the quotidian ways that they enacted development models alongside their own meanings and goals and variously interpreted and reproduced organizational characteristics through their interactions with beneficiaries and materials.

Once I had established informal relationships with beneficiaries, I visited over fifty women in their homes or places of business to speak with them about their lives, their relationships, and their experiences in the NGOs and in other organizations in their communities. I attempted to select a broad range of women to interview—from those who were less active and appeared less invested in the NGO to those who were extremely active and enthusiastic. I structured these interviews around a standard set of questions but allowed flexibility to explore new areas or tailor questions to women's responses. I conducted participant observations before formal interviews with these beneficiaries, hoping that women would feel more comfortable talking with me as a result, although I was cognizant that this decision came with tradeoffs. I was especially worried that women would be unwilling to report dissatisfaction with NGOs if they associated me with these organizations. I attempted to mitigate this possibility by repeatedly reminding beneficiaries that I was not working for or volunteering with the NGO and would not "report" to higher-ups about what I observed or heard. Interviewing women in their homes or businesses also provided a measure of separation and privacy.

These formal interviews, repeated informal conversations, long-term participant observations during NGO activities, and visits to women's communities provided rich data on women's lives, their views of the NGOs, and their experiences of development. I was often surprised when women revealed thoughts and experiences that they had shared with few others. My sense was that these women trusted me, but perhaps more so, they saw my identity as a foreigner as a benefit. Because I did not live in their communities, have strong relationships with their neighbors, or attend their churches, they were less worried that what they told me would become the latest community gossip. In other circumstances, women reported dissatisfaction with NGOs or employees, perhaps assuming that, as a foreigner, I had some authority to address their complaints. I often found myself correcting this assumption even though I sometimes benefited from it. Thus, while my identity as an "outsider" introduced important practical and ethical challenges (discussed later), in some circumstances, it also gave me advantages over "insiders."

In 2010, I conducted a survey of 264 women who operated small businesses and who fit the profile of potential beneficiaries of loan-granting NGOs and MFIs. The survey, conducted across twenty-six different communities, included questions about women's experiences with, and perceptions of, NGOs and MFIs. This survey allowed me to get a sense of the representativeness of the communities in which Namaste and the Fraternity work and to gather more data on what women outside of these two organizations thought of

NGOs and microfinance. It also provided valuable information on the factors that affected women's decision to join these types of programs.

I have maintained relatively consistent contact with funders, policymakers, and NGO leaders through email, phone, Skype, and in-person visits (in Guatemala, Toronto, and California) since the time of my initial research in 2007, though my ability to do so with beneficiaries has been limited by their lack of access to such technology. I conducted follow-up visits in 2011 and in 2013 to observe NGO activities and administer follow-up interviews with NGO workers and beneficiaries.

During the 2013 visit, I also partnered with Namaste to locate and survey sixty-eight former beneficiaries about their lives since leaving the organization two or more years prior. This type of survey would be difficult to repeat in the Fraternity because of the long duration of women's membership and the Fraternity's disinterest in record-keeping, making locating former (and even current) beneficiaries quite difficult. In addition to giving me a window into the long-term economic and social effects of women's participation in Namaste, this survey included questions about other organizations targeting women and women's experiences with other NGOs and MFIs before and after their participation in Namaste. In combination, this survey, my earlier 2010 survey, and my interviews and observations with other women's NGOs allowed me to situate my observations of Namaste and the Fraternity in a broader context and gave me a sense of how Namaste and the Fraternity compared with other NGOs targeting poor women.

Because this study was conducted over the course of seven years, it provides a unique, longitudinal view of organizations, developers, and beneficiaries— allowing me to view development from multiple perspectives and over an extended period of time. Studying development in this way presented both advantages and challenges. Ethnography, especially ethnography taking place over long periods as in this study, provides a more accurate depiction of the reality of development interventions and NGOs than do policy documents or interviews alone. Formal mission statements and policies may in fact mask diverging day-to-day practices or unstated goals, norms, or rules. Ethnography provides a window into hidden transcripts, informal institutions, and taken-for-granted (and thus unstated) priorities. Evaluation reports and data sets are often edited and focus exclusively on the outcomes intended by policymakers, thus overlooking the many other unintended effects that interventions are likely to have, and which ethnography is likely to uncover.

For obvious reasons, developers have incentives to present interventions in a positive light. Similarly, beneficiaries have incentives to downplay their complaints or overstate their levels of satisfaction in order to ensure continued benefits and avoid potential reprimands. Long-term ethnography thus allows researchers to triangulate claims made by developers and beneficiaries alike regarding the nature of development interventions. It also allows researchers to locate inconsistencies within a given intervention and observe the non-linear processes that are often eliminated in NGO leaders' and policymakers' official techno-rational presentations (Lewis and Mosse 2006).

More broadly, I found that my ethnography also served as "an antidote to the generalizations made about NGOs by their advocates and detractors" (Markowitz 2001, 42). It allowed me to move beyond the romanticization or condemnation of NGOs to see them as diverse organizations, embedded in distinct contexts and comprising real people with multiple goals, values, meanings, and biases. This allowed me to move beyond the "good NGO, bad NGO" binary (Alvarez 2009) and to appreciate NGOs and development interventions as diverse, ambiguous social forces.

Yet I also found that applying ethnographic methods to the study of NGOs and development introduced a number of practical and ethical challenges. Given the nature of their funding, relationships, and work, studying NGOs entailed "doing local fieldwork within a web of relationships that are inherently unstable among groups of people with whom one has widely varying relationships" (Markowitz 2001, 40). Studying NGOs meant studying down, up, and sideways (Nader 1974). I often found myself on dirt roads or in houses without running water, other times in well-maintained donor and NGO offices, and still others dressed up at private fundraising events. It was unsettling to move from one context to the other, and I often had to adopt very different strategies, including ways of speaking and dressing, in each setting.

In the context of the Fraternity, I often felt uncomfortable as a nonreligious person in a religious setting. When I was asked about my religious affiliation, I explained that while much of my family was Catholic, I was not actively attending any particular church. I sometimes attended services and participated in group prayers when invited to do so in order to more fully embed myself in people's lives and meanings. It was important to me that I did not mislead women about my beliefs but also did not offend them.

Throughout my research, I struggled with my identity as foreigner and outsider. This is common among researchers, especially those who pursue ethnographic methods in which the researcher herself is the data-collection instrument. But operating in the context of NGOs added unique challenges, for NGO actors often see their legitimacy as central to their survival; they are therefore reluctant to provide outsiders with unlimited access to their operations, conversations, and files. While I was granted immediate and un-restricted access to records and internal correspondences in Namaste—an organization that prides itself on transparency—it took three years for the Fraternity's director to admit that they maintained any files at all, at which point she reluctantly granted me access.

In the context of NGOs, any foreigner risks being perceived as a volunteer, a visiting donor, or even a "boss." Foreign researchers might find that staff and beneficiaries look to them informally as sources of potential donations, raising practical and ethical challenges. The potential for donations or other forms of support might give employees incentives to hide the true nature of their work or to refuse to discuss shortcomings—something I encountered with some NGOs but not others. This tendency only amplifies the importance of long-term ethnographic methods for detecting and interrogating inconsistencies between public and hidden transcripts.

Researchers embedding themselves in NGOs often confront the tension between remaining objective and their desire to intervene in situations they deem problematic. For example, as described, I found that workers and bene-ficiaries alike often looked to me as an authority figure, a perception I actively attempted to combat on a daily basis. But there were times in which I had the urge to leverage that "authority" to intervene to correct some injustice. For ex-ample, I remember vividly watching in horror as a new NGO employee scrib-bled in pen on the arm of the plush chair in a beneficiary's home. I fought the urge to stop or scold the employee, fearing that it might reinforce a perception of me as an authority figure among employees and beneficiaries, which I was trying to combat. Still, I could not stop thinking about the incident or the look on the woman's face as she uncomfortably sat watching the employee treat her furniture with such disregard. Earlier in the day, the same employee arrived late to a meeting, making women wait for some time; privately explained to me that he thought loans should be given to men, not women; and attempted to hit on me. In short, I did not like the employee and was concerned about the way he was treating beneficiaries. My personal feelings toward him seemed irrelevant, but I felt the urge to stand up for the beneficiaries, who clearly felt uncomfortable confronting the person from whom they were soliciting a loan. What to do? A few days later, I casually questioned a higher-up about his per-ceptions of the new employee. When he mentioned that they were unhappy with the employee's performance and were probably going to let him go, I mentioned the pen incident (which had been witnessed by another Namaste employee) but not the content of our private conversations. While I doubt that this conversation affected the higher-up's decision to fire the employee, to this day, I wonder whether I did the right thing by discussing the employee's behavior with his boss.

Intervening in a more positive way, however, is more common among researchers conducting ethnographies of NGOs or movements. In many cases, ethnographers offer to "help out" in exchange for access—potentially introducing bias and associating the researcher with the NGO (Markowitz 2001, 43). Like those who have gone before me, I struggled to balance my desire to make myself useful and cultivate mutually beneficial relationships with the NGOs I studied, on the one hand, while on the other hand to maintain a critical distance in my own eyes and the eyes of employees and beneficiaries. This tension was never fully resolved, and I continue to feel uneasy about my roles within the NGOs. Occasionally I offered material support—for example, helping the organizations find grants to conduct impact assessments that would be useful to both the NGO and me, donating supplies (markers, papers, copies, etc.), and, once the bulk of research had already been completed, donating small amounts for producing educational material. More often, I provided services, helping to distribute food and drinks at events, sharing information with employees about other NGOs with which they might collaborate, and providing written reports outlining my impressions at the NGOs' request.

At times I felt I was not doing enough and was just getting in the way. On other occasions I worried that I was doing too much or that my "expertise" was given too much weight. This anxiety seems to be an inevitable component of development ethnography (Gow 2008; Markowitz 2001), but it is, I hope, a sign of an aware and critical researcher. In many ways, embedding myself in these organizations and cultivating relationships with their developers and beneficiaries helped, rather than impeded, my ability to overcome the biases with which I began this project. It allowed me to see nuances that I did not anticipate and undermined romantic ideas about women, development, and "helping" that I had previously entertained. Paradoxically, studying development "up close" provided me with the critical distance that I needed to arrive at the conclusions presented here.

Another dilemma is the issue of consent and the reporting of results. Dorothea Hilhorst notes that the "notion of prior consent does not easily tally with the nature of ethnography, where the lines of analysis evolve over time" (Hilhorst 2003, 230). That is, it is difficult to explain the nature of your study, when the nature of your study is itself unfolding in ways that are not always entirely predictable. The potential for NGOs' developers and beneficiaries to feel a sense of betrayal is compounded if the researcher uncovers and reports unsavory aspects of NGOs' work. This can risk the researcher's ability to gain access to that or any NGO in the future. Furthermore, those who are involved in the daily practice of development often find academic analyses impractical. They are likely to resent the "individual appropriation of a collective experience" that renders them "'the objects of study'" (Mosse 2005, xii; see also Hilhorst 2003). Because practitioners are often focused, understandably, on outcomes, it is likely that they will dismiss as irrelevant studies like this one, which focuses on processes and resists the urge to outline the "right" or "best" way of doing development.

During the course of my research I developed close relationships with many people who championed the NGOs I studied, people whom I grew to like and respect. While I have in the past shared versions of the ideas and conclusions outlined here with many of them, I worry about how the final product will be received and the effects it will have on these relationships. I cannot claim to present the ultimate truth about these particular organizations or about development, NGOs, or microfinance more generally, and I am aware of the power that comes from choosing whose stories get told and what gets presented as reality. Still, I have done my best to provide a nuanced, honest account of how I saw development and NGO work play out on the ground and to what effect—out of respect not only for Guatemalan women as they strive for the good life but also for those who sincerely want to assist them in that quest.

The names of the NGOs studied here are real, but the names of individuals have been changed, with the exception of Namaste's founder, Robert Graham, who has spoken publicly and even written a book about his experiences with Namaste. I chose to use the NGOs' real names, with their permission and after much deliberation, so that readers would have the opportunity to judge my interpretations for themselves, based in part on the existing written material on these NGOs (Namaste is described in Graham's autobiography and a number of online publications, and the Fraternity is mentioned in a number of missionary blogs and reports). I have chosen to use pseudonyms for individuals and their communities in order to protect the identities of workers and beneficiaries and thus ensure their relationships with NGOs are not affected by their participation in the study.

NOTES

CHAPTER 1. *Social Engineering from Above and Below*

1. Community and municipality names, as well as the names of individuals other than Robert Graham, have been changed to protect women's identities, but NGOs' names have been maintained. For a discussion of the reasoning behind these decisions, see the appendix. Quoted material from individuals will feature a pseudonym and the year comments were made.

2. These terms refer to ideal types, and the positions of these actors are likely to vary across organizations and across time. For example, Namaste's policymakers have historically included the founder and board of directors, located in San Francisco. The regional director in Guatemala influenced policy but did not have the final say, and was more appropriately labeled an NGO leader. In contrast, the Fraternity's director, for the majority of its history, could be seen as both the NGO leader and the main policymaker. After her death, however, the board of directors took on a more active role in crafting formal policy, and its members could subsequently be seen as NGO leaders and policymakers (even though some of them were simultaneously beneficiaries as they continued to receive goods/services in their loan groups). The fluidity of these roles further demonstrates the dynamic and contingent nature of development on the ground.

3. The capabilities approach developed by Martha Nussbaum, for example, distinguishes between internal capabilities and external capabilities in order to demonstrate that human flourishing requires not just adequate external conditions but also people's own sense that they are actually capable and worthy of doing so (Nussbaum 2001). Arjun Appadurai similarly emphasizes developing the capacity to aspire as crucial to development, entailing the ability to link the more and less immediate objects of aspiration and to develop, articulate, and work effectively toward an expanded vision of the good life (Appadurai 2004). These works mirror earlier feminist theories of power that emphasize the "power within" (Rowlands 1997).

4. Alicia, director of Fraternity, interview with the author, 2009.

5. I thank David Lewis for this observation.

6. Some studies that have relied on in-depth ethnographies of NGOs and development interventions have begun to uncover the multiple ways that beneficiaries,

NGO leaders, and workers leverage or sidetrack development projects to produce contradictory effects that are likely to be overlooked by traditional modes of evaluation (Fortun 2001; Riles 2001; Magno 2002; Hilhorst 2003; Bornstein 2005; Mosse 2005; Olivier de Sardan 2005; Lewis and Mosse 2006; O'Reilly 2006; Hemment 2007; Murdock 2008; Fechter and Hindman 2011; Yarrow 2011; Baillie Smith and Jenkins 2012; Schuller 2012; Venkatesan and Yarrow 2012; Bernal and Grewal 2014; Krause 2014). Perhaps the clearest example of this type of research applied to NGOs is represented in Dorothea Hilhorst's *The Real World of NGOs: Discourses, Diversity and Development*, which draws on actor-oriented sociology to treat NGOs "not as things but as open ended processes" (Hilhorst 2003, 5). Recognizing that "there is no single answer to the questions of what an NGO *is*, what it *wants* and what it *does*" (Hilhorst 2003, 3), Hilhorst focuses on how various individuals involved in NGO-led projects exercise agency by leveraging competing discourses to pursue their goals. She thus depicts NGOs as power-laden networks, affected internally by status differentials and intertwining with local political and cultural struggles and histories.

7. The fact that NGOs are able to act creatively to "integrate critics and critiques in their policy discourse with limited effect on practices" (Bierschenk 2008, 10) challenges typical instrumental views of development policies in which policies address development problems and guide practice. Yet, even when they do not guide on-the-ground practices, policies continue to serve other ends, including enrolling other actors (donors, media, government officials) in one's project (Mosse 2003, 2005).

CHAPTER 2. *Repackaging Development in Guatemala*

1. Catholic Action was a movement in the Catholic Church that initially sought to combat radical, Communist politics and syncretic forms of Catholicism by providing acceptable outlets for local frustrations and teaching contemporary Catholic doctrine. Eventually, a progressive strand, influenced by the Second Vatican Council and the Medellin Conference of the Latin American Episcopal Council, focused on improving the material conditions of the poor and raising the poor's consciousness (Fischer 1996, 58).

2. For example, while U.S. investment in Guatemala represented 11 percent of FDI in the early 1970s, it only was responsible for employing 1 percent of the labor force. At that time, $100,000 of total assets on average was associated with 658 employees, compared to a measly 58 employed for the equivalent in U.S. capital (Booth 1984).

3. They also promoted tax reform, yet, to date, Guatemala's congress has failed to pass even the most basic tax reforms, maintaining Guatemala's tax rate as one of the lowest in Latin America.

4. The Law for the Promotion and Development of Export Activities and Drawback (1989) lured maquiladoras with a ten-year exemption from incomes taxes, exemptions from duties and value-added taxes on imported machinery, and suspension of duties and taxes on other inputs and packing material. Given their home country's long-standing diplomatic ties with Guatemala and Guatemala's proximity to the United States, Korean investors found Guatemala a particularly attractive place to invest. By

2007, South Korean investors owned 66 out of Guatemala's 184 textile maquiladoras, employing roughly 70,000 people, 80 percent of whom were young women. The Guatemalan government remained complicit with the labor rights violations that regularly occurred in these factories and actively assisted maquiladora companies in fighting off unionization (Petersen 1992).

5. Following the advice of the World Bank, the 1996 mining law reversed previous restrictions on foreign companies owning 100 percent of mining operations, established even more generous tax breaks for transnational companies, and dramatically reduced the royalties (to 1 percent) that transnational mining operations paid to the Guatemalan state.

6. The World Bank and IDB divided their strategies into two areas: (1) poverty alleviation and (2) macroeconomic stability and structural reform. In the latter, they provided funding and support in the country's "productive" sector—agriculture, finance, transportation, and tourism. These programs "often [resulted] in support for large, capital intensive businesses and international corporations with little or no support for small producers of basic foods and domestic products" (Ruthrauff 1998, n.p.), thus demonstrating that the tendency for large-scale, top-down development projects remained alive and well, despite talk of decentralization and participatory development.

7. Internationally backed public-private partnerships also took on government roles; see for example Elizabeth Oglesby's analysis of FUNDAZUCAR's involvement in education, health care, and local governance (Oglesby 2013).

8. Religious NGOs are defined as those who derive their identity and mission from the teachings of one or more religious or spiritual traditions, even if they do not have formal affiliations with larger religious communities (Clarke and Jennings 2008).

9. As a result of this influence, the United States ruled in 2004 that USAID could not discriminate against organizations that combined development or humanitarian with religious activities (Hearn 2002).

10. Mix Market is a nonprofit organization that collects, validates, and disseminates business information, including financial and social performance data, from participating MFIs worldwide.

11. In 2007, banks provided 36 percent of recorded microfinance loans, credit unions gave 48 percent, and microfinance NGOs provided 15 percent. Women borrowers were underrepresented among banks and credit unions but overrepresented in microfinance NGOs (representing 66 percent of borrowers) (Superintendencia de Bancos, Guatemala 2011).

12. FAPE, fundacionfape.org.

13. Fundación Génesis Empresarial, genesisempresarial.org.

14. Quotes from Mentors International, mentorsinternational.org

15. All of the Guatemalan MFIs reporting to Mix Market list women among their "target" markets, and over 80 percent of the clients of MFIs that belong to the umbrella organization REDIMIF (the Network of Microfinance Institutions in Guatemala) are women.

16. To avoid confusion, I use the term "Protestant" to generally refer to non-Catholic

Christian faiths, although in Guatemala these are generally referred to as evangelical. In Guatemala, mainline Protestants are a small minority and are represented by Presbyterians. The majority of Protestants are Pentecostals, emphasizing a direct relationship and personal experience with God and baptism through the Holy Spirit.

17. For example, in the early 1980s, Ríos Montt unveiled his *trabajos, tortillas y techo* (work, food [literally, tortillas], and shelter [literally, roof]) campaign to reconstruct war-torn areas, which was headed by Fundación de Ayuda al Pueblo Indígena (FUNDAPI), a foundation financed by U.S. fundamentalist sources and operated by a number of Protestant-affiliated groups (Martin 1990, 254–5; Garrard-Burnett 1998, 149).

18. There are wide-ranging estimates for the number of NGOs in Guatemala. Some count roughly five hundred NGOs in 2005, whereas others count as many as ten thousand just two years later (Way 2012, 186–7; Sridhar 2007). The official government registry of nonprofits includes a wide-range of associations including NGOs, credit unions, sports clubs, and parents' associations, among others. In my analysis of the 2008 registry, I found over five thousand of these organizations that appeared to be NGOs, although this estimate was based on Internet searches and analyses of organizational names alone because the list only included information on the organizations' names and locations. There were also many NGOs of which I was aware that did not appear on the governmental registry.

CHAPTER 3. *Namaste's Bootstrap Model*

1. FINCA provided a loan to a group of ten to fifty people, usually women, as well as the autonomy to manage it, so that they could eventually establish their own mini-bank, independent of FINCA. In contrast, Grameen's solidarity groups gathered smaller groups and did not incorporate internal financial management.

2. Namaste's leaders gave me open access to all past and ongoing field updates and included me in their internal emails. This provided a tremendous opportunity to observe the daily processes of decision-making and management.

3. Namaste Direct/Fundación Namaste Guatemaya, "2013–2016 Business Plan."

4. Fundación Namaste Guatemaya, "Fundación Namaste Guatemaya: The Namaste Business Development Program for NGOs and MFIs" (n.d.); emphasis added.

5. Fundación Namaste Guatemaya, n.d.

6. Namaste Direct, namastedirect.org, accessed January 6, 2010.

7. Effective interest rates for small commercial loans ranged between 22 and 28 percent. Initially, Namaste charged an effective interest rate of roughly 21 percent upon taking over the administration of loans but has since raised it to 30 percent.

8. Since the time of research, Namaste has allowed some women to access three loans and has considered allowing a fourth, slightly larger loan to act as a "bridge" to its STARZ program.

9. Since the time of this research, Namaste has shifted a good deal of decision-making roles and authority to NGO leaders in Antigua, Guatemala.

10. I use the term enroll here in reference to actor-network theory, which posits that networks become more powerful and durable as they enroll more social and material actants in order to support their own definitions and aims (Latour 2007).

11. Using Namaste's data, however, I was able to determine that implicit biases did affect loan sizes in ways that were not easily observable. Women who had more formal schooling, for example, were often awarded larger loans, controlling for a host of other personal and business-related factors (Beck, Aguilar, and Schintz forthcoming).

12. Fundación Namaste Guatemaya, n.d.

CHAPTER 4. *Women and Workers Responding to Bootstrap Development*

1. On a return visit in 2016, I attempted to visit these model communities and found that they remained half-completed. One, in fact, had been converted into a weight-loss center for well-off Guatemalans and foreigners.

2. On average, Namaste's beneficiaries have just over four years of formal schooling—slightly below the average of five and a half years for Guatemalan women nationwide (UNDP 2013).

3. Namaste operates in the departments of Suchitepéquez, Sacatepéquez, and Chimaltenango. In the past the NGO also operated in the department of Sololá, though these operations had been discontinued by the time of my research. At the time of my most in-depth research (2009–10), it was working with just over four hundred women, across fifty-six small groups. As of March 2014, the NGO had distributed just under 2,700 loans to slightly more than 1,700 women in total. Most of its beneficiaries live in semirural areas, although a minority live in areas that would be considered relatively urban, reflecting Namaste's shifting focus toward business viability as one of the most important qualifications for potential beneficiaries. Women are ladina (nonindigenous), K'iche', and Kaqchikel.

4. According to Namaste's internal records, 43 percent of women in their first loan cycle had received at least one loan from another MFI. This percentage does not include the women who applied for a Namaste loan but were turned away because they did not have a business or had already taken on too much debt.

5. Even several women who were identified by Namaste's employees as the most active participants (attending classes regularly and participating in discussions) admitted that they would not continue attending classes if it were not for the loan—saying, "It would not be worth it because I would be losing time," or "It would be hard to do the classes without the loan because it is borrowing one's time." Half of the women interviewed who were labeled as more active participants said they would not be interested in continuing with the classes without the loan.

6. Focusing only on the 60 percent of women who increased their business profits during their first loan cycle, the average increase in business profits was $175 per month. It is important to note that 40 percent of women who participated in Namaste did not see any notable increases in their monthly business incomes, even in the short

term. I argue that this can be explained by the mismatch between women's goals and policymaker's goals and by the nature of the environment in which Namaste was operating (see Beck, Aguilar, and Schintz forthcoming).

CHAPTER 5. *The Fraternity's Holistic Model*

1. Elders advise pastors, organize church projects, and make decisions regarding outreach, management, and construction. Deacons focus on the care and counsel of churchgoers, their families, and the community. Both are prestigious roles that individuals hold for three-year terms, although they maintain their titles for life.

2. The divisions that had been brewing between the conservative and progressive sections of the IENPG led to a split in the church soon thereafter, with the most conservative sections forming their own synod.

3. The average loan size in 2009 was $250.

4. At the time of my most intensive research (2009), K'iche' women on average received a loan of 3,200 quetzales ($400), whereas Mam women on average received a loan of 2,700 quetzales ($338).

5. In follow-up conversations and emails with the Fraternity's funders and board in 2015, I discovered that members of the Fraternity's board decided not to renew Antonieta's contract and instead placed a long-time board member as the new director. I have not had the chance to analyze how this change has effected the organization's structure, values, or work with beneficiaries.

CHAPTER 7: *The Implications of Socially Constructed Development*

1. For a discussion of this tendency in the sphere of microfinance, see Beck and Radhikrishnan, forthcoming

2. Double-loop learning encourages changing or rejecting "governing variables"—including central goals and underlying values and rules (or "mental models") in light of experience. It encourages people to realize that the very ways a problem/goal is defined and addressed can be sources of the problem (Argyris and Schön 1978; Argyris 1991).

Acosta, Alberto. 2010. "El Buen Vivir en el Camino del Post-Desarrollo: Una Lectura desde la Constitución de Montecristi." Policy Paper 9. Ecuador: La Fundación Friedrich Ebert, El Insituto Latinoamericano de Investigaciones Sociales.

Adams, Vincanne, and Stacy Leigh Pigg. 2005. *Sex in Development: Science, Sexuality, and Morality in Global Perspective*. Durham, NC: Duke University Press.

Adkins, Julie. 2009. "Beyond Development and 'Projects': The Globalization of Solidarity." In *Bridging the Gaps: Faith-Based Organizations, Neoliberalism, and Development in Latin America and the Caribbean*, edited by Tara Haffernan, Julie Adkins, and Laurie Occhipinti, 103–18. Lanham, MD: Rowman and Littlefield.

Agg, Catherine. 2006. "Trends in Government Support for Non-governmental Organisations: Is the 'Golden Age' of the NGO Behind Us?" Paper Number 23. Civil Society and Social Movements. United Nations Research Institute for Social Development. http://unpan1.un.org/intradoc/groups/public/documents/un-dpadm/unpan040102.pdf.

Almeyda, Gloria, and Brian A. Branch. 1998. "Microfinance in Guatemala: The Case of Credit Unions." Research Monograph Series 13. Madison, WI: World Council of Credit Unions.

Alvarez, Sonia E. 1999. "Advocating Feminism: The Latin American Feminist NGO 'Boom.'" *International Feminist Journal of Politics* 1 (2): 181–209.

———. 2009. "Beyond NGO-ization? Reflections from Latin America." *Development* 52 (2): 175–84.

Anderson, C. Leigh, and Laura Locker. 2002. "Micro Credit, Social Capital and Common Pool Resources." *World Development* 30 (1): 95–105.

Andrews, Matt. 2013. *The Limits of Institutional Reform in Development: Changing Rules for Realistic Solutions*. Cambridge: Cambridge University Press.

Angelucci, Manuela, Dean Karlan, and Jonathan Zinman. 2014. "Microcredit Impacts: Evidence from a Randomized Microcredit Program Placement Experiment by Compartamos Banco." National Bureau of Economic Research. http://www.nber.org/papers/w19827.

Appadurai, Arjun. 2004. "The Capacity to Aspire: Culture and the Terms of Recognition." In *Culture and Public Action: A Cross-Disciplinary Dialogue on Development*

Policy, edited by Michael Walton and Viayendra Roa, 59–84. Washington, D.C.:
World Bank Publications.

Apthorpe, Cris. 1997. "Writing Development Policy and Policy Analysis Plain or
Clear: On Language, Genre and Power." In *Anthropology of Policy: Critical Perspectives on Governance and Power*, edited by Cris Shore and Susan Wright,
43–58. London: Routledge.

Arce, Alberto, and Norman Long. 1993. "Bridging Two Worlds: An Ethnography of
Bureaucrat-Peasant Relations in Western Mexico." In *An Anthropological Critique
of Development: The Growth of Ignorance*, edited by Mark Hobart, 179–208. London: Routledge.

Argyris, Chris. 1991. "Teaching Smart People How to Learn." *Harvard Business Review Reflections* 4 (2): 4–14.

Argyris, Chris, and David A. Schön. 1978. *Organizational Learning: A Theory of Action Perspective*. Reading, MA: Addison-Wesley.

Armendáriz, Edna, Roberto de Michele, Osmel Manzano, and Pedro Martel. 2013.
"Reflexiones Sobre El Desarrollo de La Economía Rural de Guatemala." Washington, D.C.: Interamerican Development Bank.

Auyero, Javier. 2012. *Patients of the State: The Politics of Waiting in Argentina*.
Durham, NC: Duke University Press.

AVANCSO-IDESAC. 1990. *ONGs, Sociedad Civil Y Estado En Guatemala: Elementos
Para El Debate*. Guatemala: Asociación para el Avance de las Ciencias Sociales
en Guatemala-Instituto para el Desarrollo Económico Social de America Central
(AVANCSO-IDESAC).

Aviva, Ron. 1999. "NGOs in Community Health Insurance Schemes: Examples from
Guatemala and the Philippines." *Social Science and Medicine* 48 (7): 939–50.

Azpuru, Dinorah, Juan Pablo Pira, and Mitchell A. Seligson. 2006. "The Political Culture of Democracy in Guatemala: 2006." *Latin American Public Opinion Project
(LAPOP) Democracy Audit*, directed by Mitchell Seligson, with assistance from the
United States Agency for International Development (USAID). Accessed June 3,
2009. http://www.vanderbilt.edu/lapop/guatemala/2006-politicalculture.pdf.

Babb, Florence E. 1996. "After the Revolution: Neoliberal Policy and Gender in Nicaragua." *Latin American Perspectives* 23 (1): 27–48.

Baillie Smith, Matt, and Katy Jenkins. 2012. "Existing at the Interface: Indian NGO
Activists as Strategic Cosmopolitans." *Antipode* 44 (3): 640–62.

Bakewell, Oliver and Hannah Warren. 2005. *Sharing Faith with Donors: Does It
Make a Difference?* Oxford, UK: International NGO Training and Research Centre
(INTRAC).

Banerjee, Abhijit, Esther Duflo, Rachel Glennerster, and Cynthia Kinnan. 2013. "The
Miracle of Microfinance? Evidence from a Randomized Evaluation." Accessed
October 25, 2016. http://www.nber.org/papers/w18950.

Banks, Nicola, and David Hulme. 2012. "The Role of NGOs and Civil Society in
Development and Poverty Reduction." *University of Manchester Brooks World
Poverty Institute*, Working Paper no. 171. Accessed October 25, 2016. http://civil20
.org/upload/iblock/9b1/rolengo.pdf.

Bateman, Milford. 2013. "The Age of Microfinance: Destroying Latin American Economies from the Bottom Up." *Ola Financiera* 15. http://www.networkideas .org/focus/sep2013/Microfinance.pdf.

Bebbington, Anthony. 2004. "NGOs and Uneven Development: Geographies of Development Intervention." *Progress in Human Geography* 28 (6): 725–45.

Bebbington, Anthony, Samuel Hickey, and Diana C. Mitlin. 2008. *Can NGOs Make a Difference? The Challenge of Development Alternatives.* London: Zed Books.

Beck, Erin. 2014. "Countering Convergence: Agency and Diversity among Guatemalan NGOs." *Latin American Politics and Society* 56 (2): 141–62.

———. 2016. "Repopulating Development: An Agent-based Approach to Studying Development Interventions." *World Development* 80 (April): 19–32.

Beck, Erin, Michael Aguilera, and James Schintz. Forthcoming. "Who Benefits? The Interactional Determinants of Microfinance's Varied Effects."

Beck, Erin, and Smitha Radhakrishnan. Forthcoming. "Tracing Microfinancial Value Chains: Beyond the Impasse of Debt and Development." *Sociology of Development.*

Bending, Tim, and Sergio Rosenda. 2006. "Rethinking the Mechanics of the 'Anti-Politics Machine.'" In *Development Brokers and Translators: The Ethnography of Aid and Agencies,* edited by David Mosse and David Lewis, 217–38. Bloomfield, CT: Kumarian.

Berger, Susan A. 2006. *Guatemaltecas: The Women's Movement, 1986–2003.* Austin: University of Texas Press.

Berk, Gerald. 2009. "How People Experience and Change Institutions: A Field Guide to Creative Syncretism." *Theory and Society* 38 (6): 543–80.

Bernal, Victoria, and Inderpal Grewal, eds. 2014. *Theorizing NGOs: States, Feminisms, and Neoliberalism.* Durham, NC: Duke University Press.

Bernasek, Alexandra. 2003. "Banking on Social Change: Grameen Bank Lending to Women." *International Journal of Politics, Culture, and Society* 16 (3): 369–84.

Bierschenk, Thomas. 1988. "Development Projects as Arenas of Negotiation for Strategic Groups: A Case Study from Bénin." *Sociologia Ruralis* 28 (2–3): 146–60.

———. 2008. "Anthropology and Development: An Historicizing and Localizing Approach." Institut Für Ethnologie Und Afrikastudien Working Paper, no. 87a.

———. 2014. "From the Anthropology of Development to the Anthropology of Global Social Engineering." *Zeitschrift Für Ethnologie* 139: 73–98.

Bierschenk, Thomas, Georg Elwert, and Dirk Kohnert. 1993. "The Long-term Effects of Development Aid: Empirical Studies in Rural West Africa." *Economics: Biannual Journal of the Institute for Scientific Co-Operation* 47 (1): 83–111.

Blee, Kathleen M. 1991. *Women of the Klan: Racism and Gender in the 1920s.* Berkeley: University of California Press.

———. 2003. *Inside Organized Racism: Women in the Hate Movement.* Berkeley: University of California Press.

Blumberg, Rae Lesser. 1995. "Gender, Microenterprise, Performance, and Power." In *Women in the Latin American Development Process,* edited by Christine E. Bose and Edna Acosta-Belén, 194–226. Philadelphia: Temple University Press.

———. 2001. "'We Are Family': Gender, Microenterprise, Family Work, and Well-

Being in Ecuador and the Dominican Republic—with Comparative Data from Guatemala, Swaziland, and Guinea-Bissau." *History of Family* 6: 271–99.

Bob, Clifford. 2001. "Marketing Rebellion: Insurgent Groups, International Media, and NGO Support." *International Politics* 38 (September): 311–34.

Booth, John A. 1984. "'Trickle-up' Income Redistribution and Development in Central America During the 1960s and 1970s." In *The Gap between Rich and Poor: Contending Perspectives on the Political Economy of Development*, edited by Mitchell A. Seligson, 351–65. Boulder, CO: Westview.

Bornstein, Erica. 2005. *The Spirit of Development: Protestant NGOs, Morality, and Economics in Zimbabwe*. Stanford, CA: Stanford University Press.

Boserup, Ester. 1970. *Woman's Role in Economic Development*. London: Earthscan.

Bourdieu, Pierre. 1990. *The Logic of Practice*. Translated by Richard Nice. Stanford, CA: Stanford University Press.

Brau, James C., Shon Hiatt, and Warner Woodworth. 2009. "Evaluating Impacts of Microfinance Institutions Using Guatemalan Data." *Managerial Finance* 35 (12): 953–74.

Brigg, Morgan. 2001. "Empowering NGOs: The Microcredit Movement through Foucault's Notion of Dispositif." *Alternatives: Global, Local, Political* 26 (3): 233–58.

Brodzinsky, Sibylia. 2013. "Guatemala's Sugar Cane Land Rush Anything but Sweet for Corn Growers." *Guardian*, June 26. http://www.theguardian.com/global-development/2013/jun/26/guatemala-sugar-land-corn.

Brysk, Alison. 2000. "Democratizing Civil Society in Latin America." *Journal of Democracy* 11 (3): 151–65.

Bucheli, Marcelo. 2003. "United Fruit Company in Latin America." In *Banana Wars: Power, Production, and History in the Americas*, edited by Steve Striffler and Mark Moberg, 80–100. Durham, NC: Duke University Press.

Buvinic, Mayra. 1983. "Women's Issues in Third World Poverty: A Policy Analysis." In *Women and Poverty in the Third World*, edited by Mayra Buvinic, Margaret A. Lycette, and Paul McGreevey, 14–33. Baltimore, MD: Johns Hopkins University Press.

Canellas, Andrew A., and Cressida S. McKean. 1989. "Microenterprise Stock-Taking: Guatemala." A.I.D. Evaluation Occasional Paper 22. U.S. Agency for International Development.

Carey, David, Jr. 2009. "Guatemala's Green Revolution: Synthetic Fertilizer, Public Health, and Economic Autonomy in the Mayan Highland." *Agricultural History* 83 (3): 283–322.

Carroll, Thomas F. 1992. *Intermediary NGOs: The Supporting Link in Development*. West Hartford, CT: Kumarian.

CEIDEC. 1993. *Guatemala ONG's y Desarrollo: El Caso del Altiplano Central*. Mexico: Centro de Estudios Integrados de Desarrollo Comunal (CEIDEC).

CGAP (Consultative Group to Assist the Poor). 2006. "Good Practice Guidelines for Funders of Microfinance: Microfinance Consensus Guidelines." Washington, D.C.: CGAP. Accessed September 24, 2013. https://www.cgap.org/sites/default

/files/CGAP-Consensus-Guidelines-Good-Practice-Guidelines-for-Funders-of
-Microfinance-Oct-2006.pdf.

Chambers, Robert. 1983. *Rural Development: Putting the Last First*. London:
Routledge.

———. 2010. "Paradigms, Poverty and Adaptive Pluralism." Institute of Development
Studies (IDS) Working Paper, no. 344 (July).

Chase-Dunn, Christopher. 2000. "Guatemala in the Global System." *Journal of Inter-
american Studies and World Affairs* 42 (4): 109–26.

Chinchilla, Norma S. 1977. "Industrialization, Monopoly Capitalism, and Women's
Work Guatemala." *Signs* 3 (1): 38–56.

Chomsky, Noam. 2015. *Year 501: The Conquest Continues*. Chicago: Haymarket Books.

Christen, Robert Peck. 2001. "Commercialization and Mission Drift." CGAP Occasional Paper No. 5 (January). http://documents.worldbank.org/curated/en
/122331468265801032/pdf/334620rev0ENGLISH0OccasionalPaper105.pdf.

Clark, John. 1991. *Democratizing Development: The Role of Voluntary Organizations*.
West Hartford, CT: Kumarian.

Clarke, Gerard. 1998. "Non-governmental Organizations (NGOs) and Politics in the
Developing World." *Political Studies* 46: 36–52.

———. 2007. "Agents of Transformation? Donors, Faith-based Organisations and
International Development." *Third World Quarterly* 28 (1): 77–96.

———. 2010. "Faith Matters: Development and the Complex World of Faith-Based
Organisations." In *Poverty: Malaise of Development*, edited by Ann Boran,
198–232. Chester, UK: Chester Academic Press.

Clarke, Gerard, and Michael Jennings. 2008. "Introduction." In *Development, Civil
Society, and Faith-based Organizations*, edited by Gerald Clarke and Michael Jennings, 1–16. New York: Palgrave Macmillan.

Copeland, Nicholas. 2012. "Greening the Counterinsurgency: The Deceptive Effects
of Guatemala's Rural Development Plan of 1970: Greening the Guatemalan Counterinsurgency." *Development and Change* 43 (4): 975–98.

———. 2015. "Regarding Development: Governing Indian Advancement in Revolu-
tionary Guatemala." *Economy and Society* 44 (3): 418–44.

Copestake, James. 2002. "Inequality and the Polarizing Impact of Microcredit: Evidence from Zambia's Copperbelt." *Journal of International Development* 14 (6):
743–55.

Copestake, James, Sonia Bhalotra, and Susan Johnson. 2001. "Assessing the Impact
of Microcredit: A Zambian Case Study." *Journal of Development Studies* 37 (4):
81–100.

Cornia, Giovanni Andrea, Richard Jolly, and Frances Stewart, eds. 1987. *Adjustment
with a Human Face: Protecting the Vulnerable and Promoting Growth*. Vol. 1. New
York: Oxford University Press.

Cornwall, Andrea, and Karen Brock. 2005. "'Poverty Reduction,' 'Participation' and
'Empowerment' in Development Policy." Programme paper no. 10: Overarching
Concerns. United Nations Research Institute for Social Development. Accessed

January 29, 2014. http://www.unrisd.org/80256B3C005BCCF9/(httpAuxPages)/F25D3D6D27E2A1ACC12570CB002FFA9A/$file/cornwall.pdf.

Cowen, Michael, and Robert W. Shenton. 1996. *Doctrines of Development*. Abingdon, UK: Taylor and Francis.

Craig, David, and Doug Porter. 1997. "Framing Participation: Development Projects, Professionals, and Organisations." In *Development and Patronage*, 229–36. Oxford, UK: Oxfam.

Cultural Survival. 2010. "Poisoned by Pesticides: Honduras, Guatemala, Venezuela, Iraq." February 4. http://www.culturalsurvival.org/publications/cultural-survival-quarterly/honduras/poisoned-pesticides-honduras-guatemala-venezuela-i.

Daley-Harris, Sam. 2009. "The State of the Microcredit Summit Campaign Report 2009." Washington, D.C.: Microcredit Summit Campaign. Accessed October 25, 2016. http://www.microcreditsummit.org/resource/48/state-of-the-microcredit-summit.html.

Davidson, E. Jane. 2006. "The RCTs-Only Doctrine: Brakes on the Acquisition of Knowledge." *Journal of Multidisciplinary Evaluation* 6: ii–v.

DeHart, Monica. 2009. "Fried Chicken or Pop? Redefining Development and Ethnicity in Totonicapán." *Bulletin of Latin American Research* 28 (1): 63–82.

De Herdt, Tom, and Johan Bastiaensen. 2007. "Aid as an Encounter at the Interface: The Complexity of the Global Fight against Poverty." *Third World Quarterly* 25 (5): 871–85.

Dicklitch, Susan, and Heather Rice. 2004. "The Mennonite Central Committee (MCC) and Faith-based NGO Aid to Africa." *Development in Practice* 14 (5): 660–72.

Duffy-Tumasz, Amelia. 2009. "Paying Back Comes First: Why Repayment Means More than Business in Rural Senegal." *Gender and Development* 17 (2): 243–54.

Ebrahim, Alnoor. 2003. *NGOs and Organizational Change: Discourse, Reporting, and Learning*. Cambridge: Cambridge University Press.

Edwards, Michael. 1989. "The Irrelevance of Development Studies." *Third World Quarterly* 11 (1): 116–35.

———. 2010. *Small Change Why Business Won't Save the World*. San Francisco: Berrett-Koehler.

Edwards, Michael, and David Hulme. 1995. "NGO Performance and Accountability: An Introduction and Overview." In *NGO Performance and Accountability in the Post–Cold War World: Beyond the Magic Bullet*, edited by Michael Edwards and David Hulme, 3–16. Oxon: Earthscan.

Escobar, Arturo. 1995. *Encountering Development: The Making and Unmaking of the Third World*. Princeton, NJ: Princeton University Press.

Esteva, Gustavo. 1992. "Development." In *The Development Dictionary: A Guide to Knowledge as Power*, edited by Wolfgang Sachs, 6–25. New York: Zed Books.

Eyben, Rosalind. 2007. "Labeling People for Aid." In *The Power of Labelling: How People Are Categorized and Why It Matters*, edited by Joy Moncrieffe and Rosalind Eyben, 33–47. London: Earthscan.

Fairhead, James, and Melissa Leach. 1997. "Webs of Power and the Construction of Environmental Policy Problems: Forest Loss in Guinea." In *Discourses of Develop-

ment: Anthropological Perspectives, edited by R. D. Grillo and R. L. Stirrat, 35–57. Oxford: Bloomsbury Academic.

Faulkner, William N. 2014. "A Critical Analysis of a Randomized Controlled Trial Evaluation in Mexico: Norm, Mistake or Exemplar?" *Evaluation* 20 (2): 230–43.

Fechter, Anne-Meike, and Heather Hindman. 2011. *Inside the Everyday Lives of Development Workers: The Challenges and Futures of Aidland.* Sterling, VA: Kumarian.

Ferguson, James. 1994. *The Anti-Politics Machine: Development, Depoliticization, and Bureaucratic Power in Lesotho.* Minneapolis: University of Minnesota Press.

Fischer, Edward F. 1996. "Induced Culture Change as a Strategy for Socioeconomic Development: The Pan-Maya Movement in Guatemala." In *Maya Cultural Activism in Guatemala*, edited by Edward F. Fischer and R. McKenna Brown, 51–73. Austin: University of Texas Press.

Fisher, Julie. 1993. *The Road from Rio: Sustainable Development and the Nongovernmental Movement in the Third World.* Westport, CT: Praeger.

Fortun, Kim. 2001. *Advocacy after Bhopal: Environmentalism, Disaster, New Global Orders.* Chicago: University of Chicago Press.

Foucault, Michel. 1980. *Power/Knowledge: Selected Interviews and Other Writings 1972–1978.* Edited by Colin Gordon. New York: Pantheon.

Fox, Renée C. 2014. *Doctors Without Borders: Humanitarian Quests, Impossible Dreams of Médecins Sans Frontières.* Baltimore: Johns Hopkins University Press.

Fraser, Nancy. 1990. "Rethinking the Public Sphere: A Contribution to the Critique of Actually Existing Democracy." *Social Text* 25/26: 56–80.

Freire, Paulo. 1970. *Pedagogy of the Oppressed.* New York: Continuum.

Fundación Namaste Guatemaya. n.d. "Fundación Namaste Guatemaya: The Namaste Business Development Program for NGOs and MFIs."

Gareau, Brian J. 2012. "Worlds Apart: A Social Theoretical Exploration of Local Networks, Natural Actors, and Practitioners of Rural Development in Southern Honduras." *Sustainability* 4 (12): 1596–1618.

Garrard-Burnett, Virginia. 1989. "Protestantism in Rural Guatemala, 1872–1954." *Latin American Research Review* 24 (2): 127–42.

———. 1998. *Protestantism in Guatemala: Living in the New Jerusalem.* Austin: University of Texas Press.

———. 2004. "God Was Already Here When Columbus Arrived: Inculturation Theology and the Mayan Movement in Guatemala." In *Resurgent Voices in Latin America: Indigenous Peoples, Political Mobilization, and Religious Change*, edited by Edward L. Cleary and Timothy J. Steigenga, 125–53. New Brunswick, NJ: Rutgers University Press.

Giddens, Anthony. 1984. *The Constitution of Society: Outline of the Theory of Structuration.* Cambridge, UK: Polity Press.

Gow, David D. 2008. *Countering Development: Indigenous Modernity and the Moral Imagination.* Durham, NC: Duke University Press.

Graham, Robert E. 1997. *50–50 at 50: Going Just Beyond!* Carmel, CA: Pacific Rim Publishers.

Grandia, Liza. 2012. *Enclosed: Conservation, Cattle, and Commerce among the Q'eqchi' Maya Lowlanders*. Seattle: University of Washington Press.

Gutierrez, Roberto. 1990. "The FUNDAP/Momostenango Project: A Strategy for Development Promoted by the Private Sector (The Guatemala Case)." In *The Other Policy: The Influence of Policies on Technology Choice and Small Enterprise Development*, edited by Frances Stewart, Henk Thomas, and Ton de Wilde. London: Intermediate Technology Publications.

Haffernan, Tara. 2007. "Finding Faith in Development: Religious Non-governmental Organizations (NGOs) in Argentina and Zimbabwe." *Anthropological Quarterly* 80 (3): 887–96.

Hale, Charles R. 2006. *Más Que Un Indio (More than an Indian): Racial Ambivalence and Neoliberal Multiculturalism in Guatemala*. Santa Fe, NM: School of American Research Press.

Haque, M. Shamsul. 2002. "The Changing Balance of Power between the Government and NGOs in Bangladesh." *International Political Science Review* 23 (4): 411–35.

Hart, Gillian. 2001. "Progress Reports Development Critiques in the 1990s: Culs de Sac and Promising Paths." *Progress in Human Geography* 25 (4): 649–58.

Hashemi, Syed M., Sidney Ruth Schuler, and Ann P. Riley. 1996. "Rural Credit Programs and Women's Empowerment in Bangladesh." *World Development* 24 (4): 635–53.

Hearn, Julie. 2002. "The 'Invisible' NGO: US Evangelical Missions in Kenya." *Journal of Religion in Africa* 32 (1): 32–60.

Hemment, Julie. 2007. *Empowering Women in Russia: Activism, Aid, and NGOs*. Bloomington: Indiana University Press.

Hermes, Niels, and Robert Lensink. 2007. "The Empirics of Microfinance: What Do We Know?" *Economic Journal* 117 (517): F1–10.

Herrera Castillo, Carlos Enrique. 2003. "Guatemala: Analysis of the Lending and Credit Reporting Systems in the Formal and Agricultural Sectors." In *Credit Bureaus and the Rural Microfinance Sector: Peru, Guatemala, and Bolivia*, by Alain De Janvry et al., 54–88. Accessed April 6, 2015. http://crsps.net/wp-content/downloads/BASIS/Inventoried%202.27/13-2003-7-115.pdf.

Hiatt, Shon R., and Warner P. Woodworth. 2006. "Alleviating Poverty through Microfinance: Village Banking Outcomes in Central America." *Social Science Journal* 43 (3): 471–77.

Hilhorst, Dorothea. 2003. *The Real World of NGOs: Discourses, Diversity and Development*. London: Zed Books.

Hirschman, Albert O. 1967. *Development Projects Observed*. Washington, D.C.: Brookings Institution.

———. 1970. *Exit, Voice, and Loyalty: Responses to Decline in Firms, Organizations, and States*. Cambridge, MA: Harvard University Press.

———. 2002. *Shifting Involvements: Private Interest and Public Action*. Princeton, NJ: Princeton University Press.

Hofer, Katharina. 2003. "The Role of Evangelical NGOs in International Development: A Comparative Case Study of Kenya and Uganda." *Afrika Spectrum* 38 (3): 375–98.

Hoksbergen, Roland, and Noemi Espinosa Madrid. 2000. "The Evangelical Church and the Development of Neoliberal Society: A Study of the Role of the Evangelical Church and Its NGOs in Guatemala and Honduras." *Peace Research Abstracts* 37 (4): 37–52.

Hulme, David, and Michael Edwards. 1997. *NGOs, States and Donors: Too Close for Comfort (International Political Economy)*. New York: St. Martin's.

Illich, Ivan. 1997. "Development as Planned Poverty." In *The Post-Development Reader*, edited by Majid Rahnema and Victoria Bawtree, 94–102. London: Zed Books.

Immerman, Richard H. 1980. "Guatemala as Cold War History." *Political Science Quarterly* 95 (4): 629–53.

Instituto Nacional de Guatemala. 2009. "Census Data." Guatemala City: Instituto Nacional de Guatemala (INE).

Inter-American Development Bank. 2012. "Guatemala. The Bank's Country Strategy with Guatemala 2012–2016." Inter-American Development Bank. Accessed July 4, 2013. http://idbdocs.iadb.org/wsdocs/getdocument.aspx?docnum=37366389.

Jaquette, Jane S. 1985. "Women, Population and Food: An Overview of the Issues." In *Women as Food Producers in Developing Countries*, edited by Jamie Monson and Marion Kalb, 1–10. Los Angeles: University of California Press.

Jaquette, Jane S., and Kathleen A. Staudt. 1988. "Politics, Population and Gender: A Feminist Analysis of US Population Policy in the Third World." In *The Political Interests of Gender: Developing Theory and Research with a Feminist Face*, edited by Kathleen B. Jones and Anna G. Jonasdottir, 214–33. London: Sage.

Kabeer, Naila. 1994. *Reversed Realities: Gender Hierarchies in Development Thought*. London: Verso.

———. 2001. "Conflicts over Credit: Re-evaluating the Empowerment Potential of Loans to Women in Rural Bangladesh." *World Development* 29 (1): 63–84.

———. 2004. "Social Exclusion: Concepts, Findings, and Implications for the MDGS." Institute of Development Studies.

———. 2011. "Between Affiliation and Autonomy: Navigating Pathways of Women's Empowerment and Gender Justice in Rural Bangladesh." *Development and Change* 42 (2): 499–528.

Kabeer, Naila, and United Nations. 2009. *Women's Control over Economic Resources and Access to Financial Resources, Including Microfinance: 2009 World Survey on the Role of Women in Development*. New York: United Nations.

Karim, Lamia. 2011. *Microfinance and Its Discontents: Women in Debt in Bangladesh*. Minneapolis: University of Minnesota Press.

Karlan, Dean, and Jonathan Zinman. 2014. "Measuring the Impact of Microcredit in the Philippines." *Abdul Latif Jameel Poverty Action Lab*. Accessed March 20, 2014. http://www.povertyactionlab.org/evaluation/measuring-impact-microcredit-philippines.

Keating, Christine, Claire Rasmussen, and Pooja Rishi. 2010. "The Rationality of

Empowerment: Microcredit, Acumulation by Dispossession, and the Gendered Economy." *Signs* 36 (1): 153–76.

Khandker, Shahidur. 1998. *Fighting Poverty with Microcredit: Experience in Bangladesh*. New York: Oxford University Press for the World Bank.

Khavul, Susanna, Helmuth Chavez, and Garry D. Bruton. 2013. "When Institutional Change Outruns the Change Agent: The Contested Terrain of Entrepreneurial Microfinance for Those in Poverty." *Journal of Business Venturing* 28 (1): 30–50.

Kilby, Patrick. 2006. "Accountability for Empowerment: Dilemmas Facing Non-governmental Organizations." *World Development* 34 (6): 951–63.

Kimberly, John R. 1979. "Issues in the Creation of Organizations: Initiation, Innovation and Institutionalization." *Academy of Management Journal* 22: 437–57.

Kimberly, John R., and Hamid Bouchikhi. 1995. "The Dynamics of Organizational Development and Change: How the Past Shapes the Present and Constrains the Future." *Organization Science* 6 (1): 9–18.

Korf, Benedikt. 2006. "Dining with Devils? Ethnographic Enquiries into the Conflict-Development Nexus in Sri Lanka." *Oxford Development Studies* 34 (1): 47–64.

Korten, David C. 1990. *Getting to the 21st Century: Voluntary Action and the Global Agenda (Kumarian Press Library of Management for Development)*. West Hartford, CT: Kumarian.

Krause, Monika. 2014. *The Good Project: Humanitarian Relief NGOs and the Fragmentation of Reason*. Chicago: University of Chicago Press.

Lairap-Fonderson, Josephine. 2002. "The Disciplinary Power of Micro Credit." In *Rethinking Empowerment: Gender and Development in a Global/Local World*, edited by Jane L. Parpart, Shirin Rai, and Kathleen A. Staudt, 182–98. London: Routledge.

Latour, Bruno. 2007. *Reassembling the Social: An Introduction to Actor-Network Theory*. Oxford: Oxford University Press.

Lawrence, Felicity. 2011. "Guatemala Pays High Price for Global Food System Failings." *Guardian*, May 31. http://www.theguardian.com/global-development/poverty-matters/2011/may/31/global-food-crisis-guatemala-system-failure.

Leve, Lauren. 2014. "Failed Development and Rural Revolution in Nepal: Rethinking Subaltern Consciousness and Women's Empowerment." In *Theorizing NGOs: States, Feminisms, and Neoliberalism*, edited by Victoria Bernal and Inderpal Grewal, 50–92. Durham, NC: Duke University Press.

Levenson, Deborah. 2002. "Reactions to Trauma: The 1976 Earthquake in Guatemala." *International Labor and Working-Class History* 62 (1): 60–8.

Lewis, David. 1998. "Development NGOs and the Challenge of Partnership: Changing Relations between North and South." *Social Policy and Administration* 32 (5): 501–12.

———. 2008. "Using Life Histories in Social Policy Research: The Case of Third Sector/Public Sector Boundary Crossing." *Journal of Social Policy* 37 (4): 559–78.

———. 2009. "International Development and the 'Perpetual Present': Anthropological Approaches to the Re-historicization of Policy." *European Journal of Development Research* 21 (1): 32–46.

———. 2014. *Non-governmental Organizations, Management and Development.* 3rd ed. New York: Routledge.

Lewis, David, and Nazneen Kanji. 2009. *Nongovernmental Organizations and Development.* London: Routledge.

Lewis, David, and David Mosse. 2006. *Development Brokers and Translators: The Ethnography of Aid and Agencies.* Bloomfield, CT: Kumarian.

Li, Tania Murray. 2007. *The Will to Improve: Governmentality, Development, and the Practice of Politics.* Durham, NC: Duke University Press.

Lissner, Jørgen. 1977. *The Politics of Altruism: A Study of the Political Behavior of Voluntary Agencies.* Geneva: Lutheran World Federation.

Long, Norman. 2001. *Development Sociology: Actor Perspectives.* London: Routledge.

———. 2004. "Actors, Interfaces and Development Intervention: Meanings, Purposes and Powers." In *Development Intervention: Actor and Activity Perspectives*, edited by Tiina Kontinen, 14–36. Helsinki: Center for Activity Theory and Developmental Work Research and the Institute of Development Studies.

Long, Norman, and Ann Long, eds. 1992. *Battlefields of Knowledge.* London: Routledge.

Lund, Christian. 2001. "Precarious Democratization and Local Dynamics in Niger: Micro–Politics in Zinder." *Development and Change* 32 (5): 845–69.

Lynch, Cecilia. 2011. "Local and Global Influences on Islamic NGOs in Kenya." *Journal of Peacebuilding and Development* 6 (1): 21–34.

Macfarquhar, Neil. 2010. "Banks Making Big Profits from Tiny Loans." *New York Times*, April 13. http://microrate.com/media/downloads/2012/04/New-York-Times-Banks-Making-Big-Profits-From-Tiny-Loans-13-April-2010.pdf.

Maes, Jan P., and Larry R. Reed. 2012. "State of the Microcredit Summit Campaign Report 2012." Microcredit Summit Campaign. Accessed December 10, 2011. http://www.microcreditsummit.org/resource/46/state-of-the-microcredit-summit.html

Magno, Cathryn. 2002. *New Pythian Voices: Women Building Political Capital in NGOs in the Middle East.* New York: Routledge.

Markowitz, Lisa. 2001. "Finding the Field: Notes on the Ethnography of NGOs." *Human Organization* 60 (1): 40–6.

Markowitz, Lisa, and K.W. Tice. 2002. "Paradoxes of Professionalization: Parallel Dilemmas in Women's Organizations in the Americas." *Gender and Society* 16 (6): 941–58.

Marsland, Rebecca. 2006. "Community Participation the Tanzanian Way: Conceptual Contiguity or Power Struggle?" *Oxford Development Studies* 34 (1): 65–79.

Martin, David. 1990. *Tongues of Fire: The Explosion of Protestantism in Latin America.* Oxford, UK: Wiley-Blackwell.

Mayoux, Linda, and Maria Hartl. 2009. "Gender and Rural Microfinance: Reaching and Empowering Women." International Fund for Agricultural Development (IFAD). Accessed June 3, 2013. https://www.ifad.org/documents/10180/8551f293-2573-417d-908a-d1841359df57.

McAllister, Carlota, and Diane M. Nelson, eds. 2013. "Aftermath: Harvests of Violence and Histories of the Future." In *War by Other Means: Aftermath in Post-Genocide Guatemala*, 1–48. Durham, NC: Duke University Press.

McIntosh, Craig, and Bruce Wydick. 2005. "Competition and Microfinance." *Journal of Development Economics* 78: 271–98.

McKernan, Signe-Mary. 2002. "The Impact of Microcredit Programs on Self-Employment Profits: Do Noncredit Program Aspects Matter?" *Review of Economics and Statistics* 84 (1): 93–115.

Meyer, John W., and Brian Rowan. 1977. "Institutionalized Organizations: Formal Structure as Myth and Ceremony." *American Journal of Sociology* 83 (2): 340–63.

Michels, Robert. 1911. *Political Parties: A Sociological Study of the Oligarchical Tendencies of Modern Democracy*. New York: Hearst's International Library Co.

Micro Capital Institute. 2004. "The Commercialization of Microfinance in Latin America." Accessed October 25, 2016. http://www.microcapital.org/downloads/whitepapers/Latin.pdf.

Milian, Bayron, and Liza Grandia. 2013. "Inheriting Inequity: Land Administration and Agrarian Structure in Petén, Guatemala." Paper prepared for presentation at the Annual World Bank Conference on Land and Poverty, Washington, D.C., April.

Mix Market. 2013. "Cross-Market Analysis." Accessed November 11, 2016. http://www.mixmarket.org/.

Mohanty, Chandra T. 1991. "Cartographies of Struggle: Third World Women and the Politics of Feminism." In *Third World Women and the Politics of Feminism*, edited by Chandra T. Mohanty, Ann Russo, and Lourdes Torres, 1–50. Bloomington: Indiana University Press.

Moodie, Megan. 2013. "Microfinance and the Gender of Risk: The Case of Kiva.org." *Signs* 38 (2): 279–302.

Moser, Caroline. 1989. "Gender Planning in the Third World: Meeting Practical and Strategic Gender Needs." *World Development* 17 (11): 179–82.

Mosley, Paul. 2001. "Microfinace and Poverty in Bolivia." *Journal of Development Studies* 37 (4): 101–32.

Mosse, David. 2003. "The Making and Marketing of Participatory Development." In *A Moral Critique of Development: In Search of Global Responsibilities*, edited by Philip Quarles van Ufford and Ananta Kumar Giri, 43–75. London: Routledge.

———. 2005. *Cultivating Development: An Ethnography of Aid Policy and Practice*. London: Pluto.

———. 2013. "The Anthropology of International Development." *Annual Review of Anthropology* 42 (1): 227–46.

Mowles, Chris. 2013. "Evaluation, Complexity, Uncertainty: Theories of Change and Some Alternatives." In *Aid, NGOs and the Realities of Women's Lives: A Perfect Storm*, edited by Tina Wallace, Fenella Porter, and Mark Ralph-Bowman, 47–60. Warwickshire, UK: Practical Action.

Munson, Ziad W. 2008. *The Making of Pro-Life Activists: How Social Movement Mobilization Works*. Chicago: University of Chicago Press.

Murdock, Donna F. 2008. *When Women Have Wings: Feminism and Development in Medellín, Colombia*. Ann Arbor: University of Michigan Press.

Nader, Laura. 1974. "Up the Anthropologist—Perspectives Gained from Studying

Up." In *Reinventing Anthropology*, edited by Dell Hymes, 284–311. New York: Vintage.

Nauta, Weibe. 2006. "Ethnographic Research in a Non-governmental Organization: Revealing Strategic Translations through an Embedded Tale." In *Development Brokers and Translators: The Ethnography of Aid and Agencies*, edited by David Mosse and David Lewis, 149–72. Bloomfield, CT: Kumarian.

North, L. L. 1998. "Reflections on Democratization and Demilitarization in Central America." *Studies in Political Economy (Carleton University, Ontario)* 55: 155–72.

Nuñez, José Oscar Barrera. 2009. "Desires and Imagination: The Economy of Humanitarianism in Guatemala." In *Mayas in Postwar Guatemala: Harvest of Violence Revisited*, by Walter E. Little and Timothy J. Smith, 110–23. Tuscaloosa: University of Alabama Press.

Nussbaum, Martha C. 2001. *Women and Human Development: The Capabilities Approach (The Seeley Lectures)*. Cambridge: Cambridge University Press.

Occhipinti, Laurie A. 2005. *Acting on Faith: Religious Development Organizations in Northwestern Argentina*. Lanham, MD: Lexington Books.

Oglesby, Elizabeth. 2013. "'We're No Longer Dealing with Fools': Violence, Labor, and Governance on the South Coast." In *War by Other Means: Aftermath in Post-Genocide Guatemala*, edited by Carlota McAllister and Diane M. Nelson, 143–69. Durham, NC: Duke University Press.

Olivier de Sardan, Jean-Pierre. 2005. *Anthropology and Development: Understanding Comtemporary Social Change*. London: Zed Books.

O'Reilly, Kathleen. 2006. "Women Fieldworkers and the Politics of Participation." *Signs* 31 (4): 1075–98.

Otero, Maria. 1994. "The Role of Governments and Private Institutions in Addressing the Informal Sector in Latin America." In *Contrapunto: The Informal Sector Debate in Latin America*, edited by Cathy A. Rakowski, 177–98. New York: State University of New York Press.

Park, Albert F., and Ren Changqing. 2001. "Mircrofinance with Chinese Characteristics." *World Development* 29 (1): 39–62.

Paul, Samuel, and Arturo Israel. 1991. *Nongovernmental Organizations and the World Bank*. Washington, D.C.: World Bank.

Pawson, Ray. 2006. *Evidence-Based Policy: A Realist Perspective*. Thousand Oaks, CA: Sage.

Pearson, Ruth. 2007. "Reassessing Paid Work and Women's Empowerment: Lessons from the Global Economy." In *Feminisms in Development: Contradictions, Contestations and Challenges*, edited by Andrea Cornwall, Elizabeth Harrison, and Ann Whitehead, 201–13. London: Zed Books.

Petersen, Kurt. 1992. "Zones of Exploitation: Korean Investment on Guatemala." *Multinational Monitor*. Accessed April 22, 2015. http://www.multinationalmonitor .org/hyper/issues/1992/12/mm1292_10.html.

———. 1994. "The Maquila Revolution in Guatemala." In *Global Production: The Apparel Industry in the Pacific Rim*, edited by Edna Bonacich, Lucie Cheng, Norma

Chinchilla, Nora Hamilton, and Paul Ong. Philadelphia, PA: Temple University Press.

Philpot-Munson, J. Jailey. 2009. "Peace under Fire: Understanding Evangelical Resistance to the Peace Process in a Postwar Guatemalan Town." In *Mayas in Postwar Guatemala: Harvest of Violence Revisited*, edited by Walter E. Little and Timothy J. Smith, 42–53. Tuscaloosa: University of Alabama Press.

Pigg, Stacy Leigh. 1992. "Inventing Social Categories through Place: Social Representations and Development in Nepal." *Comparative Studies in Society and History* 34 (3): 491–513.

Pitt, Mark, and Shahidur R. Khandker. 1998. "The Impact of Group-Based Credit Programs on Poor Households in Bangladesh: Does the Gender of Participants Matter?" *Journal of Political Economy* 106 (5): 958–96.

Pitt, Mark, Shahidur R. Khandker, and World Bank. 1996. "Household and Intrahousehold Impact of the Grameen Bank and Similar Targeted Credit Programs in Bangladesh." Washington, D.C.: International Bank for Reconstruction and Development and the World Bank.

Pritchett, Lant, and Michael Woolcock. 2004. "Solutions When the Solution Is the Problem: Arraying the Disarray in Development." *World Development* 32 (2): 191–212.

Quarles van Ufford, Philip. 1993. "Knowledge and Ignorance in the Practices of Development Policy." In *An Anthropological Critique of Development: The Growth of Ignorance*, edited by Mark Hobart, 116–34. London: Routledge.

Rahman, Rushidan Islam. 1986. "Impact of Grameen Bank on the Situation of Poor Rural Women." Grameen Evaluation Project 1. BIDS Working Paper. Dhaka, Bangladesh: Institute of Development Studies.

Raxche' (Demetrio Rodríguez Guaján). 1996. "Maya Culture and the Politics of Development." In *Maya Cultural Activism in Guatemala*, edited by Edward F. Fischer and R. McKenna Brown, 74–88. Austin: University of Texas Press.

Richards, Paul. 1985. *Indigenous Agricultural Revolution: Ecology and Food Production in West Africa*. London: Hutchinson.

Richardson, David C., Barry L. Lennon, and Brian A. Branch. 1993. "Credit Unions Retooled: A Road Map for Financial Stabilisation." *World Council of Credit Unions, Madison*. Accessed July 12, 2013. https://www.woccu.org/documents /Monograph_1.

Riddell, Roger C. 2007. *Does Foreign Aid Really Work?* Oxford, UK: Oxford University Press.

Riles, Annelise. 2001. *The Network Inside Out*. Ann Arbor: University of Michigan Press.

Roberts, Adrienne. 2012. "Financial Crisis, Financial Firms . . . and Financial Feminism? The Rise of 'Transnational Business Feminism' and the Necessity of Marxist-Feminist IPE." *Socialist Studies* 8 (2): 85–108.

———. 2015. "The Political Economy of 'Transnational Business Feminism': Problematizing the Corporate-Led Gender Equality Agenda." *International Feminist Journal of Politics* 17 (2): 209–31.

Rohloff, Peter, Anne Kraemer Díaz, and Shom Dasgupta. 2011. "'Beyond Development': A Critical Appraisal of the Emergence of Small Health Care Non-governmental Organizations in Rural Guatemala." *Human Organization* 70 (4): 427–37.

Roodman, David. 2012. "Loans to Poor Rarely Transform Lives." *Journal Gazette*, March 16. http://ibankingondemand.com/2012/04/02/MicrofinanceLoansToPoor RarelyTransformLives.aspx.

Rooy, Alison Van. 1998. *Civil Society and the Aid Industry: The Politics and Promise*. London: Earthscan.

Rose, Nikolas, and Peter Miller. 1992. "Political Power Beyond the State: Problematics of Government." *British Journal of Sociology* 43 (2): 173–205.

Rossi, Benedetta. 2004. "Order and Disjuncture: Theoretical Shifts in the Anthropology of Aid and Development." *Current Anthropology* 45 (4): 556–60.

———. 2006. "Aid Policies and Recipient Strategies in Niger: Why Donors and Recipients Should Not Be Compartmentalized into Separate 'Worlds of Knowledge.'" In *Development Brokers and Translators: The Ethnography of Aid and Agencies*, edited by David Mosse and David Lewis, 27–50. Bloomfield, CT: Kumarian.

Rottenburg, Richard. 2009. *Far-Fetched Facts: A Parable of Development Aid*. Cambridge, MA: MIT Press.

Rowlands, Jo. 1997. *Questioning Empowerment: Working with Women in Honduras*. Oxford, UK: Oxfam.

Ruthrauff, John. 1998. "The Guatemalan Peace Process and the Role of the World Bank and Interamerican Development Bank." Paper presented at the 1998 Conference on Development & Democratization in Guatemala, March 26–28, Universidad del Valle, Guatemala.

Sachs, Wolfgang, ed. 1992. *The Development Dictionary: A Guide to Knowledge as Power*. London: Zed Books.

Samson, C. Mathews. 2007. *Re-enchanting the World: Maya Protestantism in the Guatemalan Highlands*. Tuscaloosa: University of Alabama Press.

Samson, C. Mathews. 2008. "From War to Reconciliation: Guatemalan Evangelicals and the Transition to Democracy, 1982-2001." In *Evangelical Christianity and Democracy in Latin America*, 63-96. Oxford: Oxford University Press.

Sanyal, Paromita. 2009. "From Credit to Collective Action: The Role of Microfinance in Promoting Women's Social Capital and Normative Influence." *American Sociological Review* 74 (4): 529–50.

Schäfer, Heinrich. 1991. *Church Identity between Repression and Liberation: The Presbyterian Church in Guatemala*. Translated by Craig Koslofsky. Geneva: World Alliance of Reformed Churches.

Schirmer, Jennifer. 1999. *The Guatemalan Military Project: A Violence Called Democracy*. Philadelphia: University of Pennsylvania Press.

Schlesinger, Stephen C, and Stephen Kinzer. 2005. *Bitter Fruit: The Story of the American Coup in Guatemala*. Cambridge, MA: Harvard University, David Rockefeller Center for Latin American Studies.

Schofer, Evan, and Ann Hironaka. 2005. "The Effects of World Society on Environmental Protection Outcomes." *Social Forces* 84 (1): 25–47.

Schön, Donald A. 1987. *Educating the Reflective Practitioner: Toward a New Design for Teaching and Learning in the Professions*. San Francisco: Jossey-Bass.

Schuller, Mark. 2012. *Killing with Kindness: Haiti, International Aid, and NGOs*. New Brunswick, NJ: Rutgers University Press.

Selznick, Philip. 1984. *Leadership in Administration: A Sociological Interpretation*. Rep. ed. Berkeley: University of California Press.

Sen, Amartya. 1999. *Development as Freedom*. New York: Knopf.

Sen, Gita, and Caren Grown. 1987. *Development, Crises and Alternative Visions: Third World Women's Perspectives*. New York: Monthly Review Press.

Sharma, Aradhana. 2014. "The State and Women's Empowerment in India: Paradoxes and Politics." In *Theorizing NGOs: States, Feminisms, and Neoliberalism*, edited by Victoria Bernal and Inderpal Grewal, 93–114. Durham, NC: Duke University Press.

Shore, Cris, and Susan Wright. 1997. "Policy: A New Field of Anthropology." In *Anthropology of Policy: Critical Perspectives on Governance and Power*, edited by Cris Shore and Susan Wright, 3–39. London: Routledge.

Silliman, Jael. 1999. "Expanding Civil Society: Shrinking Political Spaces—The Case of Women's Nongovernmental Organizations." *Social Politics: International Studies in Gender, State and Society* 6 (1): 23–53.

Sletto, Bjørn. 2008. "The Knowledge That Counts: Institutional Identities, Policy Science, and the Conflict over Fire Management in the Gran Sabana, Venezuela." *World Development* 36 (10): 1938–55.

Smith, Carol A. 1990. "The Militarization of Civil Society in Guatemala: Economic Reorganization as a Continuation of War." *Latin American Perspectives* 17 (4): 8–41.

Snow, David A., E. Burke Rochford Jr., Steven K. Worden, and Robert D. Benford. 1986. "Frame Alignment Processes, Micromobilization, and Movement Participation." *American Sociological Review* 51 (4): 464–81.

Social Venture Network. n.d. "Who We Are." *Social Venture Network*. Accessed September 13, 2010. http://svn.org/.

Soss, Nancy. 2005. "Making Clients and Citizens: Welfare Policy as a Source of Status, Belief, and Action." In *Deserving and Entitled: Social Constructions and Public Policy*, edited by Anne L. Schneider and Helen M. Ingram, 291–328. Albany: State University of New York Press.

Sridhar, Archana. 2007. "Tax Reform and Promoting a Culture of Philanthropy: Guatemala's Third Sector in an Era of Peace." *Fordham International Law Journal* 31 (1): 186–229.

Staudt, Kathleen. 1986. "Women, Development and the State: On the Theoretical Impasse." *Development and Change* 7: 325–33.

Sundberg, Juanita. 1998. "NGO Landscapes in the Maya Biosphere Reserve, Guatemala." *Geographical Review* 88 (3): 388–412.

Superintendencia de Bancos, Guatemala. 2011. "Sector Microfinanzas: Análisis de Sectores Económicos." Guatemala.

Swidler, Ann. 1986. "Culture in Action: Symbols and Strategies." *American Sociological Review* 51 (April): 273–86.

Swidler, Ann, and Susan Cotts Watkins. 2009. "'Teach a Man to Fish': The Sustainability Doctrine and Its Social Consequences." *World Development* 37 (7): 1182–96.

Taylor, Marcus. 2012. "The Antinomies of 'Financial Inclusion': Debt, Distress and the Workings of Indian Microfinance." *Journal of Agrarian Change* 12 (4): 601–10.

Thekaekara, Stan. 2013. "Development from the Ground: A Worm's Eye View." In *Aid, NGOs and the Realities of Women's Lives: A Perfect Storm*, edited by Tina Wallace, Fenella Porter, and Mark Ralph-Bowman, 47–60. Warwickshire, UK: Practical Action.

Thorp, Rosemary, Corinne Caumartin, and George Gray-Molina. 2006. "Inequality, Ethnicity, Political Mobilisation and Political Violence in Latin America: The Cases of Bolivia, Guatemala and Peru." *Bulletin of Latin American Research* 25 (4): 453–80.

Tinker, Irene. 1976. "The Adverse Impact of Development on Women." In *Women and World Development*, edited by Irene Tinker and Ester Boserup, 22–34. Washington, D.C.: Overseas Development Council.

———. 1982. *Gender Equity in Development: A Policy Perspective*. Washington, D.C.: Equity Policy Center.

———. 1990. *Persistent Inequalities: Women and World Development*. Oxford: Oxford University Press.

Trefzger, Douglas. 2002. "Guatemala's 1952 Agrarian Reform Law: A Critical Reassessment." *International Social Science Review*, spring–summer. Accessed March 4, 2015. http://www.ditext.com/trefzger/agrarian.html.

Trinh, T. Minh-ha. 1989. *Women, Native, Other: Writing Postcoloniality and Feminism*. Bloomington: Indiana University Press.

UNDP. "Guatemala: Human Development Indicators." Accessed October 23, 2016. http://hdr.undp.org/en/countries/profiles/GTM

US State Department. 2006. "Country Report on Human Rights Practices, Guatemala." Accessed October 24, 2016. http://www.state.gov/j/drl/rls/hrrpt/2006/78893.htm

Venkatesan, Soumhya, and Thomas Yarrow. 2012. *Differentiating Development: Beyond an Anthropology of Critique*. New York: Berghahn.

Ver Beek, Kurt Alan. 2000. "Spirituality: A Development Taboo." *Development in Practice* 10 (1): 31–42.

Viterna, Jocelyn, and Cassandra Robertson. 2015. "New Directions for the Sociology of Development." *Annual Review of Sociology* 41: 243–69.

Warren, Kay B. 2001. "Pan-Mayanism and the Guatemalan Peace Process." In *Globalization on the Ground: Postbellum Guatemalan Democracy and Development*, edited by Christopher Chase-Dunn, Susanne Jonas, and Nelson Amaro, 145–66. Lanham, MD: Rowman and Littlefield.

Warren, Mark E. 2001. *Democracy and Association*. Princeton, NJ: Princeton University Press.

Watkins, Susan Cotts, Ann Swidler, and Thomas Hannan. 2012. "Outsourcing Social Transformation: Development NGOs as Organizations." *Annual Review of Sociology* 38 (1): 285–315.

Way, J. T. 2012. *The Mayan in the Mall: Globalization, Development, and the Making of Modern Guatemala.* Durham, NC: Duke University Press.

Wealth-X. 2013. "World Ultra Wealth Report: 2012–2013." Singapore: Wealth-X. Accessed October 21, 2016. http://wuwr.wealthx.com/Wealth-X%20and%20UBS%20World%20Ultra%20Wealth%20Report%202013.pdf.

Weber, Heloise. 2014. "Global Politics of Microfinancing Poverty in Asia: The Case of Bangladesh Unpacked." *Asian Studies Review* 38 (4): 544–63.

Weber, Max. 1921. *Economy and Society.* Translated by Guenther Roth and Claus Wittich. New York: Bedminster.

———. 1958. *From Max Weber: Essays in Sociology.* Translated by Hans Heinrich Gerth and C. Wright Mills. New York: Oxford University Press.

———. 1978. *Economy and Society: An Outline of Interpretive Sociology,* 2 vols. Edited by Guenther Roth and Claus Wittich. 4th ed. Berkeley: University of California Press.

Werker, Eric, and Faisal Z. Ahmed. 2008. "What Do Nongovernmental Organizations Do?" *Journal of Economic Perspectives* 22 (2): 72–92.

White, Sarah S. 1996. "Depoliticising Development: The Uses and Abuses of Participation." *Development in Practice* 6 (1): 6–15.

Wieringa, Saskia. 1992. "IBU or the Beast: Gender Interests in Two Indonesian Women's Organizations." *Feminist Review* 41 (summer): 98–113.

Wood, Elisabeth Jean. 2003. *Insurgent Collective Action and Civil War in El Salvador.* New York: Cambridge University Press.

World Bank. 2009. "Guatemala Poverty Assessment: Good Performance at Low Levels." Report No. 43920-GT. Accessed October 23, 2016. http://siteresources.worldbank.org/INTLACREGTOPPOVANA/Resources/GuatemalaPovertyAssessmentEnglish.pdf

———. 2012a. "Access to Electricity (% of population)." Accessed October 23, 2016. http://data.worldbank.org/indicator/EG.ELC.ACCS.ZS?locations=GT

———. 2012b. "Improved Water Source (% of population with access)." Accessed October 23, 2016. http://data.worldbank.org/indicator/SH.H2O.SAFE.ZS?locations=GT.

———. 2015. "GNI per capita, Atlas Method (current US$)." Accessed October 23, 2016. http://data.worldbank.org/indicator/NY.GNP.PCAP.CD?locations=GT.

World Bank Independent Evaluation Group. 2010. "World Bank Support to Land Administration and Land Redistribution in Central America." IEG Performance Assessment of Three Projects: El Salvador, Land Administration Project (Loan No. 3982), Guatemala, Land Administration Project (Loan No. 4415), Guatemala, Land Fund Project (Loan No. 4432) 55341. Washington, D.C.: World Bank.

World Food Programme. 2014. "Guatemala Overview." *World Food Programme.* Accessed March 2, 2015. http://www.wfp.org/countries/guatemala/overview.

Yarrow, Thomas. 2011. *Development beyond Politics: Aid, Activism and NGOs in Ghana*. Houndmills, UK: Palgrave Macmillan.

Ybarra, Megan. 2008. "Violent Visions of an Ownership Society: The Land Administration Project in Petén, Guatemala." *Land Use Policy* 26: 44–54.

———. 2011. "Privatizing the Tzuultaq'a? Private Property and Spiritual Reproduction in Post-War Guatemala." *Journal of Peasant Studies* 38 (4): 793–810.

INDEX

168–70; language issues, 205–6; men's participation, 183–84, 219; programs and topics, 2, 143–44, 146–47; promoter classes, 178–81, 184–85, 200–201; on self-esteem, 172–76; taught by religious organizations, 158–59; women's participation, 166–67, 178–79, 216–17

education, Namaste: assumptions about women and, 91–92, 216; attendance and participation, 102, 106–7, 124, 237n5; compared to the Fraternity, 163; fees, 80, 100; hierarchical relationships in, 101–5; one-on-one mentorship, 1, 93, 106–7, 113, 121; policy and model, 74–75, 77, 85, 101–2, 105; positive experiences with, 127–28; vocational training sessions, 105, 110–11, 114–16

empowerment: disempowerment and, 27, 170, 194, 197; NGOs and, 44, 47; women's, 3, 36, 40, 50–51, 62, 74, 78, 220

entrepreneurship: Namaste's attempts to create "good," 17, 26, 80, 93, 112–13, 116, 210; poverty and, 2, 49, 73; and self-help in Guatemala's history, 31, 52, 56–57, 220; women's identities and, 78, 108. *See also* social entrepreneurship

environmental sustainability, 3, 146–47, 194–96

ethnographies: comparative, 3, 5, 10; at development interfaces, 18, 225; long-term, 227–28; of NGOs and development interventions, 233n6; practical and ethical challenges of, 228–30

families, 125–26; marital relationships, 183–84; reproductive labor or roles, 3, 51, 57, 108, 190, 216

family economy, 162–63

famine, 32, 34

FAPE. *See* Fundación de Asistencia para la Pequeña Empresa

feminists, 36, 40, 45, 190; theories, 233n3

fertilizers: chemical, 32–33, 43, 61; organic, 2, 146, 194–95, 219

Fe y Alegría (Faith and Joy), 56, 98

Fontierras, 43

Ford Foundation, 32, 57–58

foreign investment, 30, 235n5; Korean investors, 41, 234n4

Foundation for International Community Assistance (FINCA), 50, 103, 236n1; village banks, 68, 69

Foundation for the Development of Socio-Economic Programs (FUNDAP), 53, 55, 56

Fraternidad de Presbiteriales Mayas (the Fraternity): board members, 154–55, 158, 176–78, 182; charismatic structure, 14, 152, 160, 176, 178, 194; founders and leaders, 137–40, 152, 160; goals and expectations, 140, 151–52, 163–64, 217–19; influence of directors, 152–55; information collection and evaluation, 155–56, 218, 229; local and religious networks, 157–59; management of women's behavior, 161, 164, 194–98, 207; official founding, 141–42; organizational structure, 14, 15, 26–27, 156–57; origins, 12–13, 26, 60, 134–35, 157; outcomes, 27, 160–61, 199–206, 212–14; successes, 222; women's participation in, 139–40, 145, 150, 165–67. *See also* beneficiaries, the Fraternity; education, the Fraternity; holistic development model; loan program, the Fraternity; policymakers, the Fraternity

Fraternity. *See* Fraternidad de Presbiteriales Mayas

Freedom from Hunger, 85, 92, 101, 117

free trade, 41–42

Fundación de Asistencia para la Pequeña Empresa (FAPE), 100; loan repayment enforcement, 114, 116–17, 118–20; small loan program, 94–95, 110

Fundación de Ayuda al Pueblo Indígena (FUNDAPI), 236n17

Fundación Genesis Empresarial (Genesis), 53, 55, 56, 95, 119

Fundación Namaste Guatemaya (Namaste): data management system, 77, 84, 86; goals, 76, 80, 89, 132, 217–19; as "just another MFI," 26, 27, 93, 94, 100–101, 106, 215; leaders and workers, 81–82; local community ties, 86–88; measurement and evaluation, 83–84, 108, 211, 215, 218; monitoring and reporting, 81–82, 106–7, 228–29; operation departments, 237n3; organizational and bureaucratic characteristics, 14, 15, 80–85, 88–89, 236n9; origin and ideology, 12, 65, 70–73; outcomes, 212–14; successes, 222;

Fundación Namaste Guatemaya (Namaste)
(continued)
    ties with northern agencies, 85–86; wom-
    en's participation in, 106–7, 110–11, 132–33,
    227, 237n5. *See also* beneficiaries, Namaste;
    bootstrap development model; education,
    Namaste; loan program, Namaste; policy-
    makers, Namaste
funders: culturally appropriate development
    and, 8–9; definition, 4; for entrepreneurs,
    48–49; the Fraternity's, 138, 142, 153–55,
    159; humanitarian aid, 37; for infrastructure
    projects, 33; Namaste's, 86; for NGOs, 45;
    peace process and, 40; as prone to amnesia,
    21–22; quantitative measures for, 24, 47;
    USAID, 36, 42; World Bank, 33, 40–41,
    235n6

GDP growth rates, 34
gender: discrimination in churches, 135–37,
    140–41; division of labor, 112, 166; identity,
    189–90; inequalities, 9, 35, 36, 122; roles, 51;
    stereotypes, 3
Genesis. *See* Fundación Genesis Empresarial
global north, 29, 36, 65; development inter-
    vention, 7, 25, 209
global south, 9, 17, 36; assumptions of women
    in, 21; development projects, 5–7, 14, 25,
    27, 208–9, 220; neoliberal objectives in, 40;
    NGO impact in, 45
Graham, Robert: autobiography, 66, 231; Cali-
    fornia Agricultural Leadership Program
    (CALP), 66; on increasing women's in-
    comes, 76–77; at Katalysis Network, 67–70;
    on market interest rates, 79; at Namaste,
    70–71, 73–74; philanthropic inspiration,
    64, 66; social and business connections,
    67, 86
Gramajo, General Hector, 39
Grameen Bank, 50, 54, 68, 69; loan fines,
    102–3, 105
grassroots organizations, 36, 44, 57, 61, 159,
    197; foreign *vs.*, 12, 23; the Fraternity's ori-
    gins, 3, 134, 159, 164, 165
Green Revolution, 43, 62, 123, 147; technology,
    32, 34, 38, 44, 220
gringos, 86, 88, 90

Guatemala: democratic reforms, 30, 39;
    economy/economic growth, 9, 32, 34–35,
    41; foreign influence in, 9, 29, 30–31, 225;
    international funding, 40; modernization-
    inspired development, 32–35, 62; neoliberal
    transformation, 39–40; NGO movement,
    36–38, 44–47, 62–63; past development
    strategies, 29, 38–39, 220; poverty, 8,
    31, 66; tax rates, 234n3. *See also* military
    government
guerrilla forces, 32, 37, 125; church support,
    59–60, 136; women's movements and, 140–41

habitus, 7, 15, 222; of the Fraternity's policy-
    makers, 134, 176; of Namaste's policymak-
    ers, 64, 65, 77–78, 108, 215
handicrafts, 2, 9, 114, 154; cloth bags, 172,
    175–76, 194
Hatch, Jonathan, 68
health and nutrition, 146–47, 194–96; mal-
    nutrition, 8
health care, 42, 46–47, 200, 205
hegemony, 6–7, 57
Hermandad de Presbiterios Mayas (the Her-
    mandad), 137, 139
hierarchy: Catholic Church, 36; in the Fra-
    ternity, 14, 152, 154–55, 174; in Namaste, 14,
    80–81; Presbyterian Church, 136, 139; in
    social relationships, 101–2, 105, 107
Hilhorst, Dorothea, 230, 234n6
holistic development model: Christian val-
    ues, 11–12, 164; diverse experiences of, 178,
    182–83, 192–94, 198; educational activities,
    144, 163, 174; goals, 134, 160; management
    of women's behavior, 161, 164; sustained
    membership and, 150; women's well-being
    and, 2, 146–47
Honduras, 68–69

identity: as businesswomen, 93, 108, 163, 183;
    Christian, 184–87; compartmentalized,
    93, 108, 122, 133, 183; as entrepreneurs, 78;
    foreigner, 226, 228–29; the Fraternity's, 27,
    159–60, 165, 167, 206; indigenous, 60, 139;
    Namaste's, 85, 86, 111; pseudonyms, 231,
    233n1; transformation of women's, 145–46,
    164–65, 172–74, 199, 201, 206, 219

incomes: average household, 73; business profits, 121–22, 238n6; evaluating/ measuring, 217, 218; family, 162–63; the Fraternity's lack of attention to, 27, 150, 199; Namaste's specialization on, 11, 65, 76–78, 218, 222; record keeping, 205–6; successes in increasing, 75, 93, 237n6; well-being and, 135, 146, 199; women's access to, 51

indigenous populations: in controlled villages, 38–39; culturally appropriate development for, 8–9, 58; the Fraternity's inclusion of, 13–14, 145; grassroots mobilization, 60–61; labor, 30; Presbyterian Church and, 135–37; Protestantism among, 58–59; violence toward, 136. *See also* Mayans; Mayan women

industrialization, 30, 32, 34–35, 41

inequality: in church leadership positions, 135–36, 140–41; in development practices, 57, 209, 212; gender, 9, 35, 36, 51, 122; in Guatemala, 8–9, 31, 34–35; of land ownership, 43, 123; power, 16; structural, 33, 94, 151

informal sector, 8–9, 35, 79, 87; representation in Guatemala, 56–57

Inter-American Development Bank (IDB), 40, 46, 53, 61, 85, 235n6

international development, 4, 49, 61, 221; neoliberalism and, 45; trends in, 46, 208–9, 220, 225

Kaqchikel, 114–15, 145; Association, 158, 165

Katalysis Network, 67–70

Kenya, 45

K'iche' women, 137, 143, 168, 172, 181–82, 213; Association, 158, 165, 170; language, 102, 117; loans for, 2, 154, 206, 238n4

Kiva, 71, 85–86

labor: force, 34, 234n2; gendered divisions of, 112, 166; indigenous populations, 9, 30; reproductive, 51, 57, 190; rights, 234n4; wages, 107–8, 126, 131, 216; women's, 8, 51, 234n4

ladino/ladina, 30, 58, 84, 237n3

landholders, 30–31, 123, 131

land reform, 30, 32–33, 43, 58

languages, 59, 159, 173; Kaqchikel, 114–15, 145;

K'iche,' 102, 139; Q'anjob'al, 156; rights, 60; Spanish, 105, 156, 180–82

Latin America, 14, 30–31; debt crisis, 37; microfinance in, 54, 55; religious NGOs, 49

leftist politics, 31, 44–55, 58

literacy, 58, 125, 180, 204; financial, 1, 2, 75, 77, 91, 101, 149

loan program, the Fraternity: access to, 165–66; lack of emphasis on, 149; loan contracts, 194–95; loan sizes, 143, 154, 206, 238nn3–4; management, 149, 153; participation and goals, 191–94, 210, 213; religious contexts of, 166–67; repayment, 201; revolving funds, 143, 166; uneven outcomes, 199–206

loan program, Namaste: achievements, 121–22; cycles, 105, 113, 121–22, 237n4, 237n6; debt and, 101; goals and expectations of, 26, 96–101, 110, 133; group, 94, 97–98, 114–15, 118–20, 236n1; guarantees, 120; identification numbers, 83; interest rates, 13, 79–80, 121, 236n7; loan sizes, 85, 113, 236n8, 237n11; partnerships with MFIs, 71–74, 94–96; policies and strategies, 71, 73–74, 121; qualifications for, 72, 112, 237n3; relationships and, 132, 213; targeted to women, 1, 10, 71–72; total distribution of, 237n3; tracking and evaluation, 83; vocational training sessions, 105, 110–11, 113–16, 237n5

loans (general): competition for borrowers, 55; delinquency on, 56; for farmers, 79; fines, 103, 105, 117, 118; first-time, 70–71, 72; increase in borrowers, 54; interest-free, 71; interest rates, 50, 53–55; for land reform projects, 43; repayment of, 57, 103, 109, 115, 117–20; solidarity groups, 69, 236n1; targeted to women, 3, 50–51, 86; World Bank, 41, 79. *See also* microcredit/microfinance; microfinance institutions (MFIs)

Lucas García, Fernando Romeo, 37–38

macroeconomic growth, 32, 34–35, 40

Mam women, 143, 204–5; Association, 158, 165, 167, 174, 192; loan sizes, 206, 238n4; marginalization of, 181–82, 213

manufacturing, 34–35

maquiladoras, 41, 62, 234n4

markets: access to, 33; development programs and, 52; external, 34; interest rates, 55, 69, 79–80; neoliberal agenda and, 40, 60, 68; women's empowerment and, 78

Mayans: culture, 13, 146, 188–89; language, 59; pan-Mayan movement, 60, 138, 139, 147; Presbyteries, 136–37, 139

Mayan women: activism/mobilization, 12, 134–39; Christian values, 17, 194–98; the Fraternity model for, 11–12, 27, 146–50; identity, 135, 187–89; tourism and, 9

Mejía Victores, Óscar Humberto, 39, 59

Mesoamerican Committee for Peace, 146, 158, 189

microcredit/microfinance: definition of, 3; evaluation of, 211; group-based, 132; neoliberal development and, 209–10; pilot projects, 68; profits, 70, 74; providers, 54–56; targeted to women, 3, 50–52, 69, 210, 235n11. See also microfinance institutions (MFIS)

Microenterprise Multiplier System (SIMME), 53

Microfinance Information Exchange Market (Mix Market), 54, 235n10, 235n15

microfinance institutions (MFIS): credit bureaus for, 56, 112; in Guatemala, 55–57; in Honduras, 68–69; increase and commercialization of, 52–55; Namaste's partnerships, 71–74, 94–96, 117–20; organizing capacity of the poor and, 33; strategic use of, 93, 96, 99, 132; targeted to better-off clients, 70, 73; targeted to women, 51–52, 57, 235n11, 235n15; women's experiences with, 94–101

military government: citizen control, 38–39; civilian genocide, 37, 125–26; counter-insurgency campaign, 38; Mayan presbyteries and, 136; modernization programs and, 32–33; NGOs and, 37–38; Protestant support, 59–60; U.S. support, 31

mining law (1996), 41, 235n5

mobilization: indigenous women, 12, 135, 137; social, 36–37, 46

model communities, 91, 237n1

modernization theory, 32–35, 36, 40

nahual (spirit being), 187

Namaste. See Fundación Namaste Guatemaya

National Action Party (PAN), 41, 42

National Credit Union Federation (FENACOAC), 55

National Evangelical Presbyterian Church of Guatemala (IENPG). See Presbyterian Church (or IENPG)

National Women's Society, 136, 137, 140

neoliberalism: culturally appropriate development and, 58, 60–61; in Guatemala, 39–40; hegemony and, 7; microfinance projects and, 209; NGOs and, 45, 47; rural development projects and, 31; women's empowerment and, 40, 50

nongovernmental organizations (NGOs): abstract questions on, 19–20; agency of, 50, 62, 234n6; demands of, 220; development assistance for, 45, 48; development projects and, 6–7; feedback and, 222; focus on social services, 46–47; foreign vs. grassroots, 12; generalizations about, 228; goals of, 23–24, 47, 221–22; growth in developing countries, 45; in Guatemala, 38, 62–63, 236n18; interactional nature of, 18–19, 65; international trends and, 50; leaders and workers, 5, 7–8, 18, 234n6; in microfinance sector, 56; policymakers and, 4, 16; quantitative results, 24, 47; studies on, 14, 233n6; tensions, 20, 23–24. See also religious NGOs (RNGOS)

nutrition. See health and nutrition

October Revolution, 30

Oxfam, 86

participatory development projects, 23, 220–21, 235n6

peace accords (1996), 42, 55, 141; indigenous rights and, 9, 60; international funding and, 40; NGOs as a result of, 46, 142

pesticides, 33, 43, 123, 130

policymakers (general): definition, 4; goals, 24, 227; leveraging of relationships, 16; media influence on, 64; for NGOs, 4–5; as prone to amnesia, 21–22; as social actors, 15, 209; views of beneficiaries, 20, 209

policymakers, the Fraternity: assumptions about women, 216–17; complaints to,